THE HUMBER WETLANDS

The Humber Wetlands

The Archaeology of a Dynamic Landscape

Robert Van de Noort

WIND*gather*
PRESS

Published by: Windgather Press Ltd, 29 Bishop Road, Bollington, Macclesfield, Cheshire SK10 5NX

Distributed by: Central Books Ltd, 99 Wallis Road, London E9 5LN

British Library Cataloguing-in-Publication Data
A catalogue record for this book is available from the British Library

ISBN 0-9545575-4-9

Designed, typeset and originated by Carnegie Publishing Ltd, Chatsworth Road, Lancaster
Printed and bound by Cambridge University Press

Contents

Landscapes of Britain

Britain has an extraordinarily rich mix of historic landscapes. This major new series explores this diversity, through accessible and attractive books that draw on the latest archaeological and historical research. Places in Britain have a great depth of historical connections. These books show how much there is to be discovered.

Also in the series

Discovering a Welsh Landscape: Archaeology in the Clwydian Range
    Ian Brown, with photography by Mick Sharp and Jean Williamson

A Frontier Landscape: The North West in the Middle Ages
    N. J. Higham

The Peak District: Landscapes Through Time
    John Barnatt and Ken Smith

Abbreviations

BP	Before Present (= AD 1950)
cal	calibrated radiocarbon date
dGPS	differential Global Positioning System
GIS	Geographical Information System
LOEPS	Land-Ocean Evolution Perspective Study
OD	Ordnance Datum
MAREW	Monuments At Risk in England's Wetlands
MHWST	Mean High Water of Spring Tides
NWWS	North West Wetlands Survey
RIB	Rigid Inflatable Boat
PZ	Pollen Zone

Note: all radiocarbon dates used in this book were calibrated according to the maximum intercept method (Stuiver and Reimer 1986), using OxCal 3.5 (Bronk Ramsey 2000), and with end points rounded outwards to 10 years (Mook 1986).

List of Figures

Acknowledgements

This book is the result of 12 years' work in the Humber Wetlands with support from English Heritage. Within this organisation, I would like to thank chief archaeologists Geoff Wainwright and David Miles for their unwavering support for the Humber Wetlands Project. Also, I acknowledge the support and advice from many English Heritage staff, including Tim Williams, Chris Scull, Andrew Davison, Jon Etté, Keith Miller, Wendy Carruthers, Toni Pearson, Dr Helen Keeley, Dr David Weir, Claire de Rouffignac, Alex Bayliss and the members of the geophysics team. I extend my gratitude to Prof. John Coles, who acted as chairman throughout the Project, and Dr Stephen Ellis who supervised the project on behalf of Hull University, where the Project was based, and who had a major role in the production of the regional monographs and the overall success of the Project.

In the production of this book, I thank Simon Denison for checking my English, and Mike Rouillard of the University of Exeter, who produced many of the illustrations in this book, including all distribution maps, the palaeo-geographic maps of the Humber Wetlands, and the models of riverine and coastal landscapes. Photographs are my own, unless indicated by an acknow-ledgement to the copyright holder in the caption.

Finally, and most importantly, I wish to thank the members of the Humber Wetlands Project team, who have made the research possible. These are: Dr Mark Dinnin (1994–1996), Senior Palaeoenvironmentalist, responsible for designing the framework of the palaeoenvironmental surveys and leading this aspect of the work in Holderness and the Humberhead Levels; Ruth Head (1994–1998), Field Officer and responsible for the analysis of flint; Dr Malcolm Lillie (1994–2000), Palaeoenvironmentalist, responsible for work in the Trent Valley, the Vale of York, the Hull valley and the Lincolnshire Marsh and for H&S; Helen Fenwick (1994–2000), Field Officer, responsible for data pro-cessing and pottery analysis; Henry Chapman (1995–2000), Field Officer, responsible for aerial photography analysis and developing the application of GPS technology; Heike Neumann (1996–97), Senior Palaeoenvironmentalist responsible for work in the Ancholme valley; William Fletcher (1997–2000), Field Officer responsible for the analysis of archaeological wood; Benjamin Gearey (1998–2000) Palaeoenvironmentalist and palynologist; and Gavin Thomas (1998–2000), Field Officer.

CHAPTER ONE

Introduction

When the famous traveller and author Daniel Defoe visited the Humber Wetlands during his *Tour of the whole island of Great Britain* in the early eighteenth century, his impression was that of '... a wonderful conflux of great rivers, all pouring down into the Humber, which receiving the Aire, the Ouse, the Don and the Trent, becomes rather a sea than a river ...' (1726; Volume 3, letter 9). It is an image of a landscape that few people would recognize today. Indeed, the popular image of the area around the towns of York, Doncaster, Hull, Goole and Grimsby is one of rather uninspiring flatlands, given overwhelmingly to arable agriculture. The rivers in the region that turned the Humber Wetlands into the extensive delta noted by Defoe have now all been embanked and canalised.

Much of this modern landscape has been created in the last 400 years. From the seventeenth century onwards, large-scale drainage projects, some under royal patronage, transformed the wetlands into extensive tracts of land for farming. However, the drainage and reclamation of the moors and wastes were not universally embraced. In fact, commoners living in the Humber Wetlands relied for their livelihood and wealth on the myriad natural resources of the wetlands, and their resistance against 'improvement' was symbolized by the sabotage of the drainage works during the Civil War (Cory 1985).

Elements of this wetland economy go back many millennia. Beneath the sediments that were laid down by the action of water, and underneath the peat, the evidence of over 10,000 years of living and exploiting the Humber Wetlands can be found. This evidence includes well-known sites and finds such as the prehistoric 'lake-settlements' from Holderness, the Ferriby boats, the Hasholme logboat, the carved Roos Carr figurines of several men and their boat and thousands of other sites and finds, many of which are little known except to the archaeologists working in the region.

It was the remit of the Humber Wetlands Project to investigate this buried archaeological resource and to place it in its context of environmental change. The Project was commissioned by English Heritage, and operated between 1992 and 2000, based at the University of Hull. This book presents the synthesis of this Project.

Historically, the area has never been called the Humber Wetlands. One searches in vain for the name in a road atlas or on signposts, or for people referring to themselves as 'Humber Wetlanders'. In fact, the term 'Humber

Wetlands' was first used by David Crowther in 1988. In a review of the rural wetlands of England, Crowther argued for the need for an archaeological project covering all types of wetlands in the Humber basin. Such a project, modelled on similar research undertaken elsewhere in England, was needed because of a range of serious threats to the archaeological remains, such as peat extraction, coastal erosion and drainage. Since then the wetlands in the

The Humber Wetlands: The Archaeology of a Dynamic Landscape

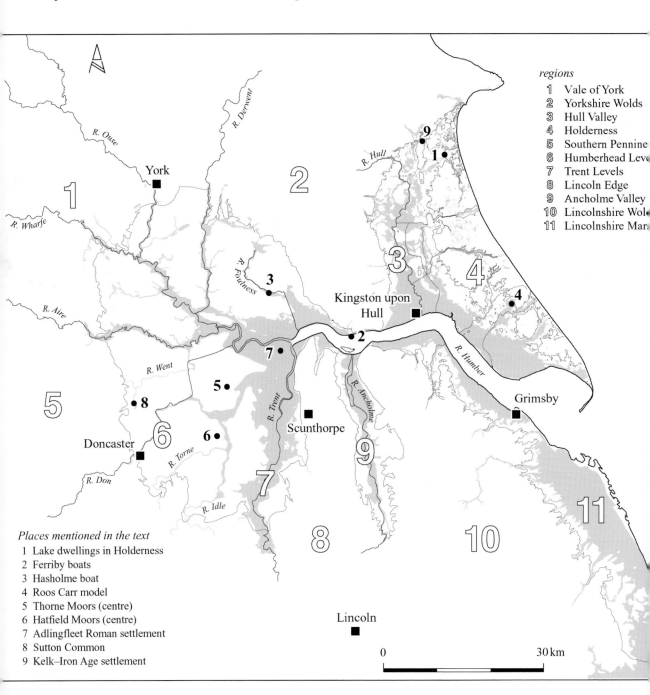

regions

1 Vale of York
2 Yorkshire Wolds
3 Hull Valley
4 Holderness
5 Southern Pennine
6 Humberhead Leve
7 Trent Levels
8 Lincoln Edge
9 Ancholme Valley
10 Lincolnshire Wol
11 Lincolnshire Mar

Places mentioned in the text

1 Lake dwellings in Holderness
2 Ferriby boats
3 Hasholme boat
4 Roos Carr model
5 Thorne Moors (centre)
6 Hatfield Moors (centre)
7 Adlingfleet Roman settlement
8 Sutton Common
9 Kelk–Iron Age settlement

0   30 km

FIGURE 2.
First impressions of
the Humber wetlands
(1): the eroding coast
of Holderness.

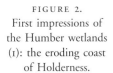

FIGURE 1 (*opposite*).
Map of the Humber
Wetlands, showing
the names of the
regions, rivers and
places mentioned in
Chapter 1. The shaded
areas indicate where
wetland deposits
(i.e. peat, alluvial silts
and clays) are in
excess of 3 m in
depth, as surveyed by
the Humber Wetlands
Project. The 10 m
OD contour defines
the maximum extent
of the Humber
Wetlands Project
research area.

Humber basin have been referred to as the 'Humber Wetlands', and the name was adopted by the Humber Wetlands Project in 1992. The concept of the Humber Wetlands has now achieved currency outside archaeological circles and has been used, for example, by the Countryside Agency in its 'Value for Wetness' initiative from the late 1990s onwards.

Some wetlands in the Humber lowlands date back to the last ice age, while others are of more recent date. The Humber Wetlands embrace a wide range of landscapes, including the estuary of the Humber, the coasts of East Yorkshire and Lincolnshire, the many rivers and their extensive floodplains, the lakes or meres in Holderness and the raised mires of Thorne and Hatfield Moors. It has been estimated that around AD 1600, that is before the large-scale drainage work commenced, these wetland landscapes totalled some 220,000 ha, or 85,000 square miles. For the purpose of this Project, the Humber Wetlands were defined as areas below the 10 m Ordnance Datum (OD) in the lowlands of the Humber basin. For practical reasons, the survey area was limited and there were cut-off points at the city of York in the north, and at Gainsborough in the south.

From the onset of the Project, we recognised seven distinct regions within the Humber Wetlands, each with their own landscape characteristics (Figure 1; see Chapter 2 for a more detailed discussion of landscape development). The landscapes of two regions, Holderness in East Yorkshire and the Lincolnshire Marsh, were largely created by the movement of ice and meltwater towards the end of the last ice age, and the southern part of Holderness and most of the Lincolnshire Marsh were subsequently buried by alluvial sediments. The characteristic wetlands of Holderness are the meres, or lakes. Active coastal erosion in this region has destroyed whatever evidence may have existed for prehistoric and historic coastal settlements and exploitation (Figure 2). The Lincolnshire Marsh contains a number of smaller river valleys, originating on the Lincolnshire Wolds, and a long and wide coastline where prehistoric landscapes have been buried beneath sediments deposited by sea and rivers. Erosion on the coast and in the Humber estuary, however, provides opportunities to investigate fragments of these prehistoric landscapes.

FIGURE 3.
First impressions of
the Humber Wetlands
(2): the lower
Ancholme valley and
Humber estuary seen
from South Ferriby.

The valleys of the Rivers Trent, Ancholme and Hull were recognised as three further distinct regions (Figure 3). These river valleys have been given their form by the changing nature of the rivers over the Holocene period. The rivers responded initially to the melting of the ice at the end of the last ice age, and subsequently to the impact of sea-level rise, impeding the run-off of freshwater which then created the wetlands.

The three valleys each have their own particular characteristics, products of their catchment, size and location. The Rivers Hull and Ancholme have both been the subject of major drainage projects. Whilst this has resulted in the disappearance of much of the original wetlands in these valleys, it permits relative easy access for research. The River Trent, for much of its length the boundary between the old county of Lincolnshire in the east and Nottingham-shire and the West Riding of Yorkshire in the west, has been embanked but survives as a river of considerable size. Outside the embanked river channel, the river's extensive floodplain is accessible for investigation, even though prehistoric landscapes tend to be deeply buried beneath alluvial sediments.

The two remaining regions, the Humberhead Levels and the Vale of York, occupy the area of the Late-glacial Lake Humber, a former massive lake of meltwater. The Humberhead Levels incorporate parts of Nottinghamshire and South Yorkshire and contain a number of wetlands. These are the Rivers Idle, Torne, Don and Went, the southern bank of the River Aire, the wetlands which developed in their floodplains and the raised mires of Thorne and Hatfield Moors. In the Vale of York, which includes parts of North Yorkshire and the East Riding of Yorkshire, the wetlands consist of the Rivers Aire (northern bank), Ouse, Wharfe and Derwent and their floodplains, the Foulness valley, and the isolated wetlands of Askham Bog and at Skipwith Common. Access to the wetlands throughout this region is relatively unproble-matic, not in the least because most of them have been drained.

The unifying feature of these seven distinct regions is the River Humber (Figure 4). As we shall see in Chapter 2, wetland development in all these regions has been determined by the evolution of the Humber in the last 10,000 years.

An archaeology of wetlands

The growing archaeological interest in wetlands in the last three decades coincides with an increasing concern for broader wetland conservation. This was initially focused on the worldwide threats to migratory bird species that relied on wetland habitats. This concern resulted in the UNESCO-sponsored Ramsar convention, so called after a meeting in the Iranian town in 1971. This convention remains in place today, and wetlands of the greatest importance across the world have received designation as 'Ramsar sites', including much of the Humber estuary and the lower Derwent floodplain.

Archaeologists' interest in wetlands is principally based on their preservative qualities. A key characteristic of many wetlands is a high groundwater table that saturates soils and sediments (Coles 1984). Waterlogging, as this is called, excludes all or most of the oxygen from the soil. This inhibits the activity of oxygenating bacteria and fungi, which form essential parts of the complex process that is responsible for the breaking down of organic remains. It results in the creation of near-equilibria in the ground, with minimal change and deterioration. In this way wetlands can preserve organic remains that are almost always absent from the archaeological record on free-draining 'drylands'. The organic remains range from objects such as baskets, wooden tools, timber-built trackways and boats, to biological remains such as insects, pollen, and human and animal bodies.

Another characteristic of wetlands is the dynamic nature of the landscape, with erosion and sedimentation constantly changing the environment. Sedimentation comprises processes such as the growth of peat or the deposition of gravels, sands or clay by rivers, estuary and sea, resulting in the burial of ancient landscapes (Figure 5). Under their cover of sediment such landscapes are protected from physical damage, notably ploughing. While on drylands such a protective cover is only encountered rarely, in exceptional contexts, in wetlands the burial of landscapes is the rule rather than the exception. For example, peat has covered the pre-Bronze Age landscapes at Thorne and Hatfield Moors, and alluvial sedimentation has resulted in deeply buried prehistoric and historic landscapes in all regions of the Humber Wetlands. The estuarine Humber has preserved fragments of the prehistoric landscape, but eroded other parts. The impact of the North Sea on the coast of Holderness has been erosive, while the prehistoric and historic landscape of the Lincolnshire Marsh has been largely buried by marine deposits (see also Chapter 2).

Wetland archaeology is not just concerned with well-preserved remains, but also with the past use of wetland landscapes. Although few wetlands now survive intact, before the large-scale drainage projects of the seventeenth century as much as 25 per cent of the landmass of England could be described as wetland (Brown and Bradley 1995). This land was exploited, lived-in and used over time for different reasons, and formed an essential part of many people's lives.

The Humber Wetlands: The Archaeology of a Dynamic Landscape

FIGURE 5.
Buried archaeology: the Humber Wetlands Project team sampling a saltern site near Ingoldmells, Lincolnshire Marsh, in 2000.

© THE HUMBER WETLANDS PROJECT, UNIVERSITY OF HULL

Nowadays, however, wetlands throughout the world are under threat. Overwhelmingly still seen as wilderness or wastelands, they are drained to accommodate urban development, or converted into agricultural land. In the Humber Wetlands, the largest single threat, drainage, has enabled the transformation of the area from a pasture to an arable landscape. This has not only brought the threat of ploughing closer to the archaeological resource but, more significantly, has lowered the groundwater table and reintroduced oxygen to previously waterlogged deposits. Other recent damaging activities include peat extraction on Thorne and Hatfield Moors, even though government intervention will safeguard relics of this landscape from future damage. Natural erosion in the Humber estuary and along the Holderness coast is also a formidable threat to the archaeological sites here. Industrial development, in particular on the outskirts of Hull and around Immingham in north Lincolnshire, contributes further to the destruction of waterlogged archaeological remains.

In recognition of the importance of the waterlogged archaeological sites, and the potential and real dangers that affect all of England's wetlands, English Heritage had already supported three other major wetland surveys in England before the Humber Wetlands Project began – the Somerset Levels Project, the Fenland Project, and the North West Wetlands Survey. Between 1973 and 1988, archaeological research on peat extraction in the Somerset Levels produced a wealth of sites, including a number of wooden trackways (e.g. Coles and Coles 1986). The Somerset Levels Project was essentially concerned with rescue archaeology and the most famous sites – such as the Sweet Track, the Abbot's Way, Walton Heath Track and the Meare Heath Track – were excavated before their destruction by peat extraction. Other sites on the Levels, including the lake settlements at Glastonbury and Meare, are suffering from desiccation and peat wastage.

Between 1981 and 1988, the survey of the Fenlands of East Anglia (Lincolnshire, Cambridgeshire and Norfolk) was undertaken. Unlike the Somerset Levels, the main threat to the archaeological resource was not (or no longer) peat extraction, but the rapid desiccation of peat, erosion and the conversion of pasture land to arable land, bringing many archaeological sites within reach of ploughing activity (Hall and Coles 1994). At the close of the project, nearly 240,000 ha (or 60 per cent of the wetlands) had been fieldwalked, with over 2,500 sites discovered, ranging in date from the Mesolithic to the medieval period.

The majority of sites identified were not waterlogged, although some included waterlogged components (Coles and Hall 1997). The Fenlands, essentially a lowland basin that had gradually become a wetland as a result of sea-level change, had through time been exploited by people living on the Fenland edge and on the 'islands' within the basin. From these places, both the wetlands and the drylands could be utilised, a practice that has been described in greatest detail for the Fengate landscape (e.g. Pryor 2001). Traces of human activity were also encountered on the 'roddons', the clay and silt sediments making up the natural embankments or levees of the former courses of tidal rivers and creeks.

The North West Wetlands Survey (NWWS) was undertaken between 1988 and 1997, focusing on the 37,000 ha of lowland peat in the counties of Cumbria, Lancashire, Greater Manchester, Merseyside, Cheshire, Staffordshire and Shropshire (Middleton and Wells 1990). The threats to the wetlands of north-west England included peat extraction, drainage and desiccation and the conversion of pasture land into arable (e.g. Leah *et al.* 1997). Nevertheless, throughout the area much pastureland remains. In the areas of Greater Manchester and Merseyside, waste disposal, urbanization and industrial development were recognized as significant threats to the wetlands.

Palaeoecology, and in particular palynology and plant macrofossil analysis, combined with high-resolution radiocarbon dating, was used extensively during the project. Its role has been portrayed as an archaeological survey tool in its own right. The (palaeo-) environmental archives contained within the peatlands were considered as 'sites' and their state of preservation and any light they might shed on past people's activity, either within or outside the wetlands, were assessed as part of the survey.

Elsewhere, research in and of wetlands has been undertaken in a wide range of places. In this book, reference will be made to important recent research in the Severn Estuary and its Welsh and English hinterlands (e.g. Bell *et al.* 2000), in the peatbogs of the Irish Midlands (e.g. Raftery 1996) and the Shannon estuary (O'Sullivan 2001), in the Low Countries (e.g. Brandt *et al.* 1987), and the North Sea basin (e.g. Rippon 2000). These projects are similarly characterised by close integration of environmental and cultural studies of the past, and by the examination of organic archaeological remains alongside inorganic finds.

The Humber Wetlands Project

The Humber Wetlands Project commenced in 1992, when Paul Davies and I were appointed as Field Officers. We produced a desktop study that established the need for an extensive survey (Van de Noort and Davies 1993). English Heritage commissioned this survey in 1994 and it was undertaken by a team of archaeologists and palaeoenvironmentalists based at the University of Hull. Over the eight years of the project, the team's members included Mark Dinnin (1994–1996), Ruth Head (1994–1998), Malcolm Lillie (1994–2000), Helen Fenwick (1994–2000), Henry Chapman (1995–2000), Heike Neumann (1996–97), William Fletcher (1997–2000), Benjamin Gearey (1998–2000) and Gavin Thomas (1998–2000). Dr Stephen Ellis of the University of Hull was closely involved with the publication of the books and other aspects of the project.

A management committee existed throughout the duration of the project, and was chaired by Professor John Coles, who also had a leading role in the other English Heritage wetland surveys. The Inspectors of Ancient Monuments represented on the committee were Andrew Davison (1992–93), Jon Etté

FIGURE 6 (*opposite*). Map of the Humber Wetlands, showing all 'mapviews' surveyed during the Humber Wetlands Project. Sites, find scatters and finds discovered during our survey were named after the mapview they were found in, i.e. Gringley–6 was found in the Gringley mapview. Numbered mapviews are:
1: Skipsea;
2: Weel;
3: Aldbrough;
4: Wheldrake;
5: Hensall;
6: Moorends;
7: Askern;
8: Hatfield Woodhouse;
9: Rossington;
10: Scaftworth;
11: Gringley;
12: Adlingfleet;
13: Whitton;
14: Melton;
15: South Ferriby;
16: Barrow;
17: Brigg;
18: Bishopbridge;
19: Grimsby;
20: Marshchapel.

(1993–2000) and Keith Miller (2000). Other English Heritage staff on the committee were Wendy Carruthers, Toni Pearson, Dr Helen Keeley, Dr David Weir and Claire de Rouffignac. The last four also acted for some time as Project Officers, and had responsibility for monitoring progress of the project (English Heritage 1991). Alex Bayliss advised the Project on the use of radiocarbon dating. A larger working party, the Humber Wetlands Forum, met several times during the early years of the project's work, and included representatives from the counties and unitary authorities, the regional museums, university departments and several individuals in addition to the members of the management committee.

The aim of the Humber Wetlands Project was the selective but systematic survey of the Humber basin lowlands over a period of six years (Figure 6). The survey was undertaken within sample areas known as 'mapviews', areas

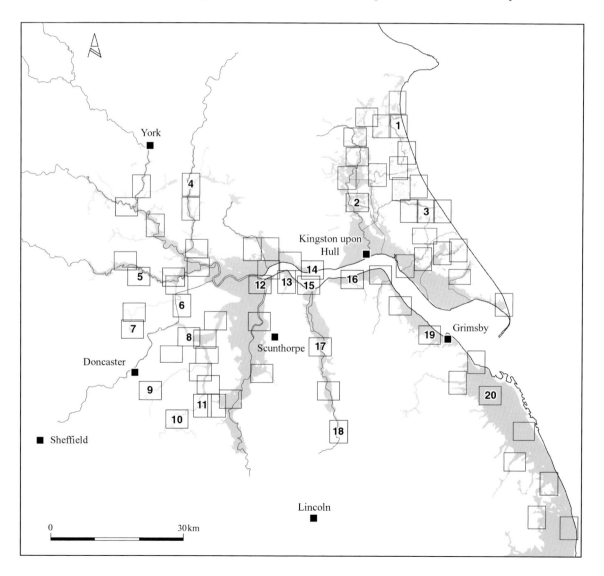

measuring 5 × 4 km centred on wetlands (e.g. Etté and Van de Noort 1997). The methods and techniques employed by the Humber Wetlands Project were by design multi-faceted. On the archaeological side, these included field-walking in transects 30 m apart, dyke survey whenever possible, systematic analysis of aerial photographs in archives, the selective deployment of English Heritage's geophysical survey team and small-scale excavations (Figure 7). On the palaeo-environmental side of the work, the methods and techniques included extensive coring programmes for lithostratigraphic analysis, and pollen analysis linked to selective but high-resolution radiocarbon dating programmes.

Obviously, such a multi-faceted approach reduced the actual acreage researched, but afforded the close integration of different techniques. Excavation of selected sites was recognized as an important tool. It served to enhance our understanding of the state of preservation of waterlogged archaeological sites and to raise the profile of the project. It also linked the finds made on the surface during field-walking to actual sites. Several excavations showed that the surface finds were all that was left of the archaeological resource, but on other occasions, important sub-surface features were discovered.

The use of geophysical survey, both magnetometer and resistivity, was successful on the sandy 'islands' within the wetlands. However, magnetometry was also found to be productive on Roman period sites sealed within the alluvium, where its application is as a rule unrewarding. The mapping of the very extensive riverside settlement of Adlingfleet at Trent Falls, at the confluence of the Rivers Trent, Don and Ouse, showed the potential of this survey technique for wetlands (see Chapter 7). However, the identification of features was dependent on the presence of 'industrial' waste, dumped in the ditches, and without such material, the ditches would not have been identified.

FIGURE 7.
The Humber Wetlands Project team field walking around Halsham church, Holderness, in 1995.

© THE HUMBER WETLANDS PROJECT, UNIVERSITY OF HULL

FIGURE 8.
The Humber
Wetlands Project team
surveying the Melton
foreshore, Vale of
York, showing dGPS
and RIB in 1996.
© THE HUMBER WETLANDS
PROJECT, UNIVERSITY OF
HULL

The Humber Wetlands Project followed the NWWS in the early adoption of a Geographic Information System (GIS). Its application was extended into the field, with palmtop computers available for data input. We were the first wetland survey to apply differential Global Positioning Systems (dGPS), which provides a new method of analysing the micro-topography that may characterize wetland sites through the process of differential desiccation, whereby peat shrinks more rapidly than silt and clay (Chapman and Van de Noort 2001). The dGPS was also used extensively in the Humber estuary and the coast for the rapid recording of sites during low tides. The part-erosive nature of the tides offered unparalleled opportunities for the discovery and excavation of many archaeological sites, many of these being waterlogged in nature. Within the estuary, however, it was our small rigid inflatable boat that revolutionised the way we worked more than anything else. The boat allowed safe and rapid transport in this sometimes treacherous environment and boosted the morale of the project staff considerably, providing a welcome alternative to field-walking (Figure 8).

In the six years between 1994 and 2000, the staff undertook an annual programme of survey, analysis and publication of one of the regions in the Humber Wetlands. In all, the Humber Wetlands Project identified over 400 archaeological sites, including 40 waterlogged sites, and many more finds and 'find scatters'. The primary results of these regional surveys were published in the 'Wetland Heritage' series. In all, six monographs were produced: *Wetland Heritage of Holderness* in 1995, *Wetland Heritage of the Humberhead Levels* in 1997, *Wetland Heritage of the Ancholme and lower Trent valleys* in 1998, *Wetland Heritage of the Vale of York* in 1999, *Wetland Heritage of the Hull valley* in 2000 and *Wetland Heritage of the Lincolnshire Marsh* in 2001 (Van de Noort and Ellis 1995, 1997, 1998, 1999 and 2000, Ellis *et al.* 2001).

Six annual reports were published alongside the monographs and these included accounts of highlights of each of the regional surveys and short reports on research undertaken in the Humber Wetlands by other organizations and individuals. The results of the project were also presented at six annual conferences, held in Hull, York and Lincoln. These brought local people, academics and the project team together, resulting in lively debate and discussion.

About this book

My intentions in writing this book are twofold. First, I aim to offer a synthesis of the results of the Humber Wetlands Project between 1992 and 2000, and to include the results of research undertaken by others in the region. Second, I hope that the synthetic review will draw out the most important themes in the archaeology of the area, rather than provide a full account of the Project's findings. The desktop study and the six monographs provide this already.

Whilst the integration of environmental and cultural data has formed a fundamental aspect of the Humber Wetlands Project, an environmentally-deterministic approach is not pursued here. Rather, the main theme throughout this book is people's perception of wetlands in the Humber lowlands in the last 10,000 years. This perception belongs, of course, to the people who are studied. As archaeologists, we interpret this perception through the evidence of material culture and environment, and our approach is therefore to a certain extent 'empathetic'.

Our approach is furthermore based on the belief that people had and have an interactive relationship with their environment and that the cultural factors, attitudes and restraints that developed over many generations determined the way they dealt with 'nature'. Reactions to environmental change may range from adaptation in subsistence strategy, to social and political change, religious inspiration or complete indifference, depending on cultural or natural influences (or both). We believe this holds true not only for the past but for modern society too. The diversity of responses to current and predicted climate change serves as an illustration.

An additional feature of this synthesis is the need to put the data collated by the Humber Wetlands Survey team into a broader context. To date, this evidence has mostly been analysed and interpreted within the framework of the wetlands themselves, but the 'contextualisation' of this data is important if we are to understand the functions of wetlands throughout prehistory and the historic period. This is achieved primarily by integrating the archaeology of surrounding higher and dryer regions. Archaeological evidence from wetland research further afield, most notably from Britain, Ireland and from the countries across the North Sea, provides another framework in which to contextualise the archaeology of the Humber Wetlands.

The study of peoples' changing perception of wetlands in the Humber lowlands attempts to identify both long-term attitudes and events. The information is therefore based on a series of themes rather than archaeological periods, although the chapters have been ordered on a broadly chronological basis. In Chapter 2, the environmental history, or palaeoenvironmental development, of the region is described with particular attention to the changing nature of the wetlands and vegetation. Chapter 3 is concerned with the prehistoric exploitation of wetlands. In early prehistory, this included fishing, hunting and gathering, but in later prehistory, the role of the wetlands changed and their contribution to farming communities was more supplementary in character.

Chapter 4 looks at wetland settlements, with particular attention to the prehistoric lake-dwellings of Holderness, first recorded by Boynton in the later nineteenth century (Smith 1911), the Iron Age sites of Sutton Common in the Humberhead Levels and Kelk in the Hull valley, and the large number of settlements that develop in later prehistory. Chapter 5 looks at wetlands as waterways, and describes the unparalleled maritime structures found in the Humber Wetlands, including the Ferriby boats, the Hasholme boat (Wright 1990, Millett and McGrail 1990) and their significance for prehistoric societies. Chapter 6 addresses the phenomenon of deposition of valuables in wet places in the Humber Wetlands. This practice has been observed throughout northern and western Europe for much of prehistoric and even historic times (Bradley 1990), and in this chapter I assess the contribution of the Humber Wetlands research to this debate.

Chapter 7 considers the Roman period, when numerous new settlements appear in the Humber Wetlands, many of these located in places at – or even below – modern sea-level, where no late-prehistoric activity had taken place. This Roman 'colonization' of the lowlands can only be understood within the wider context of the economy in the Roman period, and is also of great significance in understanding the dynamics of regional sea-level change. Chapter 8 addresses the impact of rapid sea-level rise at the end of the Roman period and the exploitation of the wetlands in the Middle Ages, which is known from both archaeological research and historical sources. Chapter 9 summarises the drainage history of the Humber Wetlands and its impact on the landscape, showing that forces residing outside the region were principally responsible for the transformation of the lowlands.

As is the case for many other wetlands across the world, the Humber Wetland presents us with a paradox. The archaeological record provides evidence of a perception of wetlands both as economically valuable and exploitable landscapes, but also as 'natural places' linked to ancestor cults and spiritual activity. In the past, as in the present, these two spheres of activity are as a rule spatially separated (e.g. Bradley 2000). The exploration of this paradox forms one of the main themes of this book. Can it be explained by examining the natural characteristics of the different wetland types, exploring their productiveness for people in the past? Or is it a result of the diverse points of view of people in the past, between for example 'insiders' and 'outsiders', or between elite and peasantry? Or can the answer be found in changing religions, or the impact of climate change on the landscape? In the concluding chapter, the many 'layers' of evidence presented here are brought together to consider this paradox, by examining the diverse perceptions of wetlands through the ages. The future of the Humber Wetlands is also considered.

CHAPTER TWO

Natural History

....

Introduction

The natural history of the Humber Wetlands is complex and the current landscape is the outcome of a range of interrelated and interactive factors (Figure 9). Nevertheless, the development of the region as a landscape is more easily explained by separating seven key factors. The first factor relates to the geology and the second to the retreat of the icesheet from the region, the subsequent creation of Lake Humber and the establishment of the river corridors. The third key factor is the rise in sea-level, starting some 11,000 years ago from *c.* 20 m below OD, with the associated changes in the character of the rivers in the Humber Wetlands. The fourth is the development of the wetlands from *c.* 5000 cal BC, a direct consequence of the Holocene sea-level change but with its own particular characteristics. The fifth key factor is climate change and the sixth is vegetation history. The seventh and final key change, that of the effect of man on the landscape, is a pivotal theme throughout the following chapters and is only introduced here. The research that enables the description of 11,000 years of landscape change has been undertaken mainly outside the framework of the Humber Wetlands Project, but the project team has enhanced our understanding of several important issues, most notably the early character of the rivers in the region, the nature of wetland development and the diversity and dynamics of vegetation change.

Geology

The pre-Holocene geology of the Humber Wetlands has been studied in the greatest detail by the British Geological Survey, and has been presented in some detail by Catt (1990) and Geoff Gaunt (1994). It has also been sum-marised by Stephen Ellis in the *Wetland Heritage* monographs. In outline, the bedrock of the Humber Wetlands and the higher grounds surrounding them consists of a number of strata that, in profile, dip generally eastwards, giving rise to a series of scarp slopes, ridges and valley lowlands (Figure 10). The oldest geological strata, marking the western limit of the Humber Wetlands, are the Permian Upper Magnesian Limestone and Upper Permian Marl. Exposures of the Upper Magnesian are visible to the west of Doncaster, for example in the Don Gorge.

The Triassic Sherwood Sandstone forms the bedrock to the east of the

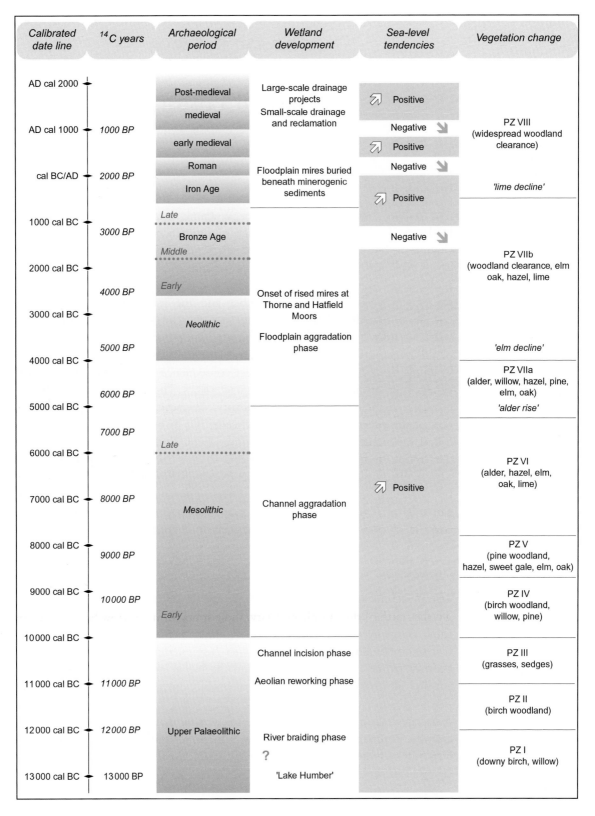

Calibrated date line	¹⁴C years	Archaeological period	Wetland development	Sea-level tendencies	Vegetation change
AD cal 2000		Post-medieval	Large-scale drainage projects	Positive	
		medieval	Small-scale drainage and reclamation	Negative	PZ VIII (widespread woodland clearance)
AD cal 1000	1000 BP	early medieval		Positive	
		Roman		Negative	
cal BC/AD	2000 BP	Iron Age	Floodplain mires buried beneath minerogenic sediments	Positive	'lime decline'
1000 cal BC		Late			
	3000 BP	Bronze Age		Negative	PZ VIIb (woodland clearance, elm oak, hazel, lime
2000 cal BC		Middle			
	4000 BP	Early	Onset of rised mires at Thorne and Hatfield Moors		
3000 cal BC		Neolithic		Positive	
	5000 BP		Floodplain aggradation phase		'elm decline'
4000 cal BC					PZ VIIa (alder, willow, hazel, pine, elm, oak)
	6000 BP				
5000 cal BC					'alder rise'
	7000 BP				
6000 cal BC		Late			PZ VI (alder, hazel, elm, oak, lime)
7000 cal BC	8000 BP	Mesolithic	Channel aggradation phase	Positive	
8000 cal BC	9000 BP				PZ V (pine woodland, hazel, sweet gale, elm, oak)
9000 cal BC	10000 BP	Early			PZ IV (birch woodland, willow, pine)
10000 cal BC			Channel incision phase		PZ III (grasses, sedges)
11000 cal BC	11000 BP		Aeolian reworking phase		PZ II (birch woodland)
12000 cal BC	12000 BP	Upper Palaeolithic	River braiding phase ?		PZ I (downy birch, willow)
13000 cal BC	13000 BP		'Lake Humber'		

16

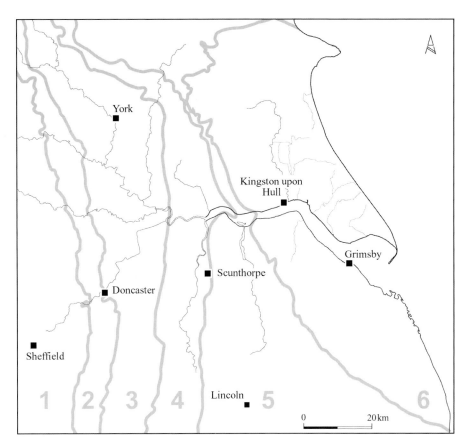

FIGURE 10.
Map of the Humber
Wetlands, showing
the underlying
geology, simplified
after Catt (1990) and
Gaunt (1994):
1: Carboniferous Coal
Measures;
2: Permian Upper
Magnesian Limestone
and Upper Permian
Marl;
3: Triassic Sherwood
Sandstone;
4: Triassic Mercia
Mudstone;
5: Jurassic marls,
limestones, sandstones
and clays;
6: Cretaceous chalk.

FIGURE 9 (*opposite*).
Table showing the
relationship between
calibrated radiocarbon
dates, radiocarbon
years, archaeological
periods, wetland
development, sea-level
tendencies and
vegetation change, as
used in this book.

Permian strata. The Sherwood Sandstone occupies the central parts of the Humberhead Levels and the Vale of York, with extensive exposures in parts of Nottinghamshire and South Yorkshire, in the area south of Doncaster. Further east, Mercia Mudstone, also formed in the Triassic, overlies the Sherwood Sandstone. Mercia Mudstone forms much of the Isle of Axholme, an area of higher ground, which forms the boundary between the Humberhead Levels and the lower Trent Valley. Further east still, the Jurassic bedrock comprising marls, limestones, sandstones and clays form the higher grounds of the Lincoln Edge between the lower Trent valley and the Ancholme valley. To the north of the Humber estuary, these strata form a narrow bench between the Triassic Mudstone and the Yorkshire Wolds.

The chalk that forms the Lincolnshire and Yorkshire Wolds was formed in the Cretaceous. It forms a distinct area of higher ground between the Ancholme valley and the Lincolnshire Marsh in the southern half of the Humber Wetlands, and between the Vale of York and the Hull valley north of the Humber. The western edge of the chalk forms a distinct escarpment, but eastwards it dips beneath glacial tills of the Quaternary era. Strata of the Tertiary period are not known from the region, suggesting that the Tertiary sea was situated to the east of the Humber Wetlands and did not form any strata in the region.

A 'veneer' of Quaternary deposits overlies major parts of the bedrock of the Humber Wetlands. Glacial till or boulder clay, deposited by the icesheets, and glaciofluvial material, deposited by meltwater, form much of the landsurface of the Lincolnshire Marsh, the Hull valley and especially Holderness. Smaller outcrops of till are present in the Vale of York and the Humberhead Levels. Throughout the Humber Wetlands, the current surface has been formed during the Late-glacial and the Holocene.

Lake Humber, the Post-glacial rivers and meres in Holderness

In the last glacial period, the Devensian, most of what has been defined as the Humber Wetlands was under ice (Figure 11). The Yorkshire and Lincolnshire Wolds and the Lincoln Edge, however, remained largely ice-free. One

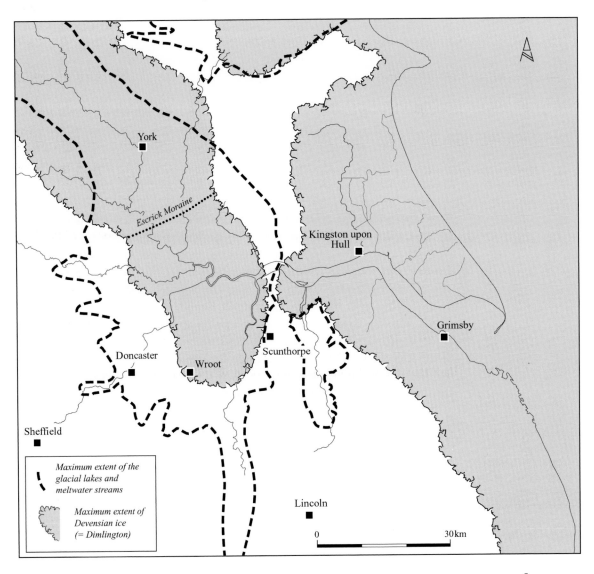

York

Escrick Moraine

Kingston upon
Hull

Grimsby

Doncaster

Wroot

Scunthorpe

Sheffield

*Maximum extent of the
glacial lakes and
meltwater streams*

*Maximum extent of
Devensian ice
(= Dimlington)*

Lincoln

0   30km

icesheet covered all of Holderness, the Hull valley and the Lincolnshire Marsh and it extended through the Humber Gap into the northern part of the Ancholme valley, depositing till (or boulder clay) throughout these regions. A second icesheet covered the lowlands to the west of the Yorkshire and Lincolnshire Wolds, including the Vale of York, the Humberhead Levels and the lower Trent valley. The maximum southern extent of this icesheet lies at Wroot, to the south of Hatfield Moors in the Humberhead Levels, indicated by a substantial end-moraine that was formed around 18,000 BP, in the early stages of the Dimlington Stadial of the Devensian. The ice-sheet wasted during the Devensian period and stabilised to the south of York, where it formed the Escrick Moraine, a distinctive ridge of till and glacial sands and gravel.

Meltwater formed lakes around the ice-sheet in the Humberhead Levels and the Vale of York, leaving lake deposits up to 33 m OD. Water entering this lake, usually called Lake Humber, was impounded by the icesheet blocking the Humber Gap between the Yorkshire Wolds and the Lincolnshire Wolds. However, by *c.* 11,000 cal BC, Lake Humber had ceased to exist, although recent research suggests that Lake Humber may have silted up by *c.* 13,000 cal BC (Bateman *et al.* 2000). Whether this is related to the unblocking of the Humber Gap with the retreat of the easterly icesheet, or to the silting up of Lake Humber, remains a matter of debate among geologists. The extensive lacustrine clays, silts and sands left behind in the Vale of York and the Humberhead Levels are called 'Lake Humber deposits' or '25-foot drift', after the maximum height of this material. A similar but much smaller meltwater lake is thought to have existed in the Ancholme valley (Neumann 1998).

The outline of the development of the rivers following the disappearance of Lake Humber was established by Geoff Gaunt (1981, 1994, 1999). Initially, rivers and streams established themselves in the Vale of York and the Humberhead Levels, including the predecessors, or proto-rivers, of the current Rivers Derwent, Ouse, Aire, Went, Don, Torne, Idle and Trent. These proto-rivers drained through the Humber Gap but their channels were not incised during this period. In view of the contemporary sea-level at more than 20 m below OD, such a process – whereby rivers cut into the Lake Humber deposits – would be expected, as their gradient would be relatively steep. Paul Davies has suggested that the absence of channel incision can be explained by the fact that the nickpoint had not eroded westwards through the Humber Gap, where the Humber flows between the Yorkshire and Lincolnshire Wolds (in Van de Noort and Davies 1993). In other words, the rivers in the Humber Wetlands flowed eastwards to a 'Humber falls' somewhere to the east of the Humber Gap, with a rather gentle gradient that did not result in the rivers incising. Instead, the proto-rivers braided, cutting multiple slow-flowing channels and forming natural embankments of clays, silts and sands, or levees. These were subsequently reworked by the wind, forming dune systems and coversands. The dates of this coversand suggest that this aeolian reworking phase was short-lived and occurred from *c.* 11,500 cal BC to 10,500 cal BC (Bateman 1995, Dinnin 1997b). At this time, which falls within the final cold

FIGURE II.
Map of the Humber Wetlands, showing Lake Humber and other glacial lakes and the maximum extent of the Devensian ice at *c.* 18,000 BC, after Catt (1990).

19

stage of the Devensian known as the Loch Lomond Stadial, the landscape of the Humberhead Levels and the Vale of York was a treeless tundra (Buckland and Dolby 1973).

When the nickpoint had eroded through the Humber Gap, the rivers responded to the very low contemporary sea-level by incising into the lacustrine deposits of Lake Humber. This created steep-sided river channels, with depths as low as −20 m OD at Trent Falls, but more commonly up to 9 m deep. The date of this channel incision stage remains a matter for further research. A postulated date for the onset of channel incision around 7500 cal BC has been challenged by work undertaken by Mark Dinnin and Malcolm Lillie, who found evidence for the start of the following phase of river development, the channel aggradation phase in which sediments are deposited within the river channel, around *c*. 10,000 cal BC, in turn reflecting rising sea-levels (Dinnin 1997c, Lillie 1997a). This early date was derived from deposits in the channel of the River Went and elsewhere in the Humberhead Levels, and was dated on the basis of pollen analysis. Further research is required to confirm this proposition, including radiocarbon dating of the deposits. Nevertheless, it appears likely that the phases described here, from the braiding of the rivers, the aeolian reworking phase, the channel incision and onset of channel aggradation, followed one another very rapidly within the Late-glacial period. Indeed, these may have overlapped to some degrees and it is likely that the individual rivers may have evolved differently.

The Post-glacial development of the Rivers Ancholme and Hull follows, in outline, the same phases as described for the rivers to the west of the Wolds. The valley floor of the Ancholme is formed from lacustrine deposits, indicating that a 'Lake Ancholme' existed here in the Late-glacial period. Ridges of reworked wind-blown sand attest to an aeolian phase comparable to that found in the Humberhead Levels and Vale of York. Channel incision occurred here too, and the Project's investigator, Heike Neumann, confirmed the believe that this phase had been short-lived too (Neumann 1998). In the Hull valley, no lacustrine deposits or wind-blown sand have been found, but the research by Malcolm Lillie and Benjamin Gearey suggests that the period of channel incision must have been equally short-lived here (Lillie and Gearey 2000). The subsequent floodplain aggradation phase and the development of the rivers during the later part of the Holocene are discussed further below.

The only type of wetland that was largely unaffected by Holocene sea-level rise were the lakes or 'meres' of Holderness. Only one such mere survives in the current landscape, Hornsea Mere, but in the early Holocene more than 70 lakes must have existed in Holderness (Sheppard 1956). These developed in depressions in the till or clay, formed by the ice and meltwater in the Devensian and Post-glacial. Flenley (1987) recognised two broad types of meres: the small, often ovoid type, developed in ice-melt features such as kettleholes or pingos, and the larger, typically elongated type, that occupy large depressions in the till, reflecting pre-Glacial valleys (cf. Valentin 1957). Several meres have provided the source material for the reconstruction of Late-glacial and early

Holocene vegetation histories, most notably the Bog at Roos (Beckett 1975), Skipsea Withow Mere (Gilbertson 1984) and Gransmoor Quarry (Walker *et al.* 1993, Lowe *et al.* 1995).

Mark Dinnin and Malcolm Lillie investigated 35 meres of both types through coring, and the date-range of the deposits and their potential to illuminate aspects of Late-glacial and Holocene vegetation and climate change were highlighted. Seven former lakes were found to have no Holocene deposits whatsoever. This has been attributed to peat cutting, drainage, oxidation and ploughing, or to the misnaming of depressions in which standing water is only a seasonal feature, as 'meres' (Dinnin and Lillie 1995a). All other meres were found to have deposits representing the Late-glacial and Holocene in part only, indicating the periods in which they functioned as lakes when sediments were laid down. The natural process of silting up, combining the accumulation of sediments within the waterbody with the accumulation of plant material on its margins, is commonly referred to as hydroseral succession.

Sea-level rise

The third key factor in the development of lowlands wetlands around the Humber is the relative regional sea-level change. The concept of the 'relative sea-level' of a region refers to the balance between eustacy (i.e. the amount of water in the world's oceans and seas, where changes result in global sea-level change), and isostasy (i.e. the movement of the earth's crust; changes here are referred to as isostatic lift or fall). At the end of the Devensian, sea-level was considerably lower than today as the water was held in icesheets. Subsequent melting of the icesheets returned water to the seas, causing a rapid relative sea-level rise. At the end of the Devensian, with sea-levels below the 20 m OD, the North Sea basin at this time was an extensive lowland. Subsequent sea-level rise submerged much of this extensive basin, and not until *c.* 6000 cal BC was the landbridge between England's east coast and the Low Countries finally broken (Shennan *et al.* 2000).

The effect of relative sea-level change on the landscape development in the Humber lowlands has been the subject of recent research by the Land-Ocean Evolution Perspective Study (LOEPS) (Shennan and Andrews 2000). The LOEPS research has produced a series of palaeogeographical maps, which show the wetland development for the Humber from 6000 to 1000 cal BC (Metcalfe *et al.* 2000), and for the North Sea basin from *c.* 6000 to 3000 cal BC (Shennan *et al.* 2000). The overall aim of LOEPS was 'to describe the evolution of coastal systems over the last 10,000 years in response to changes in natural climatic conditions, changes in relative sea-level and the changes wrought by human activities' (Shennan and Andrews 2000). The study involved a large team of scientists working on material from a number of boreholes. This multidisciplinary research included lithostratigraphic (particle size analysis, geochemistry and mineralogy) biostratigraphic (pollen, foraminifera and diatom) and chronostratigraphic (radiocarbon dating and palaeomagnetism) analysis (Ridgeway *et al.* 2000). Twenty-four new boreholes were drilled in and around the Humber estuary, and the analysis of these boreholes forms the basis for our most up-to-date understanding of the effects of sea-level change on the landscape development in the Humber Wetlands (Figure 12).

The LOEPS study indicates that at the end of the Devensian, the North Sea may have been as much as 50 m below the current sea-level, and extending southwards as far as southern Scotland only. Initial sea-level rise was extremely rapid, with depths of *c.* –20 m OD estimated for the Post-glacial period around 12,000 cal BC (Shennan *et al.* 2000). During the early Holocene, the sea-levels in the Humber basin continued to rise rapidly, but the rise was less quick in the middle and later parts of the Holocene. A curve of relative sea-level in the Humber basin shows the trend, with sea-levels around –17 m at 6000 cal BC, at –10 m OD around 5000 cal BC, at –7 m OD around 4000 cal BC, near –5 m OD around 3000 cal BC, at –4 m around 2000 cal BC and from then on rising at *c.* 1 m per millennium (Metcalfe *et al.* 2000) (Figure 13).

The methodology employed by LOEPS identifies positive and negative sea-level tendencies, rather than sea-level rises and falls or marine transgressions (the landward extension of the sea) and regressions (the seaward extension of the land). From an archaeological perspective, these palaeogeographic landscape reconstructions provide extremely useful tools for understanding landscapes and people during the Post-glacial and early Holocene, when sea-level rise was particularly rapid. However, for the later part of the Holocene such simplified reconstructions are less useful and sometimes misleading, whilst no palaeogeographical maps were produced for the last three millennia. Three methodological issues can be identified to explain this. Firstly, the study relied on the accumulation of sediments. Whilst these can be used to record sea-level rise, sea-level fall does not necessarily result in the deposition of any sediments that can bear evidence to this. Therefore, this method failed to identify any periods of sea-level fall. Secondly, practically no sedimentological and palaeo-environmental source material exists for the first millennium BC and the first and second millennia AD. Thirdly, the palaeogeographic landscape reconstructions have been built from single age-altitude models, and therefore any regional variation of the impact of sea-level change has become obscured. However, the co-existence of areas where marine transgression and regression occurred even within single catchments is well known. For example, the coast of East Yorkshire is currently rapidly eroding, but that of northern Lincolnshire is aggrading. In terms of understanding the interaction between people and their environment, this creates considerable problems, especially in the later Holocene. Additional research is required to build a basis for further palaeo-geographical maps of later Holocene date.

However, another regional-sea-level curve (but not palaeogeographical maps), produced nearly 30 years ago, shows a somewhat different model. The sea-level is shown reaching OD at *c.* 3800 cal BC and above OD after *c.* 1500 cal BC, followed by several shorter periods of relative sea-level fall and rise, including significantly a post-Roman sea-level rise (Gaunt and Tooley 1974).

FIGURE 12.
The maximum extent of wetland deposits over 3 m depth as surveyed by the Humber Wetlands Project, and the maximum extent of wetlands around 1000 cal BC according to the LOEPS model.

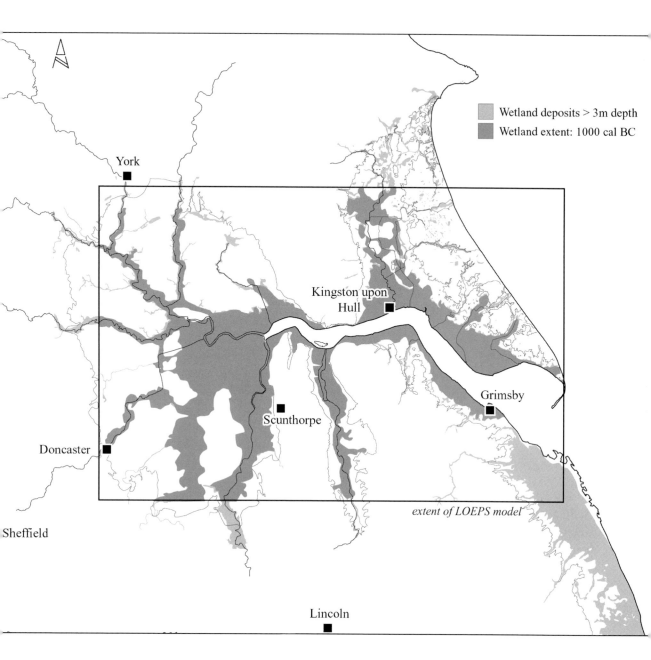

Archaeological research around the North Sea, by the Humber Wetlands Project and others, has similarly identified periods of relative sea-level fall and rise, including phases of sea-level fall in the early Roman period and towards the end of the first millennium AD (Long *et al.* 1998; Rippon 2000). The archaeological record appears to conform to this older model of regional sea-level in the Humber estuary rather than the recent model produced by the LOEPS project (see below and Chapter 7).

The effect of the Holocene sea-level rise on the rivers in the Humber Wetlands was that their gradient between source and confluence with the sea

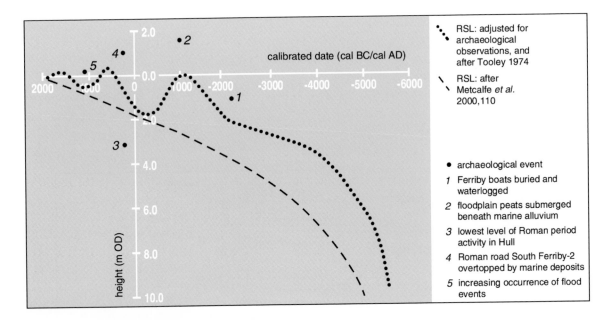

became increasingly gentle, and therefore their run-off became impeded. Whereas the Late-glacial rivers incised into the parent material creating steep-sided river corridors, the impeded run-off resulted in the deposition of material, or aggradation, within the river channels. The onset of this channel aggradation within the Humber Wetlands was variable but, as discussed earlier, the Project's work suggests that it commenced at c. 10,000 cal BC. The material deposited initially within the river channels was relatively coarse, but continued sea-level rise resulted in the deposition of increasingly fine deposits.

Over time, the sea-level rise continued to impede the run-off of the rivers further, and this resulted in regular floods in the areas outside the river channels, mainly the wider river floodplains. This phase, known as the floodplain aggradation phase, has been dated for a number of rivers by the Humber Wetlands Project. Heike Neumann's work in the Ancholme flood-plain indicates that peats developed here from around 5000 cal BC (Neumann 1998). Malcolm Lillie and Benjamin Gearey's work in the Hull floodplain suggests a date from c. 4200 cal BC and in the floodplain of the River Ouse from c. 4000 cal BC (Lillie and Gearey 1999; 2000). Throughout the region, floodplain aggradation was found to occur earlier in the lower reaches of each river than the upper reaches. Where floods occurred, sediments were laid down creating extensive tracts of level surfaces. The drainage of both rain- and floodwater on these levels was slow, and water-tolerant plant species colonised the areas, thus creating the more extensive floodplain wetlands, including carrs and fens.

The palaeogeographic maps produced as part of the LOEPS programme show extensive areas of 'eutrophic' wetlands (e.g. riparian or floodplain wetland such as carr and fen) in the lower parts of the Humberhead Levels around 6000 cal BC (Metcalfe et al. 2000). However, such a postulated early and

FIGURE 13. An age-altitude model of relative sea-level change in the Humber, showing the relative sea level (RSL) according to the LOEPS study. The dotted line reflects an alternative model based on archaeological evidence from the Humber wetlands and after Gaunt and Tooley (1974).

extensive development of the wetlands in the Humberhead Levels is erroneous. The earliest peat development outside the river channels in the area has been dated to *c.* 3300 cal BC (i.e. Dirtness Levels DL961B, Metcalfe *et al.* 2000; see also: Buckland and Dinnin 1997). New palaeogeographic maps, incorporating the results from the Humber Wetlands Project, are presented here as Plate 1.

Wetland development after c. 5000 cal BC

The fourth key factor that contributed to the landscape history in the Humber Wetlands was the development of the riparian, or riverside wetlands after *c.* 5000 cal BC. The Humber Wetlands Project set out to develop a greater understanding of the temporal and spatial aspects of the development of wetland in the river floodplains. The reasons for this emphasis were that this was a poorly studied and understood subject and because this wetland development is closely related to the preservation potential of archaeological and palaeoenvironmental organic remains. The work involved the systematic sampling and radiocarbon dating of basal peats in three river valleys in the lower estuary – the Ancholme valley led by Heike Neumann, the Hull valley run by Malcolm Lillie and the Keyingham Drain in southern Holderness directed by Mark Dinnin (Dinnin and Lillie 1995b; Neumann 1998; Lillie and Gearey 2000). Pollen and occasionally diatom analysis were undertaken on the samples from the basal peats to establish their context.

The natural processes this research revealed have been observed elsewhere, but have not been as closely dated or clearly understood. As described earlier, at some time between *c.* 5000 and 4000 cal BC floodplains aggraded in response to sea-level rise. As pollen analysis of the basal peat deposits shows, the environment established on the floodplain was alder-dominated carrland with sedge fen and oak and hazel. These carrlands would have been fringed, on the riverside, by reedswamps (Metcalfe *et al.* 2000). Over time, these alder carrs gained height, as the dead organic material did not decompose in the waterlogged soils, forming mires (i.e. peat producing ecosystems). Simultaneously, these alder carrs impeded the run-off of rainwater from the floodplain slopes and the areas beyond the limits of the floodplain, causing progressive waterlogging, or paludification. This contributed to the spread of the alder carr wetlands.

We have already seen that the onset of carr development was time-transgressive, responding to the general transgressive nature of sea-level change, with downstream areas generally affected earlier than upstream areas. However, the process by which the alder carr subsequently spread is mainly autogenic in character, meaning here that it occurred without the pressure of sea-level change. Most floodplains did not appear to develop beyond alder-dominated carrs. We assume that regular floods, introducing nutrients onto the carrs, prevented these from changing to nutrient-poor mires (cf. Waller 1994). Furthermore, many of the carrs were overtopped by tidal floods sometime during the first millennium BC, resulting in the deposition of clays and silts that changed the character of the riverside wetlands completely.

The fieldwork in the Ancholme valley was aimed at providing insight into the time-transgressive nature of wetland development across and along the valley floor. The work was principally undertaken by Heike Neumann and full details of this fieldwork were published by her (Neumann 1988). In all, 80 boreholes were set in seven transects. On the basis of the valley-wide study, a further 21 boreholes were set, which provided peat for radiocarbon dating and pollen analysis. All samples were peat samples from the interface between pre-Holocene geology and sands and basal peat. This second set of boreholes provided dated information on wetland development from three transects – Redbourne in the upper Ancholme valley, Brigg in the centre of the valley and South Ferriby close to the confluence of the River Ancholme with the Humber estuary.

A similar approach was developed in the Hull valley. Initial coring, under-taken by Malcolm Lillie, involved 212 boreholes set in 13 transects (Lillie and Gearey 2000), with two transects, one at Arram Grange, the other on Stone Carr near Wawne, subsequently sampled for radiocarbon dating of compac-tion-free basal peats. The second of these transects was adjacent to the excavations of a Mesolithic and Neolithic flint production site on a small peninsula on the east bank of the River Hull (Weel–2; Chapman *et al.* 2000).

The results of this study of wetland development is shown in Figure 14. This graph shows the calibrated date ranges of the radiocarbon date samples against the height of the sample in metres OD. The data provide a surprisingly consistent trend in the development of wetlands in these part of the Humber Wetlands. By *c.* 4000 cal BC, riparian wetlands existed at a height of around

FIGURE 14.
An age-altitude model of the growth of floodplain peats in the Hull and Ancholme valley as established by the Humber Wetlands Project, shown in relation to the relative sea-level (RSL) according to the LOEPS study.

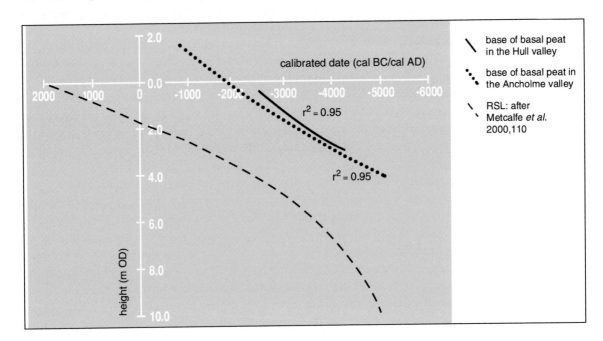

calibrated date (cal BC/cal AD)

$r^2 = 0.95$

$r^2 = 0.95$

height (m OD)

base of basal peat in the Hull valley

base of basal peat in the Ancholme valley

RSL: after Metcalfe *et al.* 2000,110

−3.8 m OD, and around 3000 cal BC these wetlands had expanded up to a height of *c.* −2.0 m OD. By 2000 cal BC, the floodplain wetlands had reached Ordnance Datum, and at 1000 cal BC extended into the lowlands up to a height of *c.* 1.5 m OD. The development of these wetlands was arrested by rapid coastal change as marine alluvium deposits sealed the floodplain peat during the first millennium BC (Long *et al.* 1998).

This consistency of the trend of wetland development in the Humber Wetlands was surprising because the Ancholme valley has been considered a part of the inner estuary and the Hull valley part of the outer estuary (e.g. Metcalfe *et al.* 2000). The effects of sea-level change and the wetland development instigated by sea-level change were thought to be rather different in the outer and inner estuary, but our research has shown that in terms of wetland development, that is not the case. The Humber Wetlands Project did not undertake any such detailed work in the Humberhead Levels and the Vale of York in the western part of the Humber Wetlands, partly out of concern for contamination of samples with 'old carbon' (Bayliss *et al.* 1999). However, basal peat from riparian wetland in the Humberhead Levels has been dated to *c.* 3300 cal BC at −2.9 m OD, and *c.* 1400–1200 cal BC from around OD, corroborating the wetland development trend studied by the Project (Metcalfe *et al.* 2000, Smith 1985).

In the Keyingham Drain, in southern Holderness, the detailed study into the time and space dimensions of wetland development had started in 1995, but the conditions were more complicated than those later encountered in the valleys of the Rivers Ancholme and Hull. The Keyingham Drain was a dry valley formed in the till, but with several meres surviving from the Late-glacial. The Holocene sea-level rise resulted in a marine transgression into the valley of the Keyingham Drain, sometime before 4000 cal BC, leaving a fine silt and clay deposit on the valley floor when the sea regressed. This deposit impeded the run-off of freshwater and an alder carr started to form in the valley. Sixty boreholes were set in six transects by Mark Dinnin and Malcolm Lillie, and ten locations were subsequently sampled for radiocarbon dating of basal peats (Dinnin and Lillie 1995b). Rather than measuring wetland development across the valley floor, the work in the Keyingham Drain was principally focused on the wetland development along the valley. Dated peats from the Keyingham Drain were obtained from Roos Carr and Halsham in the southwest of the Drain, to Sand-Le-Mere, which is now an exposure of peat on the beach of Holderness but in prehistory was the northeastern extent of the Keyingham Drain.

What does this study contribute to our understanding of sea-level change? It shows that wetlands developed and extended *c.* 3.5 to 4.0 m above the contemporary mean sea-level as reconstructed by LOEPS (Metcalfe *et al.* 2000), at or just above the Mean High Water of Spring Tides (MHWST). However, whereas the rate of sea-level rise seems to slow down during the later prehistory, the rate of peat growth in the floodplains appears to speed up. Considering that the base of basal peats have always been used to reconstruct sea-level change, this result is most surprising. Several explanations can be brought forward to explain this. For example, the sea-level curve as reconstructed by LOEPS does not show any regional variations in past sea-level within the Humber estuary, and our results may not relate to the overall picture. Also, the sea-level curve produced by LOEPS reflects very long-term changes, and it may not reflect variations to that long-term trend.

Nevertheless, an alternative explanation must be considered. After initiation, floodplain wetland development may have been, at least in part, unconnected to sea-level change. The wetlands in the Ancholme and Hull valleys 'grew' upwards at a rate of 1.5 mm/year, or 1.5 m per millennium, resulting in their lateral advance up the valley slopes. As argued earlier, the main cause of this growth was the accumulation of dead organic remains that did not decompose in the waterlogged conditions. Therefore, in periods of relative sea-level fall, there was no 'wetland regression' (or the seaward moving of the intertidal zone), although upper peats may have become drier as run-off increased. This process was seen in the Keyingham Drain where pollen analysis showed that alder gave way to bracken during dryer periods (e.g. Taylor 1995). The impediment to the run-off of freshwater from the lands caused the wetlands to 'transgress' onto the drylands. During periods of sea-level rise, the character of the lowest parts of the wetlands changed to saltmarsh, as has been noted in the Ancholme valley (Neumann 1998). Only in periods of rapid relative sea-level rise were the riparian wetlands overtopped, a process that has been observed for all sampling points in the Ancholme, Hull and Keyingham Drain valleys for the first millennium BC. Independent research in the Walling Fen area in the southern Vale of York suggests that such a major phase of marine transgression is dated to after 810–530 cal BC (Halkon and Millett 1999; see Chapter 7). The acceleration of the wetland growth may be the result of a climate with increasing wetness, or increased runoff following the widespread clearing of the indigenous woodlands by people.

What does this trend of wetland development mean in terms of landscape history? Around the sub- and inter-tidal margins of the North Sea, the Humber estuary and the lower reaches of the rivers, extensive wetlands developed consisting of marine or brackish saltmarsh and reedswamps near the waters. Alder carrs with sedge fen and stands of oak and hazel fringed the wetlands on the landward side. In the narrower valleys, for example that of the River Derwent, the extent of these wetland from the river to the dryland was seldom more than 500 m wide, but in most other areas, notably the floodplains of the Rivers Ancholme and Hull, the wetlands extended for 5000 m or more. The most extensive examples developed in the Humberhead Levels, where the floodplains of the lower reaches of the Rivers Aire, Ouse, Went, Don, Torne, Idle and Trent merged into a wetland area of some 200 km^2 or more after 3000 cal BC (cf. Metcalfe *et al.* 2000). With the overtopping and burial of these wetlands in the first millennium BC, these peatlands were replaced by minerogenic wetlands.

Apart from 'eutrophic' wetlands in river floodplains, a number of ombrotrophic (rainwater-fed) wetlands developed in the Humber basin. The two largest ombrotrophic or raised mires in the Humber Wetlands are Thorne and Hatfield Moors, with smaller communities of *Sphagnum* mosses found elsewhere (e.g. in Askham Bog in the Vale of York; Gearey and Lillie 1999). Thorne Moors originated, at least in part, as an eutrophic wetland on the Ouse floodplain. Given the gently undulating nature of the bed of the silted-up Lake Humber beneath Thorne Moors, paludification would have been localised, with the developing areas of peat subsequently combining to ever larger areas of peatland (e.g. Buckland 1979, Smith 1985, Buckland and Dinnin 1997). On Thorne Moors it is possible that this process followed the development of a series of smaller mires, dated from *c.* 3200 cal BC. The time-transgressive nature of peat development suggests that a mosaic of wetlands – including carr woodland, deciduous forest containing oak and pine trees with heathland vegetation – may have grown on the area that is now Thorne Moors. The rise in water levels effectively drowned the forest on Thorne Moors (Dinnin 1997d), and these woodlands were preserved in the peat. Hatfield Moors, on the other hand, may have its origin as an rainwater-fed wetland, developing over a woodland dominated by birch and alder. The onset of mire development at Hatfield appears to be somewhat later than at Thorne, with radiocarbon dates from the base of the peat clustering around *c.* 2700 cal BC (Smith 1985, cf. Dinnin 1997d).

Climate change

Climate change is the fifth key factor in the natural history of the Humber Wetlands. The climatic amelioration of the Late-glacial and early Holocene is relatively well understood, with evidence from the deep meres from Holderness especially in the form of insect and plant fossils indicating rapid temperature oscillations of up to 5°C in the Late-glacial (Walker *et al.* 1993). The onset of the Holocene is marked by an initially rapid and prolonged climate amelioration, with temperatures rising allowing the reforestation of the Humber Wetlands.

Research into climatic changes in the Humber Wetlands has been undertaken on Thorne and Hatfield Moors, where the onset of the mires (from *c.* 3200 to 2700 cal BC) and 'recurrence surfaces' are interpreted as periods of increased rainfall. Recurrence surfaces are boundaries between layers in ombrotrophic mires marking degrees of plant humification. These are interpreted as transitions from a relative dry mire surface to wetter conditions. Recent research on the River Ouse has identified close temporal correlation between the recurrence surface on Thorne and Hatfield Moors and the character and rate of sediment deposition in the River Ouse (Macklin *et al.* 2000). This provides collaborative support for the interpretation of the recurrence surface at Thorne and Hatfield Moors as indicators of climate, which could otherwise be simply interpreted as local climatic variations and 'bog bursts'. Recurrence surfaces occur in the Humberhead Levels' mires around 1260–820 cal BC,

820–400 cal BC, cal AD 640–980 and cal AD 1250–1410 (Smith 1985, cf. Macklin *et al.* 2000). These dates, whilst imprecise as a result of the method of dating, indicate a wet climate during the later Bronze Age and early Iron Age, a dryer period in the later Iron Age and through the Roman period, and periods of wetness in the early Middle Ages and in the thirteenth and fourteenth centuries.

The research on the River Ouse also found a wetter period in around cal AD 1400–1450, which correlates with recurrence surfaces in the North York Moors (Chiverell 1988). This coincides with the beginning of the so-called 'Little Ice Age' (Macklin *et al.* 2000). It also broadly correlates with historical data, for example from the Hull valley and Holderness, and with historical sources such as the Meaux Chronicle which records widespread flooding and loss of recently reclaimed land from the later thirteenth to the mid-fifteenth century AD (Parry 1978; Lamb 1982; 1988).

Vegetation change

The sixth key factor in the natural history in the Humber wetlands is vegetation change. This was closely associated with climatic change. After the retreat of the icesheet, the Humber Wetlands were a *tabula rasa* in vegetation terms, an area with few if any trees. Previous research into the vegetation history in the Humber Wetlands has been conducted in particular on mere-deposits from Holderness, including The Bog at Roos (Beckett 1975; 1981), at Brandesburton (Clark and Godwin 1956), and at Gransmoor (Walker *et al.* 1993; 1994). The changing vegetation is described in pollen zones (PZ), as outlined by Godwin (1940), but extensively updated with information from subsequent regional studies.

The vegetation sequence starts in the Late-glacial. In PZI (*c.* 13,600–12,000 cal BC), few trees could survive the cold climate, other than downy birch (*Betula pubescens*) and shrubs including dwarf birch (*Betula nana*), and willow (*Salix*). Seabuckthorn (*Hippophae rhamnoides*) and rockrose (*Helianthemun* spp.) have also been found in the pollen record. The detailed research in Holderness has shown some variability during the pollen zone, and between the different sites, but the overall impression is that of an open landscape with few trees. PZII (*c.* 12,000–11,000 cal BC) coincides with the Windemere or Allerød interstadial, a warmer period during which birch woodland expanded. PZIII (11,000–10,000 cal BC) represents a colder stage, the Loch Lomond or Younger Dryas stadial. The climatic deterioration and return to periglacial conditions saw the contraction of the birch woodland to sheltered areas. The Humber Wetlands during this period have been described as a tundra, with grasses and sedges the most common vegetation cover.

The Holocene commences with PZIV (*c.* 10,000–8900 cal BC). This date is obtained from various locations, including The Bog at Roos and Gransmoor, and both palynology and entymology show a rapid amelioration of the climate (Lowe *et al.* 1995). Again, regional variability appears to be considerable, but in general, the onset of PZIV is characterised initially by the expansion of birch from its refugia, the sheltered areas where it survived during the cold stages. Willow and pine (*Pinus*) also appear in the palynological record, forming a relatively dense woodland and a shade-tolerant understorey flora. During PZV (*c.* 8900 to 8250 cal BC), trees that did not survive the Late-glacial in northern England appear from their southern refugia, including hazel (*Corylus*), sweetgale (*Myrica*), elm (*Ulmus*) and oak (*Quercus*). The birch woodland of the previous pollen zone is replaced by pine-dominated woodlands on the lighter soils in the Humberhead Levels, the Vale of York and the Ancholme valley, while hazel and elm are prevalent on the heavier clay soils of Holderness and the Lincolnshire Marsh. In PZVI (*c.* 8250 to 5300 cal BC), the occurrence of alder (*Alnus*) increases, no doubt a consequence of the development of wetland landscapes in the Humber basin induced by the sea-level rise (see above). Hazel, elm and oak are the most prevalent tree-species outside the wetlands, and lime (*Tilia cordata*) appears to be the dominant tree on free-draining soils, such as the glaciofluvial and gravel outcrops.

PZVIIa (*c.* 5300–4000 cal BC) is marked by a rise in alder. This has been interpreted in previous research as indicating a wetter climate, the Atlantic epoch (e.g. Bennett 1984, Chambers and Elliot 1989), but in the Humber Wetlands, the alder rise is closely associated with the expansion of eutrophic wetlands throughout the Humber basin. The onset of non-eutrophic wetland development, including Thorne and Hatfield Moors that were dependent on a wetter climate, has been dated to the next pollen zone, *c.* 3200 cal BC (Buckland and Dinnin 1997). The ultimate dominance of alder in the eutrophic wetlands and the reductions in the pollen counts of willow, hazel, pine, elm and oak have been attributed to a complex of factors, including the non-invadable alder woodland canopy, soil development and drainage (Brown 1988, Gearey and Lillie 1999). The woodland in this pollen zone beyond the limits of the wetlands was predominantly an undisturbed mixed oak woodland, with a limited herbaceous component (Clark and Godwin 1956).

The start of PZVIIb (*c.* 4000 to 800 cal BC) is marked by the 'Elm Decline', an eco-cultural horizon in the pollen diagrams associated with the Neolithic. Although the decline of elm is no longer thought to be directly linked to extensive forest clearances by early farmers, this Europe-wide phenomenon is likely to be associated to changes in the subsistence strategies adopted in the Neolithic period. Although elm declined, oak, hazel and lime remained the dominant tree species, whilst pine dominated sandy and dry sites. During this pollen zone, the woodland was gradually fragmented by farmers (see Chapter 3). The dating evidence for woodland clearances varies from region to region. For example, the earliest evidence for small-scale forest clearance and agricultural activity is dated for Holderness to 4030–3783 cal BC (Beckett 1981), but for the Ancholme valley to 2580–2330 cal BC (Neumann 1998).

The beginning of PZVIII (*c.* 800 cal BC to the present) is marked by the decline in lime, indicating the widespread impact of people on the woodland landscapes. Although this broadly coincides with the transition of bronze to iron as the principal metal, providing more effective tools for tree-felling (cf. Turner 1962), the expansion of other tree species including beech (*Fagus*) in southern England suggests that this technological development was in comparison a minor factor. By the Roman period, the woodland had been largely cleared, and farming and pastoralism determined the vegetation throughout the region. Woodland regenerated in the Humber Wetlands after the Roman period, with oak, alder, ash (*Fraxinus excelsior*) and hazel the most common trees. Pollen analysis at Scaftworth in the River Idle identified woodland regeneration in an area of extensive agricultural activity in the Roman period (Van de Noort *et al.* 1997b; see Chapter 7). Woodland declined in the Norman period, representing the final stage in the area's vegetation history.

Recent research by Spikins (2000) has created GIS models of the vegetation history of northern England, including the Humber Wetlands, from *c.* 10,000 to 3500 cal BC. Although at a relatively low resolution, the models illustrate the dynamics of Holocene vegetation change, including the space- and time-transgressive nature of vegetation change during the early part of the Holocene.

The Humber Wetlands Project's contribution to our understanding of vegetation history in the Humber Wetlands includes detailed studies at Askham Bog in the Vale of York and at Routh Quarry in the Hull valley and also elsewhere in the regions. The work at Askham Bog involved biostratigraphic, lithostratigraphic and chrononstratigraphic analysis, undertaken by Benjamin Gearey, Malcolm Lillie and Alex Bayliss. Considerable detail was added to the vegetation history of this part of the Humber Wetlands, showing a mixed woodland with hazel, oak, elm, birch and pine, with a rise of alder after *c.* 6000 cal BC. Lime was found to be a significant element in lowland woodlands after *c.* 5700 cal BC, and the elm decline was dated to *c.* 3800 cal BC. No biostratigraphic evidence of any human activity in this region was found before the elm decline, and this is supported by a dearth of archaeological finds of this date in the area. The pollen relating to the elm decline and subsequent period show a reduction in most tree taxa. Evidence from the upper layers at Askham Bog indicates two phases of woodland regeneration and two of woodland clearance (Gearey and Lillie 1999). Unfortunately, the upper part of this deep palaeoenvironmental resource was disturbed, partly the result of peat cutting that may have started in the Roman period, partly of desiccation of the upper peat horizons and also root activity. The dating of these phases await further research (Bayliss *et al.* 1999).

The work at Routh Quarry was made possible through close co-operation with the Humber Archaeology Partnership. The detailed analysis of the sediments shows a near-complete sequence from *c.* 13,000 BP to some time in the Bronze Age, with a date of 1920–1630 cal BC available at 0.55 m depth (Lillie and Gearey 2000). Whilst the vegetational change in the Late-glacial and early Holocene resembles that from Gransmoor (Walker *et al.* 1993), the analysis from Routh shows in more detail the actual process of deforestation. It has confirmed the likely existence of natural clearances in the region from *c.* 5500 cal BC, which would have attracted game that kept the clearings open through grazing (cf. Buckland and Edwards 1979). Around 2500 cal BC, extensive parts of the woodland on the Holderness Plain had been cleared as part of the development of pastoral agriculture. By the onset of the Bronze Age, the representation of all trees and shrubs in the regional pollen record has all but disappeared and this suggests an increasing pressure on the land resource and the clearance of the more marginal parts of the landscape, such as wetlands (Lillie and Gearey 2000). Although this near-total deforestation is a time-transgressive phenomenon on the Holderness Plain, it illustrates increasing population densities and competition for land.

Human-environment interaction

The seventh and final key factor in the natural history of the Humber Wetlands is human activity. This includes a wide range of intentional and sometimes unintentional changes to the landscape. Examples include the use of fire to clear woodland, forest clearance, erosion caused by changes in agriculture and drainage, and reclamations. This interaction between people and the environment is a central theme in the following chapters.

CHAPTER THREE

Prehistoric Wetland Exploitation

....

Wetland habitats, generally speaking, are ecosystems with a high biological productivity. They are therefore considered well suited for providing food and other resources. However, this productivity varies greatly between the different types of wetland and not all resources were exploitable by people in the past. This chapter explores this theme, and includes a discussion of the main methods by which resources were exploited in prehistory – hunting and gathering, fishing, and the use of the wetlands for farming.

The resource potential of wetland habitats

After *c.* 2700 cal BC, the different types of wetlands in the Humber lowlands included the raised mires of Thorne and Hatfield Moors, reedswamps, alder carrs, sedge fens and fenwood on the river floodplains and valleys, and mudflats, saltmarshes and intertidal creek systems in the Humber estuary and along the Lincolnshire Coast. Whilst each landscape developed in response to a wide range of environmental factors, the diversity of wetlands was principally determined by the amount and quality of the water available to the plant communities (Dinnin and Van de Noort 1999; see also Chapter 2).

Where land is saturated by rainwater (i.e. ombrotrophic conditions), the resulting ecosystem in the British Isles will normally be an acidic, nutrient poor (or oligotrophic) blanket bog or raised mire. Blanket bogs and raised mires have a low primary productivity – that is, the amount of biomass generated by an ecosystem. They usually have also a low biodiversity, as only a limited number of specialised plants can tolerate the high water table, acidity and low nutrient availability. For example, *Sphagnum* mosses tend to dominate living raised mires. Where the water source includes groundwater and flood-water, the nutrients brought into the wetlands by the water create ecosystems with higher primary productivity and biodiversity. Alder carrs, sedge fens and reedswamps are examples of such 'eutrophic' or mineral rich (or minerothro-phic) wetland ecosystems. The higher primary productivity enables the development of more complex, secondary producer communities, such as fish and waterfowl that feed on the primary producers, and thus contributes to a greater biodiversity.

Ecosystems that are regularly inundated by floodwaters from streams and rivers have an even higher primary productivity and greater biodiversity. The combination of the regular supply of nutrient with the floodwater and periods of soil aeration, when water is confined to the river and stream channels, results in particularly fertile areas. The nutrient supply in rivers and streams increases downstream, which is mirrored by the increased productivity of primary and secondary producers. This is one of the reasons why estuaries are among the most productive ecosystems on earth. The very high primary productivity of estuaries is mirrored by secondary productivity (analids, molluscs, crabs, shrimps and fish) and by higher order animals, such as the large number of wildfowl that can be seen every winter in the Humber estuary.

The quantity and quality of the resources in a wetland ecosystem available to people is closely linked to its biological productivity, although human ingenuity in the past, as well as in the present, has enabled beneficial modification of these ecosystems. The exploitation of wetlands – the most common research theme in wetland archaeology in Europe and further afield – includes the hunting of a wide range of mammals and birds, gathering of plants, nuts, fruits and herbs, and fishing (e.g. Coles and Coles 1989; Louwe Kooijmans 1993). The importance of coastal exploitation is recognised in all instances where the prehistoric coastline survives, but has been progressed furthest in the regions where isostatic uplift has outpaced sea-level rise, especially in Scandinavia, enabling large-scale and systematic survey and excavation (Fischer and Myrhøj 1995; Coles 1998).

Hunting, fishing and gathering in the Mesolithic period, *c.*10,000–4000 cal BC

The earliest activity of the hunter-gatherers after the retreat of the Devensian ice in the Humber Wetlands is represented by barbed points of bone and antler from several locations in Holderness, including Brandesburton, Hornsea, Skipsea and Gransmoor (Armstrong 1922; 1923; Clark and Godwin 1956; Sheldrick *et al.* 1997). These finds are commonly referred to as 'harpoons', or arrow tips for fishing, but the barbed points may also have been used in pairs as pronged spearheads (Mellars and Dark 1998). Few barbed points have been dated, but the most recent find, from Gransmoor, provides the oldest date, at *c.* 11,400 cal BC (cf. Sheldrick *et al.* 1997).

During the Humber Wetlands Project, we found only one site with organic remains of early Mesolithic date, at Round Hill on the border of the parishes of Skipsea and Barmston in Holderness (Skipsea–25; Head *et al.* 1995a). The landscape here is dominated by an elongated depression forming part of the now-drained Bail Mere, and the site includes both a small circular till outcrop and part of the former mere. This site produced a flint assemblage of Mesolithic and Early Neolithic date and what appeared to be an unsharpened alder stake dated to 8350–7940 cal BC. This site may have been the same as the one discovered by Thomas Boynton in the 1880s, and which he described as one of the so-called 'lake settlements' of Holderness (Smith 1911; see Chapter 4). The significance of this alder stake fragment is unclear, but if Boynton's

FIGURE 15.
Detail of the Bronze Age fish-trap on the Humber foreshore near New Holland, Lincolnshire Marsh, in 1999.

© THE HUMBER WETLANDS PROJECT, UNIVERSITY OF HULL

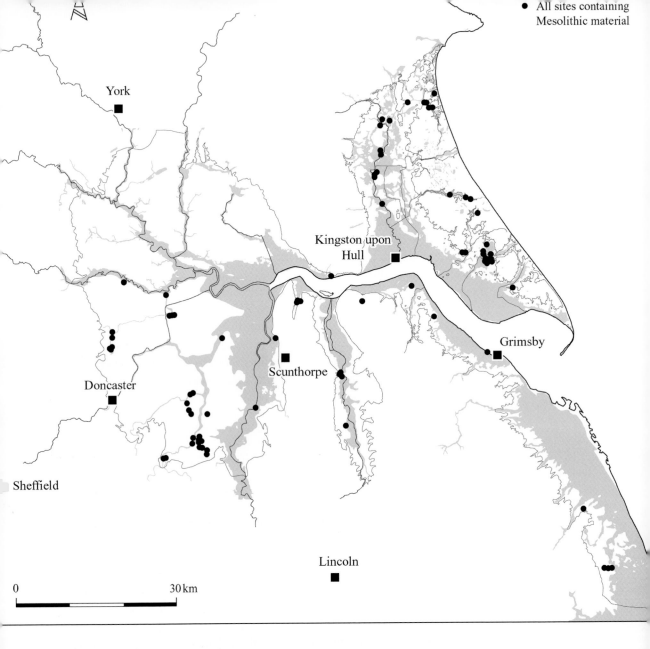

FIGURE 16.
Map of the Humber
Wetlands, showing all
sites containing
Mesolithic material.

observations of the site during the drainage works he oversaw are correct, than it may have formed an element of a platform that extended into the water.

Elsewhere, the Mesolithic period in the Humber Wetlands is mainly represented by scatters of knapped flint. During the six years of the survey, 80 flint scatters containing Mesolithic flint were identified (Figure 16). Invariably, these scatters were found near water bodies, including the larger meres of Holderness and alongside the rivers. One such flint scatter was collected from a pronounced slope on the northern edge of Lambwath Mere in Holderness (Aldbrough–11; Head *et al.* 1995a). Lambwath Mere no longer exists as a waterbody, but in the Mesolithic it was a large elongated lake probably connected to the River Hull (Dinnin and Lillie 1995a). The 182 pieces of worked flint, including

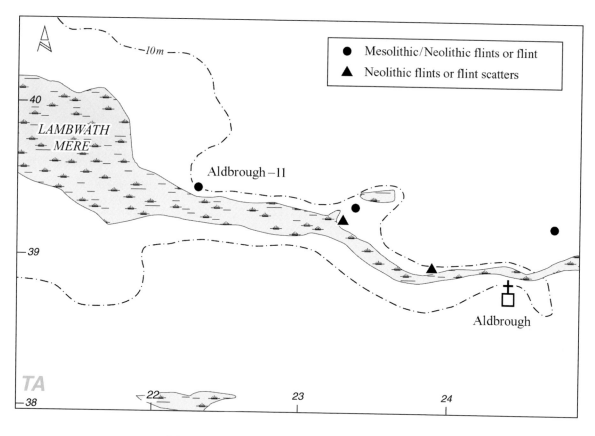

FIGURE 17.
The context of the
Mesolithic flint scatter
Aldbrough-11 (after
Head *et al.* 1995a: 169).

147 flakes, 22 chunks, seven cores, five bladelets and one scraper, represent a flint production site rather than a settlement (Figure 17). This assemblage typifies a large number of flint scatters identified during the survey of the Humber Wetlands. The location of the site and its close proximity to a contemporary lake is also typical of many other such sites and this example would have offered extensive views over Lambath Mere. It would have been well suited for spotting larger mammals that came to the water to drink.

The rivers in the Humberhead Levels were shown to have been of particular significance in the Mesolithic period. Sixteen scatters, including three sites dated to the early Mesolithic, plus an additional sixteen flint scatters dated to the Late Mesolithic and Early Neolithic were recovered during field walking from the banks of the former Rivers Idle, Torne, Don and Went. One such site, on Misterton Carr adjacent to the former River Idle, included 652 pieces of worked flint, comprising two microliths, two arrowheads, five scrapers, two bladelets, twelve cores, 594 flakes and 35 chunks (Figure 18; Gringley-6; Head *et al.* 1997b). The large number of flakes indicate that flint was knapped and worked here, but the relatively large number of finished tools implies that this was also a base- or transition camp from where the River Idle and its environment could be exploited for fish, fowl and mammals.

The importance of wetlands to the prehistoric hunter-gatherer is also illustrated in the case of the valley of the Keyingham Drain, the elongated glacial

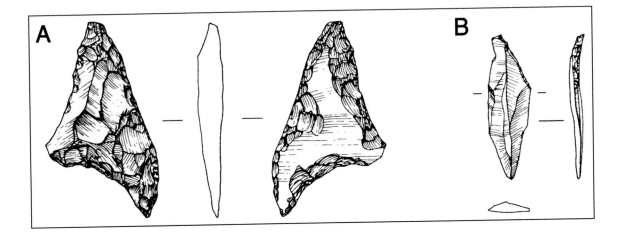

and glaciofluvial valley or depression in southern Holderness (see Chapter 2). The archaeological survey of this area was closely integrated with palaeoenvironmental work, which incorporated a radiocarbon-dated sequence of wetland development. The palaeoenvironmental survey demonstrated that the Keyingham Drain was transformed from an undulated dry valley, with possibly some small isolated meres, into a saltmarsh with creeks and brackish lagoons sometime before c. 4000 cal BC, during the later phase of the Mesolithic (Dinnin and Lillie 1995b). This transformation was caused by sea-level rise and marine transgression. Field-walking in this mapview identified 101 finds and find concentrations that included knapped flint, the highest density of finds recovery anywhere in the Humber Wetlands (Figure 19; Halsham mapview; Head *et al.* 1995b). Three finds or find concentrations were dated to the Mesolithic only, seven were dated to the Late Mesolithic or included later material with the Mesolithic flint, and an additional nine concentrations included Neolithic material (Figure 20). The remaining finds could not be dated to a specific archaeological period, but are mostly of prehistoric date. The number of flints dated to the period after the transformation of the landscape reinforces the sense that wetlands provided the focus for hunter-gatherers' activities.

During the Early Mesolithic (c. 10,000–6000 cal BC), it appears that the wetlands in the Humber basin and elsewhere were exploited to a greater extent than the uplands. Archaeological material exists here, for example at the Sheffield's Hill site north of Scunthorpe on the Lincoln Edge (Loughlin and Miller 1979), but is generally not as common as in the lowlands. Further afield, more sites of this date have been identified, for example the North York Moors (Schadla-Hall 1988). Archaeological evidence from Star Carr and Seamer Carr in the Vale of Pickering, from Holderness and the Humberhead Levels, shows a particular close correlation between waterbodies and human activity. The main reason for this correlation was the chosen hunting strategy, with hunters awaiting large mammals to come to the water to drink (Mellars and Dark 1998). Such a strategy was not possible on the higher grounds surrounding the Humber Wetlands. Grahame Clark's (1954, 1972) hypothesis

FIGURE 18.
A collection of Mesolithic flint from Gringley–6 in the Humberhead levels.
A: arrowhead;
B: microlith (scale 1:1)
(Head 1997b, 307).

FIGURE 19 (*opposite*). The context of Mesolithic, Neolithic and Bronze Age finds in the Keyingham Drain area (after: Head *et al.* 1995b, 251).

38

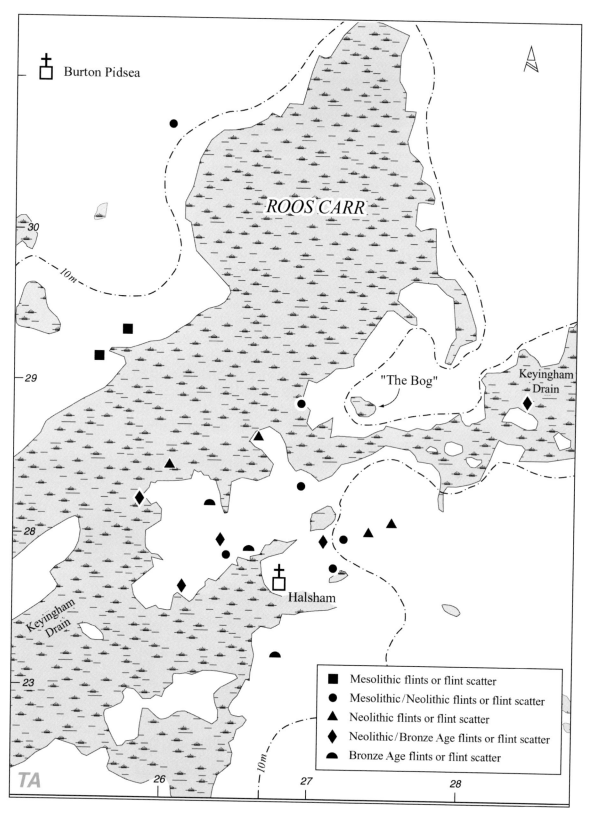

Burton Pidsea

ROOS CARR

"The Bog"

Keyingham Drain

Keyingham Drain

Halsham

TA

■ Mesolithic flints or flint scatter
● Mesolithic/Neolithic flints or flint scatter
▲ Neolithic flints or flint scatter
◆ Neolithic/Bronze Age flints or flint scatter
◗ Bronze Age flints or flint scatter

that Star Carr was a camp occupied during the winter and early spring, and complemented hunting on the North York Moors in the summer, is no longer tenable. Human activity at Star Carr is now considered to have been concentrated in the spring and summer. If seasonal movement did take place, the coastal zone of the North Sea was a more likely destination for the hunters in the autumn and winter than the North York Moors or other higher grounds (cf. Legge and Rowley-Conwy 1988; Coles 1998). We may assume that the hunter-gatherers who left their flint debitage in the Humber Wetlands followed similar patterns of seasonal movement.

During the Late Mesolithic (*c.* 6000–4000 cal BC), flint scatters in the Humber Wetlands remained closely associated to the rivers and larger waterbodies, indicating that the activities in the lowlands changed little from those of the preceding millennia. However, the archaeological evidence from the higher grounds within the Humber Wetlands, most notably the Isle of Axholme and the surrounding regions, suggest much greater levels of activity here (e.g. Loughlin and Miller 1979). Rising sea-levels, expanding woodlands and an increase in population density have all been invoked as reasons for reduced group territories, and in turn for reduced mobility and seasonality of behaviour, combined with an increase in the range of food resources exploited (e.g. Jacobi 1978). The new mobility patterns, like those of Early Mesolithic date, apparently followed river courses. It is tempting to link the Late Mesolithic activity of the Isle of Axholme with the extensive flint scatters in the Idle floodplain at Misterton, those on the Yorkshire Wolds with the Hull valley and Holderness, those on the Lincolnshire Wolds with the flint scatters in the Ancholme valley and the Lincolnshire Marsh, *et cetera*. Such tenuous links suggest seasonal movements between the wetlands and surrounding higher grounds and possibly an emerging sense of territoriality.

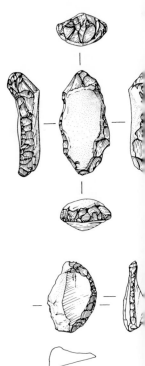

FIGURE 20.
Late Neolithic or early Bronze Age flint from Halsham–19, in Holderness.
A: fabricator;
B: scraper (scale 1:1)
(Head *et al.* 1995b, 254).

Hunting, fishing and gathering in the Neolithic and early Bronze Age period, *c.* 4000–1500 cal BC

Alongside assemblages of flint debitage and the occasional tools of Mesolithic date, we regularly found Neolithic and Bronze Age material. In the Keyingham Fleet area, for example, two finds and find concentrations were dated to the Mesolithic, Neolithic and Bronze Age (Halsham–22 and –45; Head *et al.* 1995). In the Humberhead Levels, flint concentrations dated to these periods were found near the Rivers Aire (Hensall–2), Went (Moorends–5), Idle (Gringley–4, 5 and 6, although no Neolithic material was present in the latter concentration), Don (Hatfield Woodhouse–6), and alongside the Hampole Beck (Askern–7) (Head *et al.* 1997a and b). In the Vale of York, previous research uncovered flint tools and debitage of Mesolithic, Neolithic and Bronze Age date at the site of Redcliff (Melton–29; Fletcher *et al.* 1999). And on the Lincolnshire Marsh, a multi-period assemblage was found by local amateur archaeologist Paul Greenwood, although the erosive nature of this intertidal site makes it difficult to understand what happened here in the past (Grimsby–2; Fenwick *et al.* 2001b).

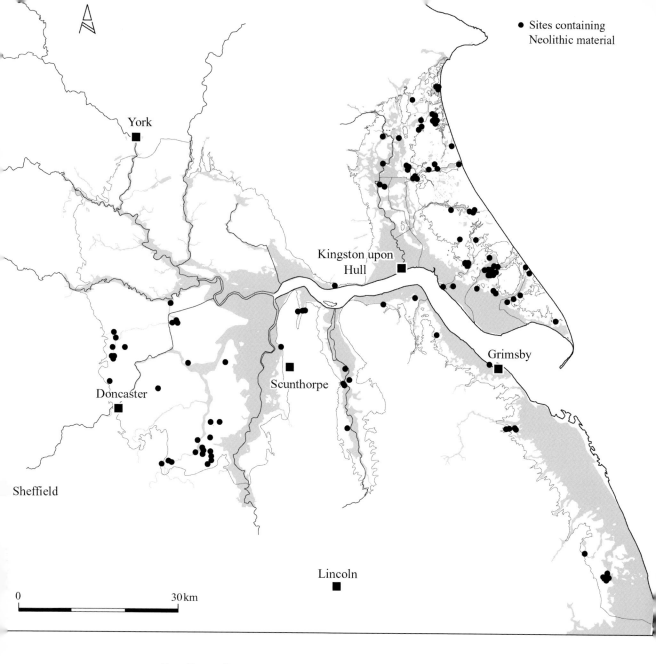

— labels within figure —

● Sites containing
Neolithic material

York

Kingston upon
Hull

Grimsby

Doncaster

Scunthorpe

Sheffield

0   30km

Lincoln

FIGURE 21.
Map of the Humber
Wetlands, showing all
sites containing
Neolithic material.

In all, 38 flint concentrations include material dating to the Mesolithic and Neolithic, and 14 contain material dated to the Mesolithic, Neolithic and Bronze Age (Figures 21, 22). The Vale of York offers a notable exception. Here, we did not find a single find scatter containing Mesolithic artefacts or debitage, although Late Mesolithic material had been recovered previously from Redcliff, where the Yorkshire Wolds and the Humber estuary meet (Melton–29; Fletcher *et al.* 1999). A satisfactory explanation for this exception has not been found, but it is worth mentioning here that flint scatters of Neolithic or Bronze Age date from the Vale of York were also virtually absent.

In a number of cases, the presence of Mesolithic debitage alongside later material may be a coincidence, but it can also be argued that these flint scatters

41

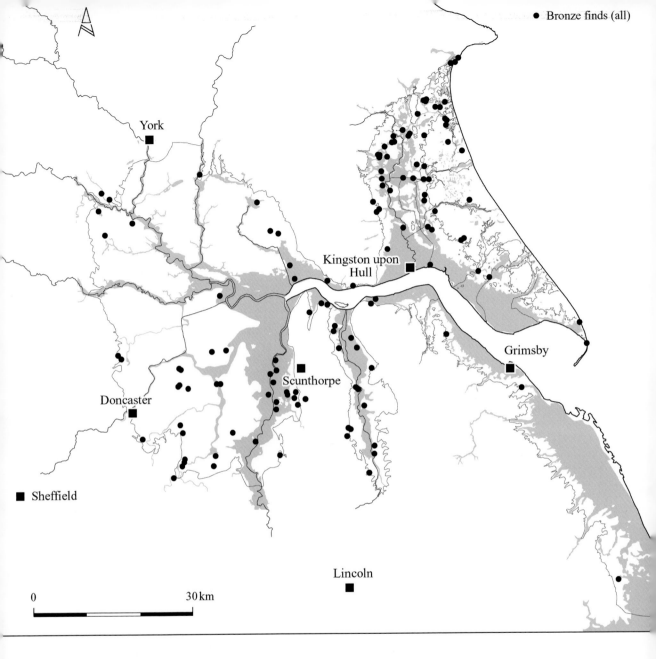

York

Kingston upon Hull

Grimsby

Scunthorpe

Doncaster

Sheffield

0   30km

Lincoln

FIGURE 22.
Map of the Humber Wetlands, showing all bronze finds of Bronze Age date.

represent the use and reuse of certain locales in the landscape over considerable lengths of time. In reviewing this phenomenon, which is widely known, Mark Edmonds has suggested that the flint tool production processes that created the flint scatters took place in temporary camps in clearances in the forests. Clearances within the predominantly closed woodland during the Late Meso-lithic and early part of the Neolithic would have been chosen for the location of the camps, and the knowledge of the location of the clearances provided opportunities and occasions for meeting with kin groups for exchange of information and goods (Edmonds 1999). These clearances attracted game that kept the clearances open through grazing (Buckland and Edwards 1979). The presence of the animals would attract hunters. Preliminary palaeoenvironmental work on such lithic scatter sites as part of the Fenland Management Project confirms the existence of smaller open areas and possibly of small-scale clearance by people within wooded catchments (Murphy in Crowson *et al.* 2000). The occurrence of Mesolithic, Neolithic and Early Bronze Age flints within many of these assemblages implies the use of these clearances for as long as hunting, fishing and gathering were important activities. Pollen analysis at Routh Quarry in the Hull valley, undertaken by Benjamin Gearey as part of the Humber Wetlands Project, has confirmed the likely existence of natural clearances in the region from as early as *c.* 5500 cal BC (Lillie and Gearey 2000).

Flint debitage and tools of Neolithic and Bronze Age date have been found in large quantities throughout the Humber Wetlands (Figure 23). In all, 41 finds and find concentrations were dated to the Neolithic and 38 to the Neolithic and/or Bronze Age. One such site was found some 800 m west of the River Ancholme north of Brigg (Brigg–3). It is one of a series of scatters (Brigg–1, 2, 4 and 5) of mainly Bronze Age material (Chapman *et al.* 1998). During the survey we retrieved here ten scrapers, five cores, 79 flakes and 16 chunks of flint. No other evidence dated to the Bronze Age was collected from here, but nearby seven pieces of Roman pottery were found. The scatter has been described as an 'activity site', suggesting that it represents a relatively short period of human presence, like a transit- or hunting camp, rather than a long-term settlement. That said, the friable nature of Bronze Age pottery, especially within the ploughsoil, may have resulted in the near-complete destruction of pottery and other kinds of material culture that we would associate with settlements.

Although the rivers and other wetlands appear to have continued to form the focus of much activity, flint scatters dated to the later part of the Neolithic and Bronze Age tend to be somewhat further away from the rivers than the Mesolithic and earlier Neolithic sites. The area around Brigg in the Ancholme valley illustrates this, but is by no means exceptional (Figure 24). The find spots dated to the Late Mesolithic and Neolithic (Brigg–7 to 9) were found within 200 m of the edge of the floodplain, but the Bronze Age material found during the survey (Brigg–1 to 5, 11 and 12) was located between 400 and 900 m from the floodplain (Chapman *et al.* 1998). It is tempting to translate the distance between flint scatter and wetland directly into a dependence on the wetlands for subsistence strategies. It would suggest that the importance of or dependence on wetlands was very high in the Mesolithic and early part of the Neolithic, but that it diminished during the later prehistory. This may be a reflection of the adoption of farming activities, if scatters such as Brigg–3 represent settlements rather than camps. Alternatively, the greater distance may reflect the opening up of the woodland and use of clearances away from the river as ideal places for hunting.

An alternative explanation may have to be sought for the focus on rivers – namely, fishing. In the Humber Wetlands, no prehistoric fishtraps had been recorded before the Humber Wetlands Project, but on the Humber foreshore at New Holland on the Lincolnshire Marsh we found a wooden structure

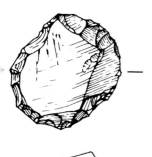

FIGURE 23.
'Anonymous flint':
a single Bronze Age
scraper from the Idle
floodplain
(Scaftworth–3; Head
et al. 1997b, 283).

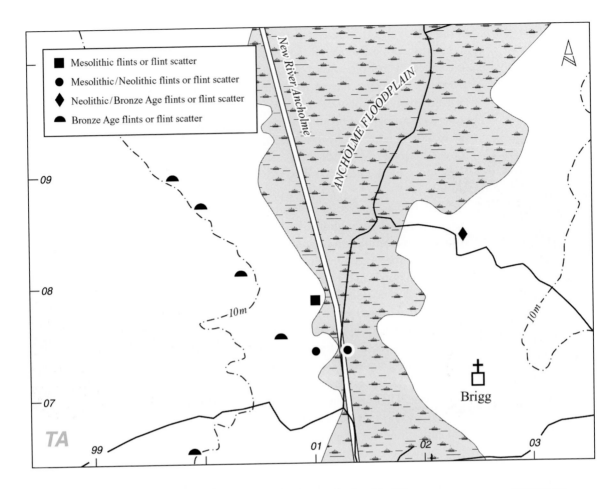

New River Ancholme

ANCHOLME FLOODPLAIN

10 m

10 m

Brigg

TA

FIGURE 24.
The context of Bronze Age and earlier finds in the Ancholme valley near Brigg (after: Chapman *et al.* 1998, 223).

dated to around 1720 cal BC (Barrow–8; Fenwick *et al.* 2001b). The structure was found located in a silted-up gully, and was interpreted as a conical fish-trap (kype or putcher). It was 1.3 m long and was made of coppiced hazel roundwood pieces lying side-by-side and one above the other in a trapezoidal arrangement, held in place by vertical stakes. This structure was found in an extremely vulnerable state of preservation and would probably have disappeared within a matter of weeks. Other traps are likely to have been destroyed by the estuary without having ever been recorded, although some of the many wooden structures dated to the Bronze Age on the Humber foreshore at Melton may have been used for fishing (Melton–5–15, 20–22, 24 and 27; Fletcher *et al.* 1999) (Figure 25). Any fishery in the Humber Wetlands pre-dating the Bronze Age must be sought at great depth, reflecting the rapid sea-level rise in the early Holocene (see Chapter 2). Future research on the Humber between 5 and 10 m OD on a sufficiently large scale may provide a wealth of new data on the early exploitation of the estuary itself.

What to eat?

What did the wetlands offer the prehistoric hunter-gatherers? As no early prehistoric camps or settlements in the Humber Wetlands with good preservation of plant and bone remains have been excavated, we do not have direct information to answer this question. Star Carr in the Vale of Pickering, just outside the Humber Wetlands, remains an early Mesolithic type-site in this respect owing to the excellent preservation of organic remains in the peat of the Late-glacial Lake Pickering. Albeit of earlier date than the vast majority of lithic sites in the Humber Wetlands, Star Carr remains the best source of evidence on Mesolithic subsistence. First excavated in 1952–3, the site is essentially the lake-edge part of a settlement or camp dated to *c.* 9000 cal BC. It contained a timber platform that included wood which had been gnawed by beaver. Artefacts included a wooden paddle suggesting the use of logboats on the lake, flint artefacts and debitage, and many bone and antler harpoon points. The bone remains revealed a dual hunting strategy, aimed at waterfowl and large mammals. A wide range of bird bones are represented, including duck, crane, stork and grebe, but the contribution of fowling in terms of food procurement was of relatively limited importance. The hunting of land mammals accounted for the overwhelming majority of meat eaten at Star Carr – as many as 80 red deer, 30 roe deer, 11 elk, nine aurochs, five pigs and the bones of many other smaller mammals were excavated (Clark 1972). Fish bones were not discovered here, and fish may not have been present in the lake at the time of occupation (Clark 1954; 1972; Legge and Rowley-Conwy 1988). Studies from elsewhere, for example the Dutch Delta, show similar hunting practices that continued into the semi-agrarian Neolithic, with hunting continuing to play an important role in food procurement (Louwe Kooijmans 1993). Here, 75–80 per cent of bones on archaeological sites are from red deer, roe deer, wild boar and beaver, although aurochs and elk were not commonly present. A range of small predators, such as otter, marten, polecat and wildcat represent species principally hunted for their fur. Fowling was common but appears not to have contributed greatly to subsistence.

A recent re-assessment of Star Carr found evidence of repeated burning of the lakeside reedbeds. This has been interpreted as a method by which the hunter-gatherers increased the biological productivity of the lakeside environment, thus attracting more game (Mellars and Dark 1998). It has also been shown that the site excavated in the 1950s was a component of a much larger site and that it was part of a complex of activity sites around Lake Pickering (Shadla-Hall 1988). In the Humber Wetlands, evidence for burning during the Mesolithic was observed in the Humberhead Levels near Westwoodside in an area called, rather confusingly, Star Carr! Here, a large amount of charcoal was found at the bottom of a relatively thin deposit of amorphous peat, found within deposits of blown sand. The base of the peat was tentatively ascribed to the early Holocene, c. 8900 cal BC, on the basis of high counts of herbaceous pollen and low counts of arboreal pollen, with birch most frequent (Dinnin 1997c). Early peat development at such locations is uncommon, and stands outside the framework of wetland development models described in Chapter 2. Its growth may have been caused by the burning episode (cf. Cowell and Innes 1994), but it remains unclear whether Mesolithic people deliberately burned the fen and reedswamp to attract game, or whether the charcoal reflects a natural fire.

Whilst fish may not have been an important resource at Star Carr, it could have become a major food source in the Humber Wetlands around the end of the Mesolithic, with the River Humber becoming estuarine from c. 6000 cal BC (Metcalfe et al. 2000). However, relative sea-level rise, coastal erosion of Holderness and the accreting nature of the Lincolnshire coast which has buried the prehistoric coastline, have all contributed to this important aspect of our past being all but lost. The prehistoric fishtrap from near New Holland in the Lincolnshire Marsh remains to date the only clear example of prehistoric fishing in the Humber Wetlands, but without any fish bones from this or other sites, it is unclear what exactly was eaten. Some clarity may be obtained from research elsewhere. For example, in the Severn estuary Late Mesolithic charcoal layers at Goldcliff included frequent fish bones, with eel the most common species (Bell et al. 2000). Leendert Louwe Kooijmans (1993) concludes that fish remains are scarce from nearly all Dutch prehistoric sites, even when preservation is optimal and the excavation techniques had been adapted for the recovery of fish bones. The three dogwood fishtraps from Bergschenhoek, all of Early Neolithic date, remain exceptional finds. In contrast, the evidence from Scandinavia where the isostatic uplift has 'outpaced' the rise in sea-level consists of a wide range of fishing tools and implements dating back to the Late Mesolithic. On Ertebølle-type sites, this included lances, harpoons, leisters, fish traps, fish hooks, nets and stationary fish weirs (e.g. Pedersen 1995).

Several broader studies have addressed the drowned archaeology of the North Sea, showing extensive evidence for Mesolithic exploitation of the North Sea plain, or 'Doggerland' (e.g. Louwe Kooijmans 1971, Verhart 1995, Coles 1999). These studies show that the exploitation of the coast, mainly for fish and shellfish, continued into the Early Neolithic period. It has been argued that the late adoption of the new farming technology in the regions around the North Sea plain may in part be attributed to the presence of an abundant coastal resource (e.g. Coles 1999; Fischer and Myrhøj 1995). Recent research on human remains involving isotope analysis, which can measure the marine component of the human diet, has tentatively suggested that marine resources were no longer exploited to the same extent in the Neolithic period (Richards and Hedges 1999).

Evidence from the Humber Wetlands for foraging in the Mesolithic and Early Neolithic remains equally elusive. Again we rely on research elsewhere, which shows that wetlands and adjacent woodlands would have provided a wide variety of foods, including nuts, roots, seeds and berries. By the later Mesolithic, wild plant foraging may have been in part replaced by wild plant production, for example through the use of fire to maintain or extend clearances in forests resulting in the increased productivity of nut and fruit trees, shrubs and wetland vegetation. Raw materials available included tree species such as birch, willow, hazel, elm, oak and alder that could have been utilised for a wide range of objects and tools, from dug-out canoes to bows and arrowshafts. The wetland vegetation included rush, reeds and grasses for basketry, ropes and possibly nets for fishing (cf. Hall and Coles 1994). Other raw materials that were utilised included flint, which was available in abundance from Flamborough Head southwards down the eroding Holderness coast (Head 1995). Only future large-scale excavations of well-preserved sites will provide the necessary information to determine these matters for the Humber Wetlands.

In the absence of assemblages from the Humber Wetlands that contain bone and plant macrofossil remains, but on the basis of much research elsewhere, we may characterise the Late Mesolithic and Early Neolithic subsistence strategy as part of what has been called a 'broad spectrum economy'. This includes hunting, fowling, fishing and foraging undertaken in the Humber Wetlands possibly as seasonal activities (cf. Zvelebil 1986). The issue of seasonality is an important theme. It has been suggested that winter settlements were predominant on coastal wetlands, and summer occupation near inland wetlands such as Star Carr or upland sites (Jacobi 1978; Mellars and Dark 1998). However, the issue of seasonality may have been confused with a more dynamic pattern of short-term visits at a range of times of year and this pattern may have taken place over very long periods (cf. Bell *et al.* 2000). The finds of many flint scatters dated to the Mesolithic, Neolithic and Bronze Age in the Humber Wetlands and elsewhere support such an explanation. We assume therefore that the vast majority of find concentrations and sites found during the Humber Wetlands Survey represent temporary or seasonal camps, which may have been revisited over considerable lengths of time. The drylands of the Isle of Axholme, the Yorkshire and Lincolnshire Wolds and the Lincoln Edge all contain evidence of Mesolithic and earlier Neolithic activity, and these may have been favoured for long-term, multi-seasonal sites. Meanwhile, the presence of hunter-gatherers in the Humber Wetlands may represent an aspect of their subsistence strategy in which the exploitation of coastal resources dominated. In both cases, it is likely that the rivers provided the paths through the lowlands. Although the oldest boat from the Humber Wetlands is Bronze Age in date, Mesolithic logboats are not infrequent finds in areas like Scandinavia, where the Mesolithic-period riverbeds are not buried by several metres of alluvium (e.g. Christensen 1990). The use of rivers as paths could also account for the repeated visits to specific locations near rivers in the Mesolithic, Neolithic and Bronze Age periods, as indicated by the multi-period flint scatters (see also Chapters 5 and 10).

In the later Neolithic and Bronze Age periods, we assume that hunting and foraging in the wetlands continued to be significant activities. One of the principal sources of evidence for this assumption is the pollen record. As argued in the previous chapter, it shows that large-scale clearance did not take place before *c.* 3900 cal BC, and that the woodlands in the Humber Wetlands were not fully cleared until much later. The limited bone assemblages dating to this period show a picture of a subsistence strategy merging farming with hunting. At the later Neolithic or Early Bronze Age site at West Furze, near Skipsea in Holderness, the bone assemblage of the 'lake dwelling' included dog, sheep, ox, pig and horse, but also red-deer, beaver, cormorant and duck (Smith 1911; see also Chapter 4). The only bone assemblage analysed as part of the survey of the Humber Wetlands, from a midden in the coastal cliffs in Holderness (Kilnsea–24; Mulville in Head *et al.* 1995b), showed that even by the Late Bronze Age or Early Iron Age hunting may have played a key role in the subsistence strategies employed. A red deer skull and antlers were present alongside the bones of cattle, pig, sheep or goat, horse and domestic fowl.

Introduction and early spread of farming in the wetlands

The introduction and spread of farming in Britain remains a matter of keen debate. Within the last four decades, the introduction of farming practices has been pinned on incoming farmers from the Continent, especially those associated with the Linear Band Ceramic (LBK), on the adoption of farming practices by indigenous hunter-gatherers and on a combination of these two concepts (e.g. Whittle 1985; 1996). In the latter model, migration was responsible for the beginning of agriculture in southern England and acculturation by indigenous hunter-gatherers for the spread of farming to other parts of Britain (e.g. Zvelebil 1986). The archaeological and palaeoenvironmental records support the notion that farming practices were adopted in a piecemeal fashion. In the Humber Wetlands, arable farming did not become the established way of life for at least another 2000 years, but the domestication of animals may have started as early as the fourth millennium BC.

The Neolithic archaeology of the lowlands of the Humber Wetlands comprises principally large number of flint production sites or transit camps of Neolithic and Early Bronze Age date. Many of these sites found during the survey of the Humber Wetlands comprise knapped flint only, contrasting with the Wolds where Neolithic pottery types, for example Peterborough Ware and Grooved Ware, have been found more frequently (Manby 1988c). This distribution pattern may have been biased by the intensity of agriculture in the lowlands that has turned prehistoric pottery into dust, or by the longer history of research on the Wolds that has resulted in an archaeological record that has accumulated over 100 years. It may also be the case, however, that the lowlands continued to be used principally for hunting and foraging for a considerable period of time after the start of the Neolithic, with the main focus of farming, settlement and ritualised activities on the Wolds. Neolithic and Early Bronze Age flint scatters found during the Humber Wetlands Project, for example in the valley of the Winterton Beck in northern Lincolnshire, include often one or two tools such as a flint knife or scraper, a core and a few flakes, suggesting short-term activity (Whitton–5 and 7; Fenwick *et al.* 1998). These sites are often identified near wetlands, sometimes in association with Mesolithic material, but more often at a distance of a few hundred metres from the expanding wetlands (see Chapter 2). This suggests that these flint

FIGURE 26.
Neolithic polished
axehead from the Aire
floodplain (Birkin–5;
Chapman *et al.* 1999,
145).

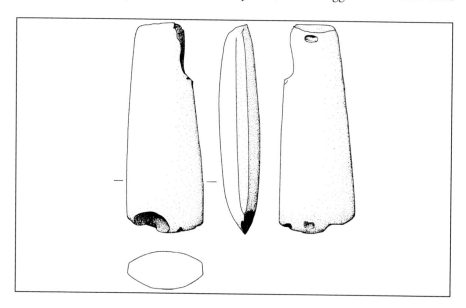

concentrations were associated to a form of wetland exploitation that was little different from that in the Mesolithic, and that the high productivity of the region's wetlands continued to be recognised.

Only one stone axe was discovered during the Humber Wetlands Survey, to the north of the floodplain of the River Aire near Gateforth in the Vale of York (Figure 26; Birkin–5; Chapman *et al.* 1999). It was made of polished epidotised tuff, or petrological Group VI. Of the 190 stone axes found in the past in the Humber Wetlands, petrological Group VI is the most common type of material, followed by petrological Group XVIII (epidotised ashy grit) in Yorkshire and Group VII (augite granaphyre) in Linconshire. The likely sources for these stone axes were Great Langdale in Cumbria, Whin Sill in Northumberland and Graig Lwyd in Caernarfon respectively (Clough and Cummins 1979). The ownership of polished axes was an important symbol, especially in its role as gift, and polished axes were frequently deposited in a ritualised manner. Polished axes, however, were also working tools, used for tree-felling and general woodworking. The debate on whether the felling of trees resulted in forest clearances suitable for arable agriculture, or whether the earliest crops were planted around tree stumps, which decayed during the subsequent decades, continues.

The palynological record indicates that the clearance of the woodland was a drawn-out process. The Elm Decline represents a European-wide eco-cultural horizon signaling the earliest occurrence of a decline of arboreal pollen dated to *c.* 4000 cal BC (see also Chapter 2). In the Humber Wetlands, the Elm Decline is dated to *c.* 3900 cal BC, for example from previous work at Gransmoor in Holderness (Beckett 1981). Pollen analysis suggests that the event was more distinct in the uplands than the low-lying wetlands. At Butterbump in the Lincolnshire Marsh, for example, a near-primeval forest is thought to have survived until 3350–2910 cal BC (Greig 1982). More convincing evidence of extensive forest clearances in the Humber Wetlands is dated to *c.* 3600 cal BC, for example at The Bog at Roos (Beckett 1981) and at Skipsea Withow Gap (Gilbertson 1984). At these sites, and elsewhere in Holderness, the initial opening up of the woodland canopy *c.* 3900 cal BC appears short-lived. Several high-resolution pollen analyses show signs of reforestation before a second and prolonged phase of forest clearance after *c.* 3600 cal BC (e.g. Flenley 1987). However, the landscape was not opened up until the Bronze Age, around 2500 cal BC (e.g. Taylor 1995), and not until *c.* 800 cal BC, the beginning of PZVIII (see Chapter 2) was agricultural land more extensive than woodland.

The Humber Wetlands show a dearth of evidence in the palynological record for arable production in the form of *Cerealia*-type (cultivated grasses) pollen and an absence of features, structures and finds that can be directly associated with cereal production. This suggests that the subsistence strategy during the Neolithic and the Bronze Age was predominantly one of pastoral farming, with probably some small-scale arable farming on the lighter free-draining soils. Hunting and foraging in the wetlands continued throughout this period and would have provided additional sources of food. However, one site in the Humber Wetlands appears to offer a very different picture. On the beach near Easington, in southern Holderness, excavations of a Bronze Age barrow by the East Riding Archaeological Society found that the mound was built over the remains of a small Neolithic house. This house also produced a large number of finds including fragments of several saddle querns and rubbing stones that had been deposited in a single pit (Mackey 1998). Although the house and the quern stones could be interpreted as evidence for arable activity in southern Holderness, the palynological evidence unequivocally indicates that this area was not under arable agriculture by *c.* 3800 cal BC, and the presence of the house's occupiers in Holderness was not for the purpose of growing crops. Mark Edmonds (1999) explains the deposition of querns and characteristically 'Neolithic' objects as a medium through which communities renewed their tenure with particular places. In the case of the Easington house, the reason for renewing the claim to the area was principally for pastoral use, hunting and foraging, rather than arable farming.

From *c.* 3500 cal BC, the archaeology of the Humber Wetlands and the surrounding higher grounds diverges. Monuments, in particular long barrows, are exclusive to the higher grounds of the Yorkshire and Lincolnshire Wolds (Manby 1988). A recent assessment of aerial photography from Lincolnshire identified 56 extant long barrows and elongated enclosures tentatively interpreted as the remains of ploughed-out long barrows (Jones 1998a). All of these sites were located on the Lincolnshire Wolds and Lincoln Edge, all above the 10 m OD contour that defines the boundary of the Humber Wetlands. Few of these sites have been dated, but the date of the Kilham Long Barrow on the Yorkshire Wolds, *c.* 3650 cal BC, has been in the main accepted as the 'start date' of the Neolithic in East Yorkshire (Manby 1976). This distinction between the lowlands and the higher grounds further increased in the later parts of the Neolithic and the Early and Middle Bronze Age (*c.* 3000 to 1000 cal BC). Round barrows, the 'Great Barrows', cursuses and henges complement what has often been described as ritual or ceremonial landscapes on the higher grounds of the Wolds during the Neolithic (see Harding and Lee 1987 for a comprehensive overview). Evidence of flint production sites and transit camps are also frequent here, although no excavation of Early Neolithic settlements has taken place. Initially, the construction of monuments may reflect the adoption of a new way of thinking, rather than a distinct new subsistence strategy, namely farming. Monument building creates a sense of time and space and, in due course, territoriality. With the exception of the barrows in the Easington and Kilnsea area of southern Holderness and those from Butterbump on the Lincolnshire Marsh (discussed in Chapter 6), the Humber Wetlands remain devoid of monumental structures.

This absence could be interpreted as suggesting that after 3500 cal BC the wetlands and their resources were probably not essential, but complementary to the way of life and food procurement strategies of the monument-builders. The relatively small size of flint scatters of Neolithic date in the Humber

Wetlands, compared to the 'flint production' sites of the Mesolithic, also suggests that the former represent hunting camps used for shorter periods, or by fewer people. The question of permanency of occupation in wetlands has also frequently arisen for the Neolithic and later prehistoric periods. In the Fenlands, such permanencies appear to have been established by the Neolithic (Hall and Coles 1994). Long barrows, such as the excavated example from Haddenham, suggest the establishment of farmers in and around the Fenlands early in the Neolithic, and the research at Fengate confirms this for the later Neolithic (Hodder and Shand 1988; Pryor 1998). However, research in the Netherlands shows a much sharper contrast between the occupation in the uplands and lowlands. Here, full-time farmers of the LBK were found occupying the fertile loess grounds of the uplands, but indigenous hunter-gatherers continued to be active in the wetlands until the Middle Bronze Age, albeit adopting some agricultural activities (Louwe Kooijmans 1993). This issue has been the subject of extensive debate. Bradley (1998), for example, has argued that in western Europe indigenous hunter-gatherers were initially opposed to, and subsequently only very slowly won over by, the new 'Neolithic' way of life, and that in the first instance only pastoral activities were adopted alongside hunting and gathering activities. This is, in turn, reflected in a dispersed pattern of settlement. It is contended that only in the late second millennium BC was farming, and particular arable farming, adopted as the predominant subsistence system, and that the political changes often associated with the introduction of farming only emerged between 1300 and 800 cal BC. If this proposition is applicable to the east of England, it would provide an alternative explanation for the nature of human activity in the Humber Wetlands, with the wetlands inhabited by indigenous groups representing the former hunter-gatherers who now also engaged in pastoralism, whilst the higher ground was occupied by farmers.

There is no doubt that the period around 1000 cal BC saw significant socio-political changes. These were far-reaching, affecting the structures of hierarchy, territoriality and possibly distribution mechanisms. This is reflected in the emergence of new settlements, notably the ringforts and hillforts such as Thwing, Grimthrope, Devil's Hill and Staple How on the Yorkshire Wolds (Manby 1980; 1988c), or in the form of the extensive built boundaries. Aerial reconnaissance has identified a range of constructed boundary systems, including pit-alignments and single, double and multiple-ditched linear boundaries on the Yorkshire Wolds and to a lesser extent in Lincolnshire, but such boundaries remain conspicuously absent from the Humber Wetlands (Stoertz 1997, Boutwood 1998). The oldest of these structures are thought to originate in the Late Bronze Age, and during the Iron Age their form was enhanced and their function may have changed. Whereas some boundaries are interpreted as 'estate' or 'ranch' boundaries, providing parallels to the boundary systems of late prehistoric Wessex, others are thought to have formed boundaries between territories or political units. Few believe that these linear structures acted as physical boundaries against enemies. Rather, their function was essentially symbolic, defining individual or communal ownership, status and social cohesion.

Nevertheless, sufficient evidence exists to argue that the Humber Wetlands remained integrated into the wider region rather than representing an isolated place where the last vestiges of indigenous hunting and gathering survived. This is most clearly reflected in the material culture. For example, the distribution of polished axes in the region shows that the same source material of the axes (epidotised tuff, see above) dominated both in the wetlands and on the higher ground. Also, the objects chosen for the votive deposition in 'wet places' – from the Neolithic jadeite axe from Wroot to the many bronze and occasional golden objects of Bronze Age date (Chapter 6) – suggest an interconnection between the people living in the Humber Wetlands and those who had formed regional exchange networks. The integration of wetlands and higher ground is also indicated by the density of Bronze Age structures on the Humber foreshore (presented below). These have been found in the greatest concentrations near the foot of the Yorkshire Wolds, and it is reasonable to suggest that this aspect of wetland exploitation was undertaken from the higher ground. Similarly, the sewn-plank boats from North Ferriby and Kilnsea, which are likely to have played a part in the expansion of the exchange networks, also suggest levels of integration between the Humber Wetlands and the wider region (Chapter 5). It is also worth noticing that the boundary-earthworks on the Wolds delineate the areas of higher ground, not the wetlands–dryland interface. Access to the wetlands from the Wolds, and exploitation of the wetlands, was therefore enabled, not obstructed.

Pastoralism in the Humber estuary

Principally on the basis of pollen analysis, it is assumed that farming in the Humber lowlands in the Neolithic and Bronze Age was predominantly focused on stockbreeding, rather than arable production. Unlike areas such as the Thames valley or Fengate, on the margins of the East Anglian Fens near Peterborough, the Humber Wetlands do not appear to contain extensive field systems comprising fields and droveways, which could illuminate the range of farming activities undertaken here. Francis Pryor (1996) has argued, on the basis of a detailed examination of Fengate's stockyards and gates, that these field systems were predominantly used for sheep breeding. The field systems hint at an intensive exploitation of the wetland edge and floodplains as summer pasture. The high biological productivity of the river floodplains and fen edge would have provided a significant resource. The absence of similar field systems in the floodplain of the River Trent has been interpreted as evidence for a less intensive use of this ecosystem in the Bronze Age (Pryor 1998). Whilst in the lower Trent such field systems may remain undiscovered beneath deep alluvial sediments, their absence in the middle and upper reaches of the Trent is significant.

The absence of pre-Iron Age field systems in the Humber Wetlands may have an alternative cause. We have seen that in the river floodplains of the Humber Wetlands, the wetland edge extended laterally during the Neolithic and the Bronze Age (see Chapter 2). The pollen assemblages of the vegetation on the edge of the river floodplain, including that of the Trent, were invariably dominated by alder. The opportunities to exploit these ecosystems as grazing ground would have been severely thwarted. Wet alder carrs are nearly inaccessible and offer little in terms of food to larger mammals, nor do they provide fodder material. Could it be the case that in the Humber Wetlands, marine transgression and the expansion of riparian 'eutrophic' wetlands created physical barriers that ruled out the use of the floodplains for intensive stockbreeding, thus precluding the development of wetland-edge field systems? I believe it did.

If pastoral farmers in the Humber Wetlands were to exploit the wetlands as grazing grounds, the Humber estuary would have provided a more suitable environment than the river floodplains with their carr woodlands. In the Humber estuary, the tides overtopped eutrophic wetlands from *c.* 4000 cal BC (cf. Metcalfe *et al.* 2000), and in the third and second millennia BC extensive saltmarshes developed over the former peat landscapes. The importance of

FIGURE 27. Plan of a Bronze Age trackway on the Humber foreshore (Melton–25; Fletcher *et al.* 1999: 231).

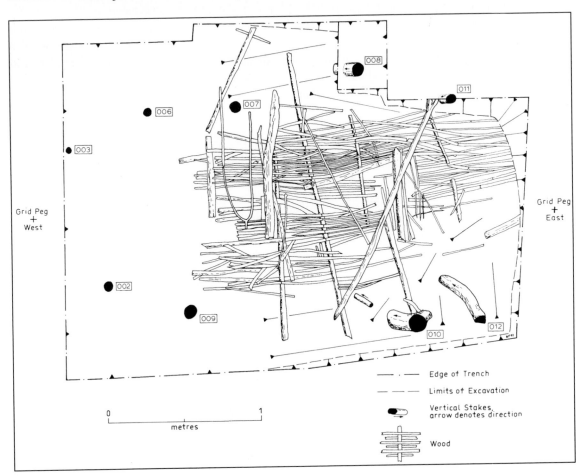

FIGURE 28.
Detail of the Bronze
Age trackway
Melton–26, Vale of
York, in 1998.

© THE HUMBER WETLANDS
PROJECT, UNIVERSITY OF
HULL

estuarine feeding grounds lies not only in the very high biological productivity of this ecosystem, but also in the fact that the growing season in the estuary is longer than elsewhere in the region, whilst salt helps prevent foot rot (Rippon 2000). In the northeast of England, the growing season is on average below 300 days per year in the drylands (cf. Fowler 1983). If a similar figure was correct for the Bronze Age, the stockbreeders would be faced with considerable problems in how to feed their stock during the winter months. The saltmarshes, however, could have solved much of the winter feeding problem.

The discovery during the survey of trackways dated to the Bronze Age on the Humber foreshore near Melton did not come as a surprise. Wooden structures had been recorded from the foreshore, both at North Ferriby and at Melton. Nevertheless, the density of archaeological sites on the intertidal zone was surprising. On the first day of the intertidal survey as part of the Humber Wetlands Survey we identified 16 waterlogged sites, the majority of which turned out to be of Bronze Age date. Following the discovery and initial recording, we decided to target two sites for further excavations. Both were exposed and clearly eroding. The first trackway (Figure 27; Melton–25; Fletcher *et al.* 1999) was made of hurdles, built in the same manner as a wattle fence (cf. Raftery 1990). The wood used for the hurdle comprised hazel, with some alder, willow or poplar and a single oak branch. Hazel is not tolerant of very wet conditions and we may assume that the hurdle was fabricated on the drylands, possibly from coppiced material. The complete hurdle, measuring

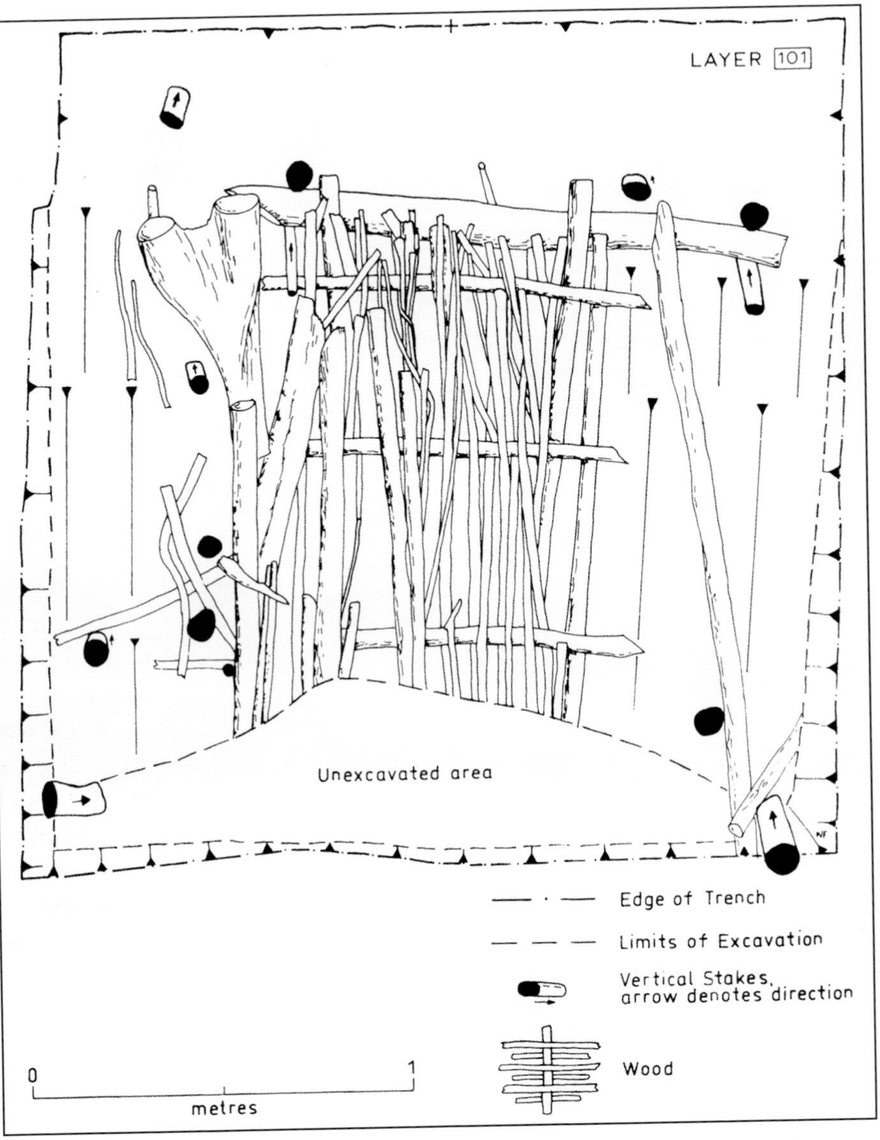

LAYER 101

Unexcavated area

—·— Edge of Trench

— — — Limits of Excavation

Vertical Stakes, arrow denotes direction

Wood

0   1

metres

FIGURE 29.
Plan of a Bronze Age trackway from the Humber foreshore (Melton–26; Fletcher *et al.* 1999: 235).

c. 1.8 × 1.0 m, was placed on the saltmarsh with a downward slant of 10° and probably fixed in its place by a number of 1 m long stakes, although we could not ascertain this. The hurdle was dated to 1440–1310 cal BC. The second site (Figure 28, 29; Melton–26; Fletcher *et al.* 1999), was located 12 m from the first site, and was in many respects very similar. This trackway was undoubtedly fixed in its place by vertical stakes, but may have been younger, with two dates of 1429–1120 cal BC and 1100–840 cal BC.

What puzzled us most about these trackways was their function. Both trackways were aligned east-west, that is parallel to the river. Thus, they provided neither access to the waterfront or water edge for fishing or fowling, nor access to boats as has been suggested for similar structures at nearby North Ferriby (Wright 1990; see also Chapter 5). Furthermore, the sites were found within silted up tidal creeks and their slanting suggested that they were placed across these. One such tidal creek, East Clough, is recorded in this area on older Ordnance Survey maps. We hypothesised that the trackways may have played a role in the exploitation of the intertidal zone as grazing grounds, similar to the exploitation of the floodplains and fen edge at Fengate and in the Thames valley. Research in the Severn estuary found that during the Iron Age saltmarsh was used as summer grazing ground for cattle. The many footprints of cattle and evidence of seasonality of occupation identified from the Goldcliff area put this type of use of the intertidal zone beyond any doubt (Bell *et al.* 2000). Tentative indications that the saltmarsh in the Humber estuary may have been used as a grazing ground for cattle rather than sheep comes in the form of the discovery of aurochs or cattle bones elsewhere on the Humber foreshore (B. Sitch pers. comm.), information from a local farmer who remembered his father setting cattle on the foreshore during the winter (Mr. Holtby pers. comm.), and on the way in which the hurdles had been positioned on the ground, suggesting some sort of 'heavy traffic'. A recent archaeological experiment involving replica hurdles confirmed that such a function was practicable (Bidgood 2002). Nevertheless, we did not find unequivocal evidence for this. No hoofprints were found associated with the trackways.

Outside the Humber Wetlands, ample evidence exists for the exploitation of saltmarshes in prehistory. For example, Bronze Age trackways in the Thames basin may have had similar functions as those on the Humber foreshore (Meddens 1996). The research at Goldcliff in the Severn Estuary found square buildings and trackways dated to the fourth and third centuries BC, which have been interpreted as seasonal use of the coastal wetlands as pasture, in a 'pattern of local transhumant land use' (Bell *et al.* 2000: 344). Short trackways providing access to areas and wetland resources have been identified in the Shannon estuary in Ireland (O'Sullivan 2001). Iron Age wetland exploitation is also well attested for the Assendelfder Polder in the Netherlands, where settlements were located on peatlands that were raised above the coastal wetlands. Detailed research on the dung found at 'site Q' found that the settlement was specialised in livestock rearing, with cattle grazing the saltmarshes and levees, and sheep and/or goats the peatlands (Brandt and Van der Leeuw 1987). Similarly, the *terpen* in the Waddensee of the northern parts of the Netherlands and Germany emerged from the third century BC, and exploited the extensive saltmarshes as pasture grounds. Stockbreeding as a specialised activity implies a degree of differentiation and dependency on exchange, reflecting interdependencies that have also been noted for the Humber Wetlands (Chapter 4).

Iron Age field systems

As stated above, the palynological record for the Humber Wetlands indicates that large-scale clearances and the evidence for an arable economy date to the later Bronze Age and Iron Age, traditionally associated to the start of pollen zone VIII, from *c.* 800 cal BC (see Chapter 2). Many examples of field systems identified through aerial photography remain undated, but as yet no single field system within the Humber Wetlands is considered to have been constructed before the later Iron Age, i.e. before 300 BC. Derek Riley's work (e.g. 1980, 1983) in the Humberhead Levels and surrounding areas has provided the most systematic mapped landscape. He recognised three types of field systems: one with a brickwork pattern, one with a nuclear pattern and one with a irregular pattern. Double-ditched features have been recognised and these were more frequent in the field systems with irregular patterns than those with the brickwork patterns. These double-ditch features appear to encompass two different structures. On excavation, some ditch infills were considered to have been derived from a bank that was situated within the two parallel ditches, indicating a boundary (Samuels and May 1980). Others revealed evidence of erosion from trampling stock or cart wheels, indicating droveways (Merrony 1993; Chadwick and Cumberpatch 1995). In both cases, the field systems have been dated to the Roman period, but may have been in use for several centuries by the time of the deposition of Roman cultural material that has provided the date for the structures.

The work on field systems by Derek Riley was mainly concentrated on the free-draining soils of the Sherwood Sandstone (see Chapter 2). Here, landscapes have not become buried beneath clays and silt and are therefore more easily visible through aerial photography. If we consider all aerial photographic work in and around the Humber Wetlands over the last two decades (Chapman 1997, 1998, 1999, 2000, 2001), the image of prehistoric farming described above is reinforced. It appears that field systems indicating an intensive and socially highly organised agricultural economy did not exist until the later Iron Age or the early Roman period. For the Yorkshire and Lincolnshire Wolds, which have both benefited from recent systematic recording of aerial images within the National Mapping Programme (Stoertz 1997; Bewley 1998), the aerial archaeological record includes a wealth of sites identified as settlements, cemeteries or territorial boundaries, but no field systems predating the later Iron Age.

And what about wetland exploitation in this period? Iron Age field systems have been identified on floodplains, most notably in the Ancholme and Hull valleys (e.g. Kelk–3 in the Hull valley; Chapman *et al.* 2000). Such sites usually comprise rectilinear enclosures, double-ditch features such as droveways and single-ditch features interpreted as field boundaries. These could be interpreted as field systems facilitating mixed farming, with the droveways being used to move livestock from the floodplain meadows to the higher grounds without the risk of the animals straying into the small arable fields. Such a use of the floodplains would have become feasible, following the burial of the extensive alder carrs some time in the first millennium BC, with sea-level rise resulting in the deposition of minerogenic sediments over these riparian woodlands (see Chapter 2). Few of these sites identified through aerial reconnaissance have been dated, but many are presumed to belong to the later Iron Age or Roman period (see also Chapter 7).

Conclusion

To summarise, throughout the Mesolithic, Neolithic and Bronze Age periods, the wetlands in the Humber lowlands were perceived as productive ecosystems for hunting, fishing and gathering. As far as can be ascertained on the basis of the research in the Humber Wetlands and elsewhere, the exploitation of the wetlands always formed part of a broader subsistence strategy. The flint scatters of Mesolithic and Early Neolithic date appear to represent transit camps of family groups, or flint-production sites. Those dating to the later Neolithic and Bronze Age are characteristic of shorter-term camps for a group of hunters. On the basis of the diminishing size of the flint assemblages found during the survey it appears that the importance of the wetlands diminished over time, and that the higher and dryer areas became the focus of later prehistoric settlement. However, it is worth bearing in mind that the evidence presented here is principally based on the results of field-walking, and is thus limited to flint scatters. Excavation of these or other sites may reveal a greater diversity of material, and aspects of the story of the earliest exploitation of the Humber Wetlands which have, to date, been underexplored.

It appears that prehistoric farming in the Humber Wetlands during most of prehistory was limited to a predominantly pastoral economy. The absence of field systems before the Iron Age does not mean that the wetlands were considered of little importance, rather that their use was not socially structured and probably less intensive than in the case of Fengate, the Thames, the middle reaches of the Trent valley and elsewhere. Alternatively, the prehistoric farmers may not have perceived the riparian wetlands as a productive environment. The existence of alder-dominated carr woodland on the dryland–wetland interface would have created a physical boundary preventing animal movement to and from the floodplains. The exception is provided by the estuarine wetlands. If the Bronze Age trackways on the Humber foreshore were constructed to enable cattle to be moved across creeks, it would follow that the saltmarshes in the Humber estuary provided an important wetland resource. And if the saltmarshes were used for winter grazing, this resource could have transformed the stockbreeding practices of prehistoric farmers in the Bronze Age. The farmers' perception of the estuarine wetlands would, in that case, have been diametrically opposed to their perception of the riparian 'eutrophic' wetlands.

In the later part of the Iron Age, aerial photographic evidence shows the development of a range of field systems. This is particularly visible for the free-draining Sherwood Sandstone areas of South Yorkshire and North Nottinghamshire. Additional examples of field systems within, and adjacent to, the major floodplains, in particular those of the Rivers Hull and Ancholme, show that the use of wetlands for farming increased. Marine transgression may have played a significant role in this development, with a higher sea-level burying the alder carrs during the first millennium BC.

CHAPTER FOUR

'Lake Dwellings' and Prehistoric Wetland Settlement

The Mesolithic, Neolithic and Bronze Age flint scatters were discussed in Chapter 3, and we concluded that these scatters mostly represent 'tool production sites' and 'transit camps' – in other words relatively short-term camps rather than long-lived settlements. Whether this observation is real or the result of limited archaeological visibility remains a matter of debate.

In terms of material culture that could indicate prehistoric settlements, little pottery and other materials have survived on the intensively farmed fields in the Humber Wetlands. Consequently, field-walking may simply have been an inappropriate tool for the identification of prehistoric settlements, and it may be that our current knowledge of prehistoric settlements falls somewhat short of their real number and distribution. Even so, aerial photography has similarly shown little in terms of settlements predating the Iron Age. The burial of prehistoric landscapes beneath alluvial sediments could account for this, but where the visibility is known to be good, unambiguous evidence for pre-Iron Age settlements is still rare. The circular crop-marks that occur infrequently have been interpreted either as Bronze Age ploughed-out barrows or later houses (e.g. Chapman 2001). The geophysical survey of areas where the potential for prehistoric settlement had been considered to be good, for example Westwoodside–2 near the River Idle in the Humberhead Levels (Head *et al.* 1997b) did not produce any evidence for surviving settlement remains. Finally, excavations of a number of 'promising' flint scatter sites during the Humber Wetlands Survey, for example in the Hull valley at Weel–2 (Chapman *et al.* 2000), failed to find *in situ* features such as hearths and post holes or stake holes, confirming that the excavated sites were probably tool production sites and transit camps. In this context, we can assume that within the wider landscape the overwhelming majority of permanent settlements were located on higher and dryer grounds such as on the Yorkshire Wolds. The single Neolithic house at Easington in Holderness (Mackey 1998), overlooking the estuarine Kilnsea Fleet, may be an important exception to the rule that the pre-Iron Age settlement in the Humber Wetlands comprised principally short-term occupation sites.

Nevertheless, several late prehistoric settlements are known from the wetlands in the Humber basin, and we will look at these again in this chapter (Figure 30).

FIGURE 30.
Map of the Humber Wetlands, showing prehistoric settlement sites and salterns of prehistoric date and the names of the sites mentioned in the text.

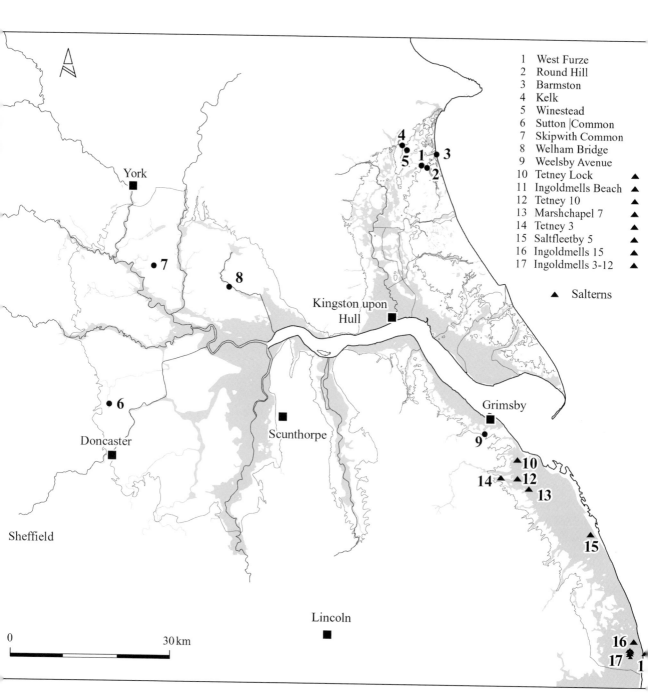

1	West Furze
2	Round Hill
3	Barmston
4	Kelk
5	Winestead
6	Sutton |Common
7	Skipwith Common
8	Welham Bridge
9	Weelsby Avenue
10	Tetney Lock	▲
11	Ingoldmells Beach	▲
12	Tetney 10	▲
13	Marshchapel 7	▲
14	Tetney 3	▲
15	Saltfleetby 5	▲
16	Ingoldmells 15	▲
17	Ingoldmells 3-12	▲

▲   Salterns

So, why did people choose to live in the wetlands? In the past, as in the present, there are a number of good reasons for avoiding living in a damp or wet location. Structures or platforms were required to raise the living surface above the high watertable and capillary fringe. Dampness is not, as a rule, conducive to healthy living or efficient storage of foodstuffs. Glastonbury Lake Village, the most famous British wetland settlement, has been described by John Coles and Stephen Minnett (1995: 207) in the following way: 'The site selected was almost deliberately difficult: difficult to establish a foundation, difficult to keep dry, difficult to maintain, and impossible to guarantee against natural disaster'. This statement is also true for many other prehistoric wetland settlements.

Yet there are also a number of positive reasons for living in wetlands. These include a degree of security created by the inaccessibility of wetlands, particularly important in the case of many crannogs in Ireland and Scotland (O'Sullivan 1998). Riverside and lakeside locations provided opportunities for communication and trade across waterways, a case argued for the Alpine lake settlements (Schlichterle 1979). Wetlands may also have been perceived as marginal areas that were not yet held in the possession of individuals or communities, thus providing opportunities for pioneering individuals and groups, or for outcasts, to find land – an argument made for some early historic lowland farms in the Low Countries (Brinkkemper 1991; Halbertsma 2000). A number of these arguments appear relevant for the late prehistoric settlements in the Humber Wetlands.

Lake-dwellings in Holderness?

The drainage commissioner Thomas Boynton undertook one of the earliest ventures into wetland archaeology in the Humber Wetlands. Overseeing maintenance work on the Skipsea Branch Drain and elsewhere in Holderness and the Hull valley in the 1880s, he discovered five sites containing waterlogged wood. The results were initially published by him in *The Yorkshire Post* (26 July 1883) and by T. M. Evans in the *Standard* (20 October 1883) and *The Hull Quarterly and East Riding Portfolio* (1885), and eventually by Reginald Smith, Keeper of British and Mediaeval Antiquities at the British Museum in *Archaeologia* in 1911 as 'The Lake-dwellings of Holderness, Yorkshire'. Renewed investigation of Boynton's sites was included in the design of the Humber Wetlands Project. In 1994, during the survey of Holderness, we looked at the sites known as West Furze and Round Hill, both in the parish of Skipsea and Ulrome, and at Barmston Drain on the coast (Van de Noort 1995). In 1999, during the survey of the Hull valley, we investigated the two remaining sites, at Kelk and Gransmoor (Chapman *et al.* 2000).

Thomas Boynton's discoveries were all characterised by the discovery of archaeological wood. Despite the problems with desiccation of this material, it appeared that at least one site remained exposed for a considerable period. The West Furze site was discovered in 1880 and excavated the following year, but the section drawings by R. T. G. Abbott of the British Museum show the waterlevel in the Drain dated to April 21st 1884. It is also evident that information as presented by Reginald Smith was a compilation of material collected over several years, ranging at least from 1880 to 1884. Nevertheless, the descriptions provide an unparalleled insight into these early discoveries.

The most important site was West Furze, discovered in 1880 on Boynton's own farm. West Furze is situated at a constriction of the Bail and Low Mere

FIGURE 31.
A photograph of a
saddle quern from
Ulrome, Holderness.
The inscription reads
'Ulrome lake dwelling,
1881, TB' = Thomas
Boynton.

complex, an elongated depression created by glaciofluvial activity. The excavations in the 1880s revealed two layers of activity. The lower layer was devoid of pottery, and the upper layer devoid of bone implements, but included a bronze spearhead assigned to the 'Heathery Burn industry', or the Late Bronze Age. Further material from the site included a range of animal bones, including beaver, and several human skulls. The site is described as a settlement which '… would thus be protected by water or marsh from wild animals, and the adjoining pasture for domestic animals would be surrounded by a palisade' (Smith 1911: 606). The finds association dated the lower layer to the pre-metal age, and the upper layer to the Bronze Age.

The second site described by Smith at length was Round Hill, to the south of West Furze and situated in Bail Mere (Figure 31). Here, Thomas Boynton had found more wooden piles, and finds from the site included a human skull, a jet armlet, charred wood, flint flakes, a macehead and pottery. Unfortunately, no plans of the excavation exist, only a fanciful 'section', but the Round Hill site was described as a lake-dwelling and a settlement, although '… the construction was found to be inferior to that of the West Furze settlement' (Smith 1911: 605).

The three remaining sites were merely mentioned by Reginald Smith. The Barmston lake-dwelling included archaeological wood. The site found during maintenance work near Brunton Hill comprised a 'settlement extending 200–300 yards [which] can still be traced by the piles in the Drain at Gransmoor' (Smith 1911: 606). And the final site, in Gransmoor Drain near Kelk, was described as containing worked wood and pottery.

The publication by Smith has been regarded, for a considerable time, as the definitive description of the lake-dwellings in Holderness. The only archaeological activity on any of these sites prior to the Humber Wetlands Project was a small-scale excavation of the Barmston lake-dwelling site by William Varley, with students of Hull College of Education (Varley 1968). The excavations identified hearths, a cobbled floor, cooking pits and posts. The latter were dated by radiocarbon essay to 1550–800 cal BC and 1450–750 cal BC (BM–122; BM–123). This work concluded that the Barmston site was not a pile-dwelling or crannog, '... but a settlement of sorts within a marshy hollow' with the peat formation submerging the settlement (Varley 1968: 20).

The work undertaken as part of the survey of the Humber Wetlands included both small-scale excavations on all five sites and the analysis of existing publications and data. The scale of excavations varied greatly. At West Furze, Round Hill and Barmston the excavations comprised two trenches measuring 2 × 2 m each, but at Brunton Hill near Gransmoor and at Kelk longer trenches were excavated by JCB. Apart from the work at Brunton Hill, where no archaeological remains that could be associated to the lake-dwelling mentioned by Smith were identified, each of the other four excavations provided some surprising results, challenging the existence of prehistoric lake-dwellings in Holderness.

At West Furze, our excavations linked the natural and archaeological stratigraphy with Reginald Smith's descriptions of the site. This, alongside a critical analysis of publications by Thomas Boynton and T. M. Evans in the early 1880s, made it clear that West Furze was not a lake-dwelling. Rather, in its early phase (or lower floor) it was actually a trackway of Neolithic or Early Bronze Age date, comprising two parallel rows of stakes that linked both sides of the water. In fact, T. M. Evans had already come to that conclusion in 1885, writing that 'the causeway is formed by parallel timbers about 5 ft [1.5 m] apart, carefully hewn and staked pretty regularly' (page 60). The function of the upper floor or platform, which includes a Later Bronze Age spearhead, remains somewhat elusive. It may have functioned as a makeshift crossing point, but alternatively may have originated as a logjam or even a beaver dam. There must have been a settlement nearby, judging from the pottery found on the site. This may have slipped down the banks into the former mere, which through the process of hydroseral succession had turned into an elongated mire. A similar explanation may be attributed to the presence of complete saddle querns and rubbing stones, but alternatives are discussed in Chapter 6.

At Round Hill, our excavations produced a single find, a short wooden stump that may have been hammered into the basal clay. As was the case for the Round Hill piles described by Smith (1911), there was no evidence of any working of the wood. The stump was dated to 8600–7950 cal BC, in the Early Mesolithic. It predates the cultural finds from this site reported by Smith by several millennia (Chapter 3). The flint found during the survey dated to the Late Mesolithic and Early Neolithic, also too young to be associated to the stump. It is possible that the piles described by Thomas Boynton to Reginald Smith were altogether different from our wooden stump, but if they belong to the same group then the site would not have been a lake-dwelling, but rather a water-edge platform of sorts, possibly paralleled by the platform at Star Carr.

Our excavations at the Barmston lake-dwelling re-excavated part of William Varley's trenches. We are quite sure about this as we found some of his labels used to mark the different layers, still legible after 30 years. Whilst Varley had dated two posts to the Bronze Age, we dated the peat. A basal peat sample was dated to the Early Mesolithic, with radiocarbon dates of 11,200–10,350 cal BC and 10,700–9300 cal BC. A macrofossil from higher in the peat layer was dated to 8740–8290 cal BC (930±70 BP, GU–5450). In other words, the peat Varley considered to be younger than the Bronze Age settlement was in fact of Post-glacial and early Holocene date, comparable to the fills formed in many meres in Holderness through hydroseral succession (see Chapter 2). Rather than the peat submerging the settlement, the posts and pits had been dug or driven into the peat from above, when the peat surface had dried sufficiently to provide suitably dry ground for habitation.

The results from Kelk were the most surprising. The wetland is confined here to a long but narrow depression, and the location of Thomas Boynton's sharpened posts or piles was only broadly known. Whilst field-walking the area, we found a large amount of pottery on a till outcrop. This included material of Iron Age and Roman date and also material indicating metallurgical activity (Figure 32). A geophysical survey and trench excavations revealed the remains of a Late Iron Age enclosure on the edge of the narrow wetland where bronze artefacts had been cast (Kelk–6; Chapman *et al.* 2000). We extended one trench, but it emerged that the settlement did not extend into the wetland.

FIGURE 32. An Iron Age sprue cup, the funnel-shaped top of moulds into which molten bronze was poured, from Kelk–6 in the upper Hull valley (scale 1:1) (Chapman *et al.* 2000, 129).

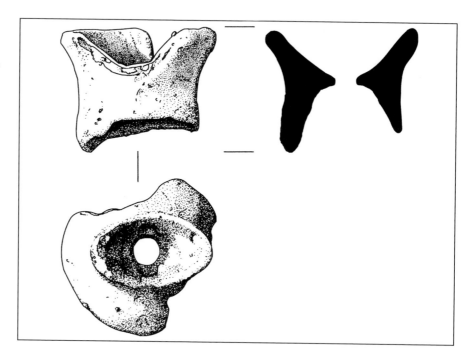

It is more likely that the stakes found by Boynton were part of a waterfront structure such as a jetty, or a trackway across the wetlands. Alternatively, the wood had been used within the settlement but had been later discarded and thrown into the water.

If none of these five sites were lake-dwellings, why were they interpreted as such? In the late nineteenth century, archaeological discoveries from wetlands remained largely unreported. Following the publication of the English translation of Frederik Keller's highly influential book on the settlements in the Alpine lakes in 1878, the concept of lake-settlements gained credence and respectability. Elsewhere on the British Isles, Robert Monroe published his *Ancient Scottish Lake-dwellings or Crannogs* in 1882 and Lt.-Col. Wood-Martin published *The Lake-dwelling of Ireland* in 1886. In England, Arthur Bulleid discovered the Glastonbury lake village in 1892; his search for a lake-settlement had been inspired by Keller's book. His analysis of the results of the excavation was similarly affected by the concepts of lake villages (cf. Coles and Minnitt 1995). It can come as no surprise that Thomas Boynton and Reginald Smith were similarly inspired to discover lake-dwellings. The presence of ancient worked timbers, pottery, animal bone remains and human skulls must have been considered sufficient evidence for the identification of lake-dwellings. More recent research has illustrated the diversity and variety of types of sites found in wetlands, but in the late nineteenth century the concept of a wooden trackway or platform was less well-known. In view of this, the interpretation of the West Furze structure as a causeway by T. M. Evans, a reporter and not an archaeologist, is particularly laudable.

Lake dwellings and other settlements located within wetlands predating the Iron Age are not known from the Humber Wetlands. The archaeological evidence points to a lifestyle pattern in which the wetlands were exploited from base-camps and settlements that were principally located on relatively higher ground, and to a perception of the wetlands as simply unsuitable for long-term or permanent settlement. The occurrence of the five 'lake-dwellings' in Holderness is in part the result of an uncritical analysis of the data. Only two of Boynton's sites were settlements. The Barmston site was located on a silted-up mere, and the Kelk site was situated on a till outcrop.

Sutton Common

One of the best-known archaeological sites in the Humber Wetlands is Sutton Common. The site, near Askern in the Humberhead Levels, was identified as early as the 1880s, and in the 1930s the Reverend Charles Whiting excavated a large number of narrow trenches through the upstanding earthworks and ditches, believing they were the remains of two Roman camps (Whiting 1936). Sutton Common comprises two enclosures, positioned on opposite sites of the Hampole Beck. The Hampole Beck is no longer a river, but in the Late-glacial and early Holocene it played an active role in the discharge of meltwater from the Magnesian Limestone to the west. The enclosure to the west of the Hampole Beck is much smaller than the one to the east, and the latter earthwork is altogether more complicated, with multivallate earthworks defining its extent. During the 1930s, the site included considerable amounts of wet-preserved archaeological remains. In the 1980s, the bulldozing of the earthworks of the larger enclosure and a small part of the smaller enclosure, and the installation of a field drainage system, resulted in deterioration of the site.

Following these developments, a number of small-scale assessments were undertaken to determine the state of preservation of the waterlogged remains at Sutton Common. This work, undertaken by the South Yorkshire Archaeology Service and the University of Sheffield, showed that parts of the site were suffering from desiccation, or the drying out of the previously waterlogged remains. The academic analysis that accompanied these assessments and subsequent publication provided the first comprehensive re-evaluation of the site since the 1930s (Parker Pearson and Sydes 1997). In summary, the most important findings were that the site was not Roman, but was constructed in the Iron Age, between *c.* 550 and 200 cal BC. The site was occupied on two occasions and beneath the earthworks of the larger enclosure, posts forming a palisade could now be interpreted as belonging to an earlier phase. It was believed that the two enclosures had been linked by a causeway across the Hampole Beck, although no clear evidence for this was found. Palaeo-environmental analysis suggests that the immediate environment of the enclosures became less wooded during the Iron Age, which may have been the result of the area becoming wetter.

On the function of the site, no clear conclusions were drawn. Although several characteristics of Sutton Common are paralleled in Bronze and Iron Age hillforts, the defensibility of the Sutton Common enclosures was questioned. The authors pointed out that the timbers of the palisade were too widely spaced to prevent people from squeezing through and the shallow ditches were not a strong deterrent. The paper also suggested that the smaller enclosure on the west of the Hampole Beck was an annex to the larger enclosure, which was the focus of activity in the Iron Age. The authors concluded that 'people seem to have been living in the large enclosure but it may also have had important ceremonial and high status significance' (Parker Pearson and Sydes 1997: 255).

Whilst the function of the Sutton Common site is still something of an enigma, the problems with the preservation of the site and its waterlogged remains were patently clear and this required urgent action. Initially, this involved the purchase of the whole of the Common and the transfer of ownership to the Carstairs Countryside Trust (CCT). In a co-operative partnership that also involved English Heritage, the Countryside Commission, English Nature and the drainage engineers Grantham Brundell and Farran, and with funding from these organisations and the Heritage Lottery Fund, the Common is now managed to provide the best possible protection for the site, including its waterlogged components.

As part of the new management of Sutton Common, further survey was undertaken in 1997, and excavations were conducted in 1998, 1999, 2002 and 2003, undertaken by staff of the Universities of Exeter and Hull (Figure 33). These were designed to resolve the 'Sutton Common enigma' – that is, to try and understand the function of the site. Was it a refuge, a settlement, a ceremonial site used for one or two specific occasions, or a lowland fort?

Although we await the outcome of the post-excavation analysis, we already know a great deal more about the site than in 1997. For example, through the application of dGPS and GIS, we know that the plans of the site drawn up in the 1930s are inaccurate in a number of important details – for example, the smaller enclosure had only one entrance (Chapman and Van de Noort 2001). We also know now that a causeway linked the two enclosures and that this was not a narrow path, but a nine metre-wide 'avenue', lined with large posts. The Hampole Beck was in the Iron Age not a flowing river, rather an 80 m wide sinuous wetland that would have been very difficult to cross on foot. The palisade may in fact have been the timber front of an earthen rampart, providing a barrier that was certainly defensible. But even after these excavations, the material culture from the site that can be directly associated to the Iron Age structures consists of little more than wooden remains.

In terms of the location of Sutton Common, the site utilised the local wetlands to maximum effect. The focus of activity, in the larger enclosure, was confined behind the wetlands that had formed in the Hampole Beck.

FIGURE 33. Detail of the excavations at Sutton Common in the Humberhead Levels in progress in 1999, showing one of the main entrance posts in advanced state of desiccation.

Access to the larger enclosure from the Magnesian Limestone area was through the smaller enclosure, crossing the wetland in the Hampole Beck on the possibly ceremonial causeway. The larger enclosure has two additional entrances, one facing north, the other east. In these directions, the enclosure was shielded from its wider environment by an eight metre deep wetland, which survives today as Rushy Moor and Shirley Pool. During the Iron Age the presence of these wetlands would have contributed to the status of the Sutton Common site as a very distinctive and significant place.

One other site in the Humber Wetlands appears similar in morphology to Sutton Common. At Skipwith Common, in the Vale of York, the Yorkshire Antiquaries Club identified a large enclosure (*c.* 160 × 130 m) in the mid-nineteenth century, which appeared to have been formed by single, double and triple banks and a ditch. The site was presumably flattened when a runway for the airfield at the Common was constructed in 1941. The site lies close to an Iron Age cemetery, comprising square-ditch burials of the 'Arras culture', characterised by its distinctive burial practice and mostly concentrated on the Yorkshire Wolds (Stead 1979; see Chapter 6). As was the case for Sutton Common, the enclosure at Skipwith Common was situated on what appears to have been relatively dry ground, within an area of small wetland habitats (Finney 1994).

Multivallate earthwork sites of Iron Age date are represented in other areas in England, where such enclosed sites are usually interpreted as 'central-places', providing a range of services including the articulation of exchange mechanisms for the wider area (Cunliffe 1991). Several sites within the Humber Wetlands appear to be more complex in character, such as those at Little Smeaton (Manby 1988) or Moorhouse Farm to the south of Bawtry (Riley 1980), which were together with Sutton Common recently described as 'marsh forts' (Chadwick 1999), and which could have acted as central places. However, several recent summaries of the Iron Age in northern England have described society at this time as working within a largely self-sufficient economy with limited development as time passed, and with evidence of an 'egalitarian' society (e.g. Robbins 1999, Chadwick 1999). If such a vision is correct, that the Sutton Common site is more likely to have fulfilled symbolic and communal functions, rather than representing the interest and control of some sort of ruling class (cf Hill 1995).

Metal production and working

While living in wetlands may have been difficult from many points of view, the relative emptiness of this landscape appears to have been very suitable for some industrial types of activity in the Iron Age. The evidence for metallurgy comes from two areas.

In the Vale of York, the East Riding Archaeological Society and the University of Durham have investigated the area around Holme-on-Spalding and the surrounding land. The location of settlement remains, as identified through field walking and the analysis of aerial photographs, suggests a clear preference for the higher and dryer locations within this landscape. The area became considerably wetter following marine transgression in the Iron Age, creating the extensive Walling Fen (Halkon and Millett 1999, see also Chapter 2). The research found some evidence that earlier occupation sites were present in the region. In the absence of pottery for dating, however, it is not clear when exactly the earliest settlements in the Holme-on-Spalding Moor area were established.

What makes this research so fascinating is the evidence for large-scale iron production. Martin Millett and Peter Halkon have argued that the most likely source for iron was peat, in the form of bog ore. An experiment involving peat from Hotham Carr in the Vale of York and a replica Iron Age furnace proved beyond doubt that extracting iron from peat was possible. It has been estimated that at Welham Bridge, where the biggest slag heap was found, some 800 iron 'currency bars' could have been produced. Welham Bridge is just one of eighteen known slag heaps from the Holme area. Apart from the bog ore, the lowlands offered extensive woodlands that provided the charcoal, an essential ingredient in the iron smelting process. It has been estimated that to produce the Welham Bridge slagheap, a minimum of 33,600 kg of charcoal were needed, which equates to the annual production of 47.32 ha of coppiced woodland.

Apart from bog ore and fuel, the wetlands offered one additional component to the Iron Age economy of the Holme area: a transport route. With the Iron Age marine transgression, Walling Fen extended deep into the southern Vale of York, and provided opportunities to trade the iron that was produced with the wider region. The Hasholme logboat, excavated in 1984, proves that exchange was important, and that vessels such as this logboat were designed to carry large loads, as well as emphasise the status of its owners (Millett and McGrail 1987, see also Chapter 5). In addition to iron smelting, woodland management and trade, the people living in the Holme area also engaged in mixed farming activities. Evidence for this comes from aerial photography, which has identified droveways and paddocks that are presumed to have enabled the efficient use of the meadows for stockbreeding. Palynology shows an increase of cereal type pollen from a sequence from Hasholme, dated to the Late Bronze Age and Early Iron Age, again reinforcing the image of an active farming community in this area.

Whilst iron smelting was the focus of activity in the Vale of York, we discovered during the survey the Late Iron Age site of Kelk in the upper part of the Hull valley, which includes evidence for bronze artefact production (Kelk–6; Chapman *et al.* 2000). The site was found as part of our efforts to reinvestigate one of the lake-dwellings described by Thomas Boynton (in Smith 1911; see above). Initially, we found large amounts of Iron Age and Roman pottery whilst field-walking the margins of the Gransmoor Drain. With this pottery, we found the first evidence of metallurgical activity in the form of fragments of crucibles. Subsequent geophysical survey showed the outline of a small settlement. This comprised positive magnetic anomalies representing filled-in double ditches forming three sides of a near-rectangular enclosure. The fourth side was formed by the wetlands flanking Gransmoor Drain. In the centre of the enclosure, an area with intense magnetic anomalies was found, indicating past industrial activity.

The site was further assessed through the excavation of three trenches, representing 1 per cent of the enclosure's total surface area. This identified a series of ditches and pits, and a large amount of Iron Age pottery and metalworking debris. Although the character of the enclosure ditches was established, the internal features remained confusing – they require large-scale excavation to be fully clarified. The metalworking debris included fragments of crucibles (vessels in which metals are melted), moulds and sprue cups (funnel-shaped hollows at the top of a mould into which the molten metal is poured) alongside fuel ash slag and fragments of fired clay. X-ray fluorescence analysis identified the types of metal that had been in contact with these fragments, including zinc, copper, tin, lead and arsenic. This indicates that non-ferrous metal working occurred on this site, most probably bronze casting.

A third Iron Age site in the Humber Wetlands that has produced evidence for metal working is Weelsby Avenue, now on the outskirts of Grimsby (Figure 34). Situated on a till spur above a small stream, the Goosemans Drain, the site was examined and excavated between 1970 and 1990. This revealed a rectangular enclosure ditch with two roundhouse gullies, a four-poster structure and various pits. The enclosure ditch contained large amounts of bronze-casting debris, and within the enclosure discrete dumps of firebrick and another of crucibles and slag were found. The enclosure was in use during the Middle and Late Iron Age, with a few pottery sherds suggesting that it continued to be in use in the Roman period (John Sills, in Fenwick *et al.* 2001).

Although Iron Age metalworking is known from a wide range of dryland and wetland sites, the examples from the Humber Wetlands clearly show that the wetlands were perceived as suitable environments for these industrial activities. As argued before it seems that sometime during the Bronze Age the soils most suitable for agriculture had been appropriated for that purpose. Pollen analysis has additionally shown that during the later Bronze Age and throughout the Iron Age most of the remaining primeval woodlands on the higher grounds disappeared (see Chapter 2). It has also been suggested that intensive wetland exploitation for stockbreeding did not commence before the Iron Age (see Chapter 3). In the case of iron production, the presence of bog iron was unquestionably a prime factor in the location of the settlements. However, it was the importance of fuel and the requirement for extensive woodlands that could be managed for fuel production, that may have been the decisive factor in the choice of sites that specialised in bronze casting. The importance of wetlands for fuel continued into the Roman period, when a large number of pottery kilns were located in the Humber Wetlands (see Chapter 7).

Who, then, was the metalwork produced for? Halkon and Millett (1999)

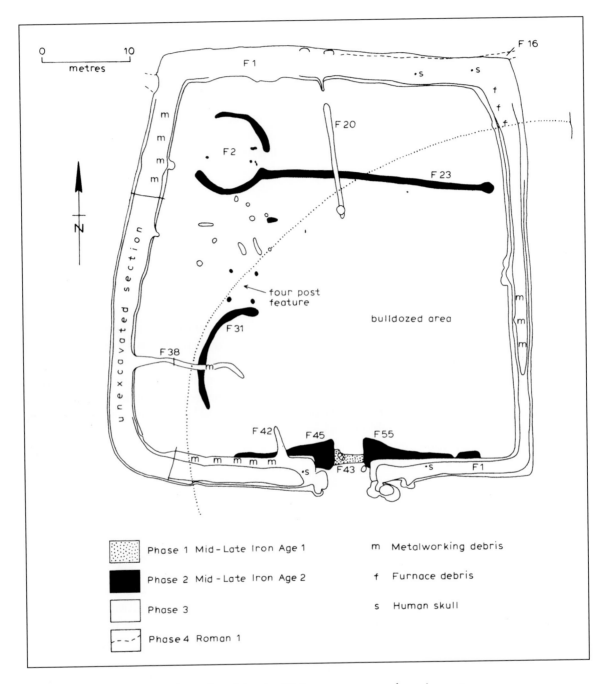

have argued that the metal produced in the Holme area was at least in part destined for use outside Holme-on-Spalding Moor, with evidence of cross-Humber trade or exchange, for example in the form of a Corieltauvian gold stater and Dragonby-type pottery found in the Holme area. The Hasholme logboat and similar craft would have been well-suited for this type of exchange. Similarly, the bronze casts from Weelsby Avenue and Kelk were the produce of highly specialised craftsman, with bronze working taking place at dedicated sites and the casts being traded with high-status sites. Whilst some of the produce was undoubtedly traded outside the eastern Yorkshire region, the people of the 'Arras culture' on the Yorkshire Wolds were the most likely recipients of the iron produced in the Holme area and of the bronze casts from Kelk.

The 'Arras culture,' or Arras tradition, is the term used to describe the people who lived from the fourth to the first century BC in what is now the East Riding of Yorkshire, in particular the Yorkshire Wolds. Their culture was characterised by cemeteries of square-ditch burial mounds, which frequently included bronze casts as grave goods – such as weapons and dress adornments – and, famously, the two-wheeled chariots or carts (Stead 1979). Their settlements were found in the dry valleys of the Wolds, such as the Gypsey Race, and their extensive field boundary systems are thought to indicate the maximum limits to which agriculture extended across the Wolds (Dent 1982). Towards the end of the Iron Age, Roman sources tell us that the name for the people living here was the 'Parisi', with their capital presumed to be at Redcliff near North Ferriby on the Humber estuary (Creighton 1990).

The land to the south of the Humber was occupied by the Corieltauvi, with their presumed capital or *oppidum* at Dragonby on the Lincoln Edge, which towards the end of the Iron Age expanded to some 6 ha (May 1996). The produce from Weelsby Avenue may have found its way to elite groups here. A relationship between specialised centres of metal production and high-status settlements has been argued for southern England in the Iron Age, for example in the case of Gussage All Saints and Bury Hill hillfort, both in Dorset – the former being where the bronzes were cast, and the latter the main recipient of the casts (Wainwright 1979; Cunliffe 1991). Similarly, the industrial activities undertaken in the wetlands at Holme-on-Spalding Moor and Kelk may have been an integrated part of the Arras culture (cf. Halkon and Millett 1999, see also Chapter 5).

Salt making

In areas adjacent to the North Sea, and to a smaller extent around the Humber, salt was produced from at least the Late Bronze Age, and by the later Iron Age this industry was being conducted on a large, near-industrial scale. Salt making in prehistoric and Roman Britain involved the evaporation of seawater by the sun and the subsequent heating or boiling of brine to obtain salt crystals. Alternatively, wet salt may have been poured into crude 'moulds' of coarse pottery in which the salt dried and was subsequently transported to its place of use, although evidence for this practice is not well-recorded for England (cf. Riehm 1961, Van der Broecke 1995). The use of salt increased with the increasing dependence on arable produce (Simmons 1999). It was used for the preservation of food, in particular fish, red meat and dairy produce, and as part of the human diet. Furthermore, salt was used in the preparation of leather, dyeing of textiles and in medicinal preparations (Rippon 2000).

The earliest discoveries of salt-making sites, or salterns, in the Humber Wetlands long predate our survey and significant discoveries and contributions have been made by Grant (1904), Swinnerton (1932), Baker (1960), Damien Grady, Betty Kirkham and others. Outside the Humber Wetlands, especially in the Fens of East Anglia, research into salterns has also been advanced (e.g. Lane and Morris 2001), helping us to understand how the salt industry in the Humber region developed. The survey of the Humber Wetlands found several new salt-working sites in the Lincolnshire Marsh dating to the Iron Age and Roman periods (e.g. Marshchapel–1, Ingoldmells–3 to 12 and 16; Fenwick *et al.* 2001), and one saltern site dated to the Late Saxon period (Marshchapel–2; Fenwick *et al.* 2001; see also Chapter 8).

The material culture of prehistoric salt production in Britain is dominated by 'briquetage', a term that encompasses a wide range of fired clay artefacts which were fashioned to facilitate the production of salt, and the evidence has been summarised by Gavin Thomas and William Fletcher (2001) (Figure 35). On the Marsh, the most common forms of briquetage remains are clay evaporation vessels and 'hand bricks' – pedestals for supporting the vessels. The concentrated dumping of the briquetage waste created artificial mounds which could have been used in subsequent years for seasonal settlement. The huts, houses or settlements that may be expected to accompany the salterns have remained largely elusive, the result of the seasonal or temporary nature of the salt making process and the use of ephemeral structures that have not been identified to date through archaeological research.

The oldest saltern from the Humber Wetlands date to the Late Bronze Age, and was excavated in 1992/3 by the Lindsey Archaeology Unit near Tetney

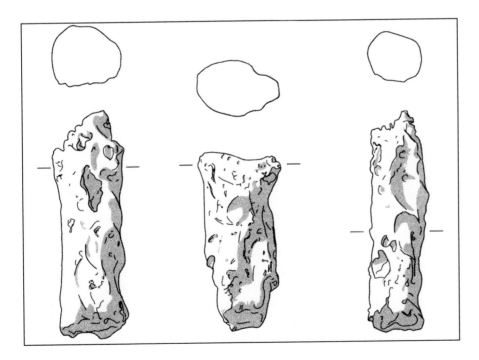

FIGURE 35.
Collection of 'hand-bricks' from Ingoldmells in the Lincolnshire Marsh, used for salt-making (scale 1:2) (Ingoldmells–6, Fenwick *et al.* 2001: 226).

FIGURE 36.
Recording and
sampling of a feeder
channel of saltern
Ingoldmells–16,
Lincolnshire Marsh in
2000.

© THE HUMBER WETLANDS
PROJECT, UNIVERSITY OF
HULL

Lock on the Lincolnshire Marsh (Palmer Brown 1993). The site comprised a natural settling pond and associated briquetage. The overwhelming majority of saltern sites on the Lincolnshire Marsh are, however, of Iron Age date. As the Iron Age briquetage mounds were constructed within a saltmarsh environment, and were buried in large numbers by marine clays and silts, Iron Age salt production appears to have coincided with a prolonged period of marine transgression (see Chapter 2). The burial of many of these salterns by marine deposits has prevented the emergence of a clear distribution or patterning of these sites in the landscape. We do not know, for example, how many salterns existed in the Iron Age on the Marsh, nor do we have information on the longevity of salt production.

As indicated above, it has been assumed that salt making was a seasonal activity, relying on the sun to evaporate most of the seawater. We may also assume that the salterns were situated alongside tidal creeks and that channels were excavated to feed ponds, pans or tanks, such as at Tetney Lock, where the seawater could settle or was turned into brine. Our survey may have found such a channel exposed on Ingoldmells beach, in July 1999, which was associated with briquetage (Figure 36; Ingoldmells–16; Fenwick *et al.* 2001). Research into the Roman saltern at Holbeck St James suggests that the flow of seawater through the channels was regulated by a simple sluice (Gurney 1999). Seasonal salt production in the Iron Age must have been linked to permanent settlement on the Lincolnshire Wolds and possibly formed part of

FIGURE 37.
A selection of
'hand-bricks' from the
salterns in the
Lincolnshire Marsh.

© THE HUMBER WETLANDS
PROJECT, UNIVERSITY OF
HULL

regional exchange networks that involved sites such as Dragonby, or small hillforts such as Yarborough Camp (May 1996; Challis and Harding 1975).

Whilst it remains difficult to distinguish Iron Age briquetage from that made in the Roman period, the existence of a number of Roman-period settlements in what had previously been a saltmarsh, suggests that the nature of salt production on the Marsh had changed (Figure 37). Much of the Roman period coincided with a period of marine regression (Chapter 2). Among the Roman settlements, several were identified as of relative high status or of a military character, indicated by the high proportions of fine wares such as Samian or colour coated wares (e.g. Tetney–10 and Marshchapel–1; Fenwick *et al.* 2001). Others were 'lesser' sites, dominated by locally produced grey wares (e.g. Tetney–3, Saltfleetby–5 and Ingoldmells–15; Fenwick *et al.* 2001, adding to previously identified examples). The existence of Roman settlement sites on the low-lying ground of the Lincolnshire Marsh is reflected throughout the Humber Wetlands (see Chapter 6). Although admittedly conjectural, it can be argued that salt making in the Roman period was of a more long-term nature than that in the Iron Age. The Roman-period marine regression focused salt production on the deepest tidal creeks and any adjacent settlement would have been less prone to flooding than its Iron Age predecessor. Moreover, the emerging settlement hierarchy would have provided mechanisms for a year-round salt trade. In the Fens of East Anglia, a number of high status sites developed in the second century AD, for example the stone tower of Stonea Grange near March, and at Langwood Farm near Chatteris (Jackson and Potter 1996; Crowson *et al.* 2000). The development of towns, from nearby Horncastle and Lincoln to York and others further afield, would have provided a ready market for the salt. Alternatively, the Roman army may have been involved in salt production or its distribution and the high-status sites may have been military settlements.

Salt making in Britain was not confined to the Lincolnshire Marsh. Indeed, late prehistoric or Roman period salterns have been identified in the Fens of East Anglia, on the Essex coast, on the south bank of the Thames estuary, in Kent, along the south coast of Britain (e.g. Langstone Harbour; Allan and Gardiner 2000) as far as the Lizard peninsula, and in the Somerset levels (e.g. Rippon 2000). Whilst the evidence from the Lincolnshire Marsh is therefore by no means without parallel in coastal Britain, the quantity of saltern sites on the Marsh remains one of the most striking and important prehistoric uses of coastal wetlands in the Humber region.

Conclusion

The archaeological evidence from the Humber Wetlands shows little evidence for permanent or long-term settlements predating the Iron Age. Although the fragile nature of prehistoric pottery may hide a much greater existence of settlement sites, our own survey, the full re-analysis of existing aerial photographs and research by others underpin this general conclusion. Any prehistoric settlements on the highest ground in the area, frequently favoured as the location of medieval settlement, may also have gone unnoticed. Nevertheless, for the Neolithic period only the single house at Easington in Holderness can be considered to represent long-term settlement. For the Bronze Age the Barmston 'lake-dwelling', in fact occupying a dried-out lake surface, is the most convincing example of a settlement. Our research into the five so-called lake-dwellings of Holderness has conclusively shown that only the sites at Barmston and Kelk were settlements. The latter, a settlement enclosure of Late Iron Age date with extensive evidence for metallurgical activity, forms part of a considerable number of sites that appear to have been established in the Humber Wetlands in this period.

The majority of these settlement sites are closely linked to the exploitation of resources for industrial activities that were readily available in the wetlands, but possibly no longer on the surrounding dryland. These resources included extensive woodlands for charcoal production that was essential for the production of iron and the casting of bronze and the sea for salt production. The mounds formed by the purposeful dumping of briquetage and other waste produced during the salt making processes became small artificial islands, ideally suited for temporary and seasonal occupation within the intertidal landscape. The Sutton Common site remains, for the time being, something of an enigma.

CHAPTER FIVE

Wetlands as Waterways

The Humber Wetlands are famed for the large number of prehistoric boats that have been found there (Figure 38). This rich maritime heritage is partly the result of the enthusiasm and persistence of local archaeologists – most notably Ted Wright – but, as we will see below, the Holocene development of the Humber has particularly favoured discoveries of later prehistoric craft. Two types of boats are present in the archaeological record, sewn-plank boats and logboats or dugout canoes, but it is likely that a third category was used in prehistory, namely hide boats or coracles (McGrail 2001). Such boats can only be preserved in particularly acidic conditions, for example in raised mires such as Thorne Moors, but boats were unlikely to be used here and it is doubtful if we will ever find prehistoric hideboats.

It has already been suggested that the proximity of many Mesolithic and Early Neolithic flint scatters to the contemporary rivers may be a direct consequence of the use of boats, either logboats or hideboats, by hunter-gatherers (see Chapter 3). Unfortunately, no boats of such early date have been found in the Humber Wetlands. The great age assigned to a dugout canoe from near Withernsea in Holderness, destroyed before radiocarbon dating was developed, remains unproven. The wooden paddle from Star Carr in the Vale of Pickering provides as yet the only physical evidence in the region that some type of boat was used in the early Holocene.

Research elsewhere in Europe has been more productive, for example in Scandinavia (Christensen 1990). The isostatic uplift of Scandinavia has compensated for the global rise in sea-level following the last ice age (see Chapter 2), and archaeological research there into Mesolithic sites in coastal wetlands and shallow waters has produced a number of logboats and paddles. At the coastal site of the Ertebølle culture Tybrind Vig, for example, the remains of three lime boats and up to 15 paddles have been found. Four of the paddle blades had been beautifully decorated with geometric patterns. The concept of hunter-gatherers travelling long distances through the landscape using boats is supported by the presence of 'ember places' on the floor of two of the boats (Andersen 1987). Other Mesolithic logboats have been found in the Netherlands, France and in the Alpine Lakes (Coles and Coles 1986).

In view of this evidence, we must ask why there are no very early boats from the Humber Wetlands. The main reason lies in the depth of the Mesolithic sea and rivers. The relative sea-level was around −4 m OD towards

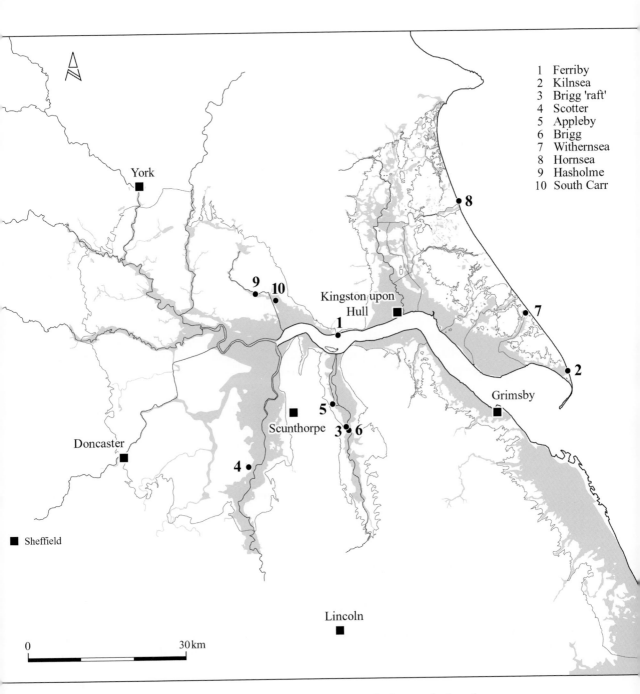

1	Ferriby
2	Kilnsea
3	Brigg 'raft'
4	Scotter
5	Appleby
6	Brigg
7	Withernsea
8	Hornsea
9	Hasholme
10	South Carr

0   30km

the end of the Mesolithic, around 4000 cal BC, and much deeper during the
earlier Mesolithic. For a Mesolithic boat to be preserved, for example in the
River Hull, it must lie below −4 m OD, or in excess of −5 m below the
current ground level. Such a boat could only be found during very large-scale
and deep excavations and such works have not been taken place on any
Mesolithic or Early Neolithic sites in the Humber Wetlands. However, the
Humber Wetlands have produced a considerable number of boats dated to

the Bronze Age and Iron Age. These include at least three sewn-plank boats from North Ferriby, one from Brigg and the fragmentary remains from Kilnsea. Prehistoric logboats have been found in the past at Hasholme, Appleby, Scotter, Brigg and elsewhere. By the Early Bronze Age, MHWST was near modern OD (Metcalfe *et al.* 2000). This means that prehistoric boats which were abandoned at their contemporary natural landing places near the upper limit of the tidal zone can now be found at relative shallow depths of 1 or 2 metres. Such natural landing places were subsequently buried beneath minerogenic sediments during phases of marine transgression. Large-scale land drainage and the shrinking of the former wetlands, and an increased tidal range and amplified erosion in the embanked Humber estuary, have enabled the prehistoric boats to be identified. No Roman or early medieval boats have been found in the Humber Wetlands. In part, this can again be attributed to sea-level change, with the natural landing places of Roman and early medieval boats being too high to have been preserved in waterlogged environments. Nevertheless, there is always the chance that some boats sank during these periods, and we should not discount the possibility that in future the maritime archaeology of the Humber Wetlands will be further enlarged.

The sewn-plank boats from North Ferriby and elsewhere in the Humber Wetlands and the considerable number of logboats from the region form an unparalleled collection of sometimes advanced and highly sophisticated craft. This chapter looks at these finds and their significance in a wider archaeological context.

Sewn-plank boats: Ferriby, Kilnsea and Brigg

The sewn-plank boats from Britain form a distinctive type of craft. They all date to the Bronze Age and, as no nails or clinkers existed, the wooden planks were sewn together with withies made from yew. The edges of the planks were bevelled so that adjacent planks interlocked in a form of 'tongue and groove' work. Mosses were used to caulk the hull, filling the seams between the planks. Without further structural constraints, the hull of such a craft would collapse under the pressure of the water and an ingenious system of cleats, integral to the planks, and transverse timbers provided structural integrity to the hull. Inserted frames, which may have doubled as seats for the rowers, would have provided additional strength. Prehistoric sewn-plank boats are unique to the coastal water of England and Wales, contrasting with the distribution of logboats of prehistoric date, which have been found on rivers and streams but are exceptional in coastal and estuarine contexts. No Bronze Age sewn-plank boats are known from the Continent and it is reasonable to suggest that this innovative design was originated in Britain.

The oldest sewn-plank boat is 'Ferriby 3', or F3. The Ferriby boats (F1, F2 and F3) were discovered on the intertidal foreshore of the Humber near North Ferriby between 1937 and 1963 (Wright 1990). They were initially believed to be of 'Viking Age', but were later dated by radiocarbon assay to the Middle

FIGURE 38.
Map of the Humber Wetlands, showing all prehistoric boats and the names of the sites mentioned in the text.

Bronze Age around 1500 cal BC (Switsur and Wright 1989). This prompted a programme of redating all the boats. Redating the Ferriby boats had become an important concern to Ted Wright who, with his brother Chris, was responsible for the discoveries. Concern for the accuracy of the dates had grown with the realisation that previous dating programmes had not taken sufficient account of the chemicals that had been used since the 1930s to preserve the timbers, and as part of the new programme researchers aimed to remove 99 per cent of these chemicals. A full description of the methodology used to achieve this is published in Wright *et al.* (2001). This recent research shows that F1 is dated to 1880–1680 cal BC, F2 to 1940–1750 cal BC and F3 to 2020–1780 cal BC, and thus all three boats were made in the Early Bronze Age.

FIGURE 39.
F1 in Greenwich Dock.
THE NATIONAL MARITIME MUSEUM

None of the boats was found intact. F1, the earliest and best-preserved discovery, comprises the near-complete keel-planks, two outer bottom planks and fragmentary remains of the side strakes, showing considerable detail in the construction (Figure 39). In the past, various reconstructions of the Ferriby boats have been made, but the least controversial reconstruction shows F1 as a 15.9 m long boat with a 2.5 m beam. Such a boat could have accommodated up to 18 paddlers plus a steersman with a freely-held paddle near the stern of the boat to act as a rudder or, alternatively, a smaller crew with greater load capacity (Coates in Wright 1990). F2 consists of two keel planks, joined amidships similar to F1. F3 is formed by an outer bottom plank stitched to the remains of a lowest side strake. Interestingly, the remains of F3 were found to be placed on lengths of roundwood, as if they had been put aside, and the keelplank of F2 rested on a single alder log. Together with the many oak chips with axe marks found on the foreshore, this has been interpreted as evidence of either boat manufacture or repair, and the Ferriby foreshore is therefore the world's oldest known boatyard.

Depending on reconstructed design and requirements for freeboard, F1 would have had a maximum load between 6.9 and 11 tonnes (Coates in Wright 1990). With a maximum load of 6.9 tonnes, for example, F1 could have a maximum cargo of 5.1 tonnes, allowing for a crew of 18 paddlers and two steersmen, each with an average weight of 75 kg and an additional weight of 20 kg for paddles and personal gear. Simply on the basis of its carrying capacity, F1 was therefore well equipped as an inshore or coastal craft. It could carry 22 cattle (weighing 225 kg each) or a staggering 102 sheep (at 50 kg each), if these could be fitted onto the boat. In reality, and allowing for bilge water, the actual cargo would have been considerably below this theoretical carrying capacity. When in use as a seacraft under favourable conditions, carrying a much lighter cargo of prestige items and passengers, the boat would have had a much greater freeboard and would therefore have been considerably safer.

In addition to the Ferriby boats, a single plank from the beach of Kilnsea in Holderness has also been identified as forming part of a sewn-plank boat (Figure 40). The plank is of oak and its maximum dimensions are 1995 mm long, 440 mm wide and *c.* 75 mm thick (not including the cleats). On discovery in 1996, by members of the Hull Natural History Society, it was already severely damaged through desiccation, and tool marks were only distinguishable on the upper side of the plank. Nevertheless, the presence of an integral projecting cleat and two mortised holes, in dimensions very similar to those of F1, put it beyond doubt that it was part of a sewn-plank boat. The find was dated by radiocarbon assay to 1750–1620 cal BC, or the Early Bronze Age (Van de Noort *et al.* 1999).

A paddle discovered in 1995 provides one of three prehistoric examples from the Ferriby foreshore. No other specimens are known from the Humber Wetlands. The paddle was dated to 1420–1260 cal BC, and the blade measures 450 mm long and has a lanceolate form (Fenwick 1995). This paddle is considerably smaller than a replica made of the first paddle found on the foreshore in 1939, which was destroyed in 1943 and therefore never dated.

Near Brigg in the Ancholme valley, a sewn-plank boat was discovered in the late 1880s during clay diggings and it is generally known as the Brigg 'raft'. The boat was initially interpreted as a pontoon bridge, raft, or flat-bottomed boat (Thropp 1887). The first re-excavation took place in 1907/8 by Rev. Alfred Hunt, who described the craft as a Viking raft or Pontoon Bridge. In 1973, a second re-excavation was undertaken by the National Maritime Museum. This research provides a seminal example of close integration of archaeological and palaeoenvironmental research (McGrail 1981). It showed that at the time when the Brigg 'raft' was built, the Ancholme floodplain around Brigg had become inundated with brackish water and that, as a consequence of the sea-level rise, the river had become tidal. The shore vegetation included expanses of reed (*Phragmites communis*), whilst insect analysis indicated that the 'raft' itself was abandoned at or around the high water mark of spring tides. As discussed in Chapter 2, the floodplains of the rivers in the Humber Wetlands reached their maximum extent during the so-called floodplain aggradation phase, which had been reached around 1500 cal BC. At Brigg, the floodplain of the Ancholme narrows to *c*. 400 m and this narrowing provided the natural place to cross the river.

The Brigg 'raft' resembles the sewn-plank boats from North Ferriby in a number of ways – the integral cleats and transverse timbers, similar arrange-

FIGURE 40.
The remnants of a peat bed over blue-grey estuarine clay on the Holderness coast near Kilnsea explain the context of the Kilnsea boat.

© THE HUMBER WETLANDS PROJECT, UNIVERSITY OF HULL

84

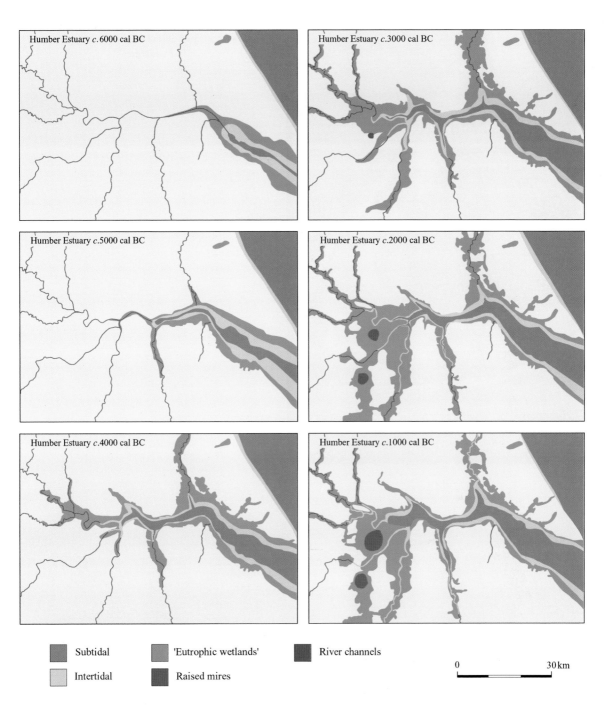

Subtidal

Intertidal

'Eutrophic wetlands'

Raised mires

River channels

0   30 km

PLATE I. Palaeogeographic maps of the Humber Wetlands, from 6000 cal BC to 1000 cal BC
(after Metcalfe *et al.* 2000: 120, but with significant modifications).

PLATE 2. Spurn Head, at the southern tip of Holderness.

NEIL MITCHELL © APS (UK)

PLATE 3. Aerial photograph of the River Ouse, flooded in 1999.

NEIL MITCHELL © APS (UK)

PLATE 4. Aerial photograph of Sutton Common in 1997.

NEIL MITCHELL © CCT & APS (UK)

PLATE 5. The 'Inclesmoor' map, dated to *c.* 1405. The vegetation on Thorne Moors is symbolised, and the various drainage, transport and farming features are shown in great detail. This was intended as a tabletop map, and the words are to be read whilst walking around the table.

PUBLIC RECORD OFFICE

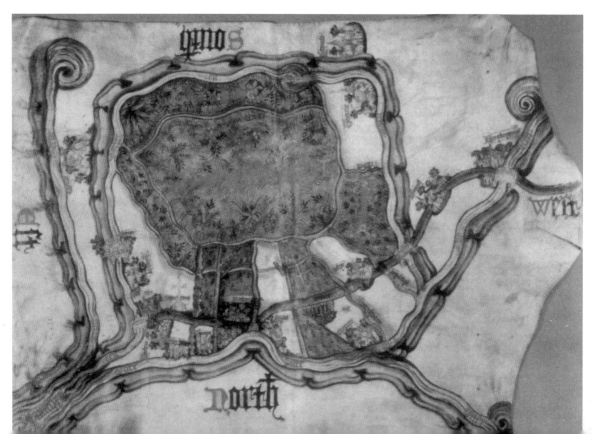

PLATE 6. All Saints' at Aughton, protruding into the Derwent floodplain. Over the centuries, a record has been kept of the highest floods by adding inscriptions to the tower; the inscription illustrated is of 1747.

ments to make the hull watertight and similarities in the woodworking techniques used. However, unlike the Ferriby boats, the planks of the Brigg 'raft' had been sewn using continuous rather than individual stitches and the 'raft' had a flat-bottomed profile. The flat-bottomed 'raft' could take the ground on a falling tide and would have been especially useful for inland and inshore waters, but was unlikely to function well in open water. Therefore, the most likely function of the Brigg 'raft' was not as a seagoing vessel but to ferry people and goods across the Ancholme floodplain (McGrail 1981). The 'raft' may also have been used for north–south transport within the Ancholme valley, travelling with the tides. Although this interpretation has been challenged (e.g. Roberts 1992), the location of the Brigg 'raft' at the constriction of the River Ancholme at Brigg suggest that its primary use was as a 'ferry' across the Ancholme, rather than a 'raft', but the term Brigg 'raft' is now an archaeological convention. A series of radiocarbon dates show that the Brigg 'raft' was much younger than the Ferriby boats, dating to *c.* 825–760 cal BC (cf. Switsur in McGrail 1981) in the Late Bronze Age. John Coates (in McGrail 1981) reckons that the Brigg 'raft' had a safe maximum load of 7.16 tonnes, equalling 20 men and 100 sheep, or 10 men and 29 cattle, indicating a potential volume of transport that exceeded the requirement for the exchange of selected prestige goods.

Also from this Late Bronze Age and Iron Age period are two more fragmentary remains from the foreshore at North Ferriby, possibly forming parts of sewn-plank boats. F4 and F5, as these remains are called, were dated to 800–200 cal BC and 410–200 cal BC respectively (Wright and Switsur 1992). If the identifications are correct, then these finds extend the period of boat building using the sewn-plank method well into the Iron Age, also indicating the long-term importance of the North Ferriby site for exchange and trade, spanning the period from *c.* 2000 to *c.* 200 cal BC.

Logboats

Prehistoric logboats are the most commonly known craft from the Humber Wetlands. Built from a single hollowed out oak tree trunk, the bow and stern of the logboats were sometimes cut directly from the trunks, but several examples include transoms – planks that closed the open ends of the trunks. In length, the logboats vary from less than 8 m to more than more than 16 m, although it is likely that many smaller logboats were in use but were not identified when found in the past. The logboats in the area all date from the Late Bronze Age and Iron Age, with the possible exceptions of the example from Withernsea that has been attributed to the Mesolithic. This bias to the later prehistoric era is principally a result of sea-level change in the region as described above and it seems likely that both before and after the Late Bronze and Iron Age periods logboats were relatively common craft for inshore and riverine use.

From the Humber Wetlands, logboats are known from Scotter in the Trent valley, Appleby and Brigg in the Ancholme valley, and from Withernsea and Hornsea from Holderness (McGrail 1990). All these craft were discovered at the end of the nineteenth or the early part of the twentieth century. The Appleby logboat, found in 1943 during dredging of the River Ancholme, is one of the oldest dated logboats in England, with a radiocarbon age of *c.* 1100 cal BC. It measures *c.* 8 by 1.35 m and was fitted with a transom. It is one of the smaller such craft from the Humber Wetlands. No dates exist for the remaining examples, but on the basis of descriptions made at the time of discovery, the logboat (or two boats) from Scotter are also considered to be of Bronze Age date.

The logboat from Brigg in the Ancholme valley (known as the Brigg boat to distinguish it from the Brigg 'raft') was found in 1886 during excavations for the Brigg Gas Works, but was largely destroyed by fire in 1942. The boat was made from a single oak log, 14.8 m long and 1.4 m wide, and the stern was fitted with a two-piece transom. At the bow, remains of a wooden shelf were identified and this has been interpreted as a small deck for a bowman who could steer the boat with a pole (Atkinson 1887; McGrail 1978). Fragments of the Brigg logboat were radiocarbon dated to 1260–800 cal BC, in the later Bronze Age (McGrail 1981). The logboat, longer than the example from Hasholme (see below), would have been capable of transporting significant cargoes.

Two years before the discovery of the logboat, a trackway had been found nearby. It lay some 1.2 to 1.5 m below the level of the 'raft' and wood from the level of the trackway has been dated to 950–350 cal BC (Godwin and Willis 1960). The trackway consisted of large oak planks laid side by side transversely across the road, resting on brushwood, and held in position by posts driven through mortised holes (Wylie 1884). Its 'oversized' construction and width suggest that it had been designed and built to carry a considerable volume of traffic and its relative smooth surface would have enabled the movement of carts. It is not clear whether the Brigg trackway provided access to the River Ancholme as a jetty, or to a bridge across the river. No evidence of either a trackway or a bridge on the east side of the River Ancholme has been discovered, suggesting that the former explanation is more likely than the latter. The evidence from the 'raft', logboat and trackway from Brigg points to prehistoric exchange and trade involving a high volume of goods, and to a regional exchange network from at least the Late Bronze Age (see below).

Only one logboat in the Humber Wetlands has been excavated by archaeologists – the Hasholme logboat in the Vale of York, discovered during land drainage works in 1984 (Figure 41). Subsequent research, by the University of Durham and the National Maritime Museum, integrated the archaeology of the boat with detailed investigations of the contemporary environment, showing the extension of the intertidal Walling Fen complex into the southern parts of the Vale of York (Millett and McGrail 1987). The logboat itself was built from a single tree, felled between 322 and 277 BC. In all, it was over

FIGURE 41.
The Hasholme
logboat, showing the
stern transom with
the carved 'U'.
PETER HALKON

12.5 m long. A single-piece transom closed the stern and a two-part transom the bow. The boat was probably propelled by paddlers, and could accommodate a maximum crew of 20. In contrast to the 'sophisticated' sewn-plank boats, logboats are usually seen as utilitarian craft, but the Hasholme example was decorated, and it was evidently an item of status (e.g. Millett in Halkon and Millett 1999). The Hasholme logboat had a carrying capacity of 8.9 tonnes, a potential load greater than the Brigg 'raft'. The cargo of the Hasholme logboat on its final journey included sides of beef and timbers.

Undoubtedly, more boats remain buried beneath the alluvial and marine sediments of the Humber wetlands and when these boats are dug up, they may not be recognised for what they are. This is especially true for the smaller logboats, which are easily mistaken for 'bog oaks'. The recent discovery of the South Carr logboat, near North Cave in the Vale of York, serves as a reminder of this. It was found during drainage works, believed to be another bog oak and left to dry out before detailed analysis could be undertaken (Halkon 1997).

Prehistoric exchange and trade

The wealth of prehistoric boats from the Humber Wetlands provides an opportunity to assess the role of these craft in exchange and trade, and also the wider social and economic significance of rivers and boats to prehistoric society. Prehistoric exchange and trade remain an important topic in archaeological debate, but the modes of transport of the goods exchanged have been treated as a rather ephemeral topic.

On the basis of material culture, it has been assumed that from the Early Neolithic the communication networks in Britain had been widening and that by the later Neolithic regional exchange networks existed. The distribution of polished axes exemplifies this. Axes of the Borrowdale Volcanic Series (or petrological Group VI) are the most numerous in the Humber basin (see Chapter 3). The origin of this type of axe lies in Cumbria and it probably comes from the 'axe factories' in the Great Langdale and Scafell areas (Chapter 3). The great distances over which these polished axes were traded in the early part of the Neolithic reflect complex networks of communication, with axes exchanged as gifts or commodities in a 'hand-to-hand movement' rather than by boat around England and Wales (Edmonds 1995). This practice may have played a role in the subsequent development of regional traditions and regional exchange networks (Bradley and Edmonds 1993). However, polished axes from this source are the most numerous type on both sides of the Humber estuary and the confluence of rivers to the west, showing that this network encompassed both the north and south banks of the Humber and their respective hinterlands. It is inconceivable that boats of some sort were not involved in the development and maintenance of this network, even if they were not part of the long-distance transport from Cumbria. The oldest boat from the Humber Wetlands known to us, F3, is too young to have played a role in the distribution of polished axes and there is no archaeological evidence that indicates what type of boat could have been used for cross-estuary and inland shipping. Logboats are the most likely candidates, but the possibility that the most advanced craft of the Neolithic period were hide-boats should not be discounted (cf. McGrail 1997).

By the later Neolithic or Early Bronze Age, these exchange networks appear to have extended into continental Europe. The material culture of Late Neolithic and Early Bronze Age Britain includes, for example, amber from the Baltic (Beck and Shennan 1991), bronzes of continental origin (Rohl and Needham 1998), and jewellery of gold, faience and jet. The exchanged material culture accompanied the exchange of ideas, particularly visible in the parallel development of Beaker-type pottery in the British Isles and on the Continent, but which included a broad spectrum of sacred and profane concepts (e.g. Kristiansen 1987). The archaeological evidence suggests that members of the elite in the British Isles frequently travelled to continental Europe, to gain knowledge and partake in reciprocal gift-exchange, thus forming elite networks (e.g. Roymans 1990).

These networks continued to exist in the Middle and Late Bronze Age and Early Iron Age. During this period, the ritual deposition of weapons, ornaments and ornamental weapons in wetlands on both sides of the North Sea has created treasures which are displayed in many museums (Burgess 1990; Bradley 1990; see Chapter 6). The existence of a class or elite after *c.* 2500 cal BC that could have driven the extended exchange networks is not questioned, but the evidence for this is not primarily found in the Humber Wetlands but on the drylands, such as the Yorkshire Wolds where the 'Great Barrows' and early ringforts are constructed in this period (Manby 1980; 1988). Further afield, the emergence of an elite, or at least its material manifestation, is shown in the rich graves in Wessex for the period 2000–1400 cal BC (what used to be called the 'Wessex Culture'). Only the barrow cemetery at Butterbump in the

Lincolnshire Marsh may indicate the presence of an elite in the lowlands at this time.

Direct evidence proving that the earliest sewn-plank boats such as those from North Ferriby and Kilnsea were engaged in the development or maintenance of this European exchange network does not exist. This type of Bronze Age boat remains unique to Britain. Nevertheless, the development of sewn-plank boats around 2000 cal BC is significant for our understanding of the method of exchanging goods across the Channel and the North Sea. Until recently, it was believed that sewn-plank boats were used for inland water transport only. However, following the discovery of the sewn-plank Dover boat in 1992 (Clark forthcoming) and the plank of the Kilnsea boat in 1996, the suggestion that these craft were involved in seafaring has become more widely accepted. This is supported by the fact that all early sewn-plank boats, including the remains from Caldicott in the Severn estuary (McGrail 1997), have been found within distinct coastal or estuarine contexts. This contrasts with the distribution of prehistoric logboats, which have been found in a range of waters, but predominantly in rivers. Their relative instability limited their use to inshore waters only.

What, then, was the reason for the innovative design of these boats? The only type of boat, before the development of sewn-plank boats, that was capable of coastal sailing or seafaring was a boat made of hide around a wooden or timber frame. But hide boats are unlikely to survive in the archaeological record (McGrail 1997). If, as suggested elsewhere (Wright *et al.* 2001), the sewing of hides for the building of hide-boats inspired the Ferriby boat builders to sew the planks, than it is likely that it was their aim to build more robust craft. With the archaeological evidence for cross-Channel or North Sea exchange in mind, it is furthermore reasonable to suggest that the increased contact with continental Europe provided the incentive for this innovation or, alternatively, that sewn-plank boats provided the mechanism for regular continental travel and the extension of the exchange networks.

Whilst the exchange of prestige goods is evident in the archaeological record from the Neolithic onwards, the exchange or trade in high value bulk goods, including livestock, may have existed as early as *c.* 2000 cal BC – as both prehistoric sewn-plank boats and logboats were capable of carrying considerable loads. On the north bank of the Humber, the settlement of Redcliffe, *c.* 1 km west of the North Ferriby foreshore, may have played a key role in this trade, and continued to do so in the Iron Age where it developed to become an important 'port of trade' in the early Roman period (Creighton 1990, Millett 1999, see also Chapter 7). On the south bank of the Humber, a similar trading settlement may have existed at South Ferriby Cliff, where the Lincolnshire Wolds meet the River Humber. Here, Iron Age coins and other metal objects have been found in considerable numbers, but no excavations have taken place to ascertain the nature of the settlement. Where the Lincoln Edge meets the Humber estuary, at Winteringham, coins and metal objects of Iron Age date have been found, but this site is not believed to have developed into one of the Iron Age 'ports of trade' and was abandoned before the establishment of the Roman settlement here, at the *terminus* of Ermine Street (Creighton 1990; see Chapter 7).

The role of logboats in late prehistoric exchange and trade is easily underestimated. Despite their lack of sophistication in comparison to the sewn-plank boats, their enormous load capacity allowed logboats to undertake the majority of transport in later prehistory. The logboats' likely cargoes included high value bulk goods such as animals, passengers and most probably the iron produced in the Holme area and, as the Hasholme boat showed, meat and timber. The recently discovered logboat from Shardlow, Derbyshire, in the Trent valley included large blocks of stone, a rare commodity in the lowlands around the Humber. The archaeological record provides clear insights into the distribution of 'exotic' artefacts, but the trading of organic goods, including livestock and people, is more difficult to identify.

Nevertheless, this exchange or trade of goods may have been controlled by elite groups in society, and have developed from existing networks involved in prestige goods exchange. The carved 'U' decoration on the transom of the Hasholme boat conceivably identifies the boat as belonging to a particular group in society, such as an elite family or to a 'tribe'. If boats were controlled by elite groups and expressed their power and prowess, than it would provide an explanation for the concentration of boat finds at North Ferriby for the Early Bronze Age, and of the boats and 'oversized' trackway at Brigg for the later Bronze Age. The North Ferriby boats could have been controlled by, or could have provided the mechanism for exchange to, elite groups based on the Yorkshire Wolds. The Brigg boats and trackway could have similarly been controlled by elite groups based on the Lincolnshire Wolds or Lincoln Edge. It is probable that smaller logboats would have been used by other families for everyday activities, including the exchange of food but, as argued before, these difficult-to-identify objects are not well-represented in the archaeological record of the Humber Wetlands.

Conclusion

Throughout the world, hundreds of logboats have been found from all wetland contexts and considering that the discovery of such craft is nearly always a matter of chance, we may safely suggest that only a fraction of the logboats used in the Humber Wetlands over the millennia have been found. The sewn-plank boats, on the other hand, are unique to Britain; and outside the Humber wetlands have been found at Caldicott and Goldcliff in the Severn estuary and at Dover. On the basis of the discoveries of these craft and on the available contextual information – and with a clear understanding of the archaeological biases involved – it becomes possible to review the role of wetlands as waterways in the prehistoric Humber Wetlands.

From the Early Mesolithic onwards, logboats and possibly hideboats were used for daily movements and travel using the many inland waters of the region. With the possible exception of the Withernsea logboat, such early craft are not known from the archaeological record of the region. However, the paddle from Star Carr and the close geographical association of the rivers and flint concentrations throughout the region clearly supports such a notion. The advantages of travelling by boat rather than on foot are apparent. It allowed for the transport of a larger range and quantity of material including tents, clothing, baskets, left-over food, hunting equipment, embers and any raw materials required, such as unknapped flint nodules. Hunter-gatherers travelling by boat would be able to locate any watering places used by the larger mammals, which were ideal hunting places. And boat travel provided access to the rich resources of wildfowl and fish.

As woodlands developed in the early Holocene, travelling by boat was not only easier, but the rivers offered familiar paths through the rapidly changing landscape and thus offered opportunities for groups of wandering hunter-gatherers to meet up to exchange goods and gossip. People's perception of the region would have comprised an intimate knowledge of the rivers bounded by deciduous forests, with frequent watering locations where hunting was most promising, and occasional clearances where people returned for short visits over extended periods of time. We may also assume that the areas at some distance from the rivers remained *tabula rasa*, or unknown lands.

It seems likely that in the Neolithic and Bronze Age, logboats, such as the example from Appleby, and presumably hideboats, continued to be used for hunting expeditions or the exchange of goods, but the changing focus on agriculture and on permanent settlements in areas of relatively higher ground can only have resulted in diminishing use of the boats in everyday life. Nevertheless, the developing networks in the Neolithic, Bronze Age and Iron Age required craft that enabled regional exchange of goods and the development of large logboats may be associated with this process. These logboats, with examples from Brigg, Scotter and Hasholme, were capable of carrying considerable cargoes and crews of more than 20 men. Such craft were no longer built and operated by family groups. Rather, they required the involvement of larger groups of people, presumably under the direction of an emerging or established elite. This concept is supported where the cargo has been recovered. The cargo of the Hasholme boat, for example, is described as 'prime' cuts of beef and building timbers, rather than objects used in everyday activities. The return cargo may have been iron produced in the Walling Fen area (Chapter 4).

Sewn-plank boats such as those from North Ferriby and Kilnsea represent an important innovation, probably developed from techniques used at that time for hide boats. This innovation was aimed at building more robust boats in order to develop or maintain exchange networks that extended into continental Europe. The use of these craft in long-distance exchange must have been controlled by elite groups that, around 2000 cal BC, must be sought in the northern half of the Yorkshire Wolds rather than within the Humber Wetlands. This long-distance exchange may well have been associated with an important rite of passage, for example with the coming to age of young male members of the elite. The long journeys would have provided such aspiring leaders with sacred and everyday knowledge that would support their future roles, alongside the exotic objects such as beakers, jewellery and weapons that attested to this knowledge. Besides, the landscape in which the Kilnsea boat was found, which includes a range of monuments dated to *c.* 2000 cal BC and earlier periods, suggests that journeys across the North Sea may have been linked to the ancestors or ancestral rites. Nevertheless, sewn-plank boats may well have been used in more local activities, especially cross-Humber exchange, using the natural havens of North and South Ferriby.

CHAPTER SIX

Late Prehistoric Ritualised Activity in Wetlands

Over the past three decades, archaeological research has contributed greatly to our understanding of the economic aspects of life in wetlands in the past – especially food procurement strategies. Another established theme in wetland research has been the concept of wetlands acting as special and sometimes sacred places where ritualised activities took place (e.g. Coles and Coles 1989; Bradley 1990; 2000; Van der Sanden 1996). Wetlands were, of course, not the only landscapes that could be interpreted as sacred or ritual, but the archaeological evidence suggests that in later prehistory certain types of wetland were seen in a particular way that did not apply to drylands. The evidence is formed principally by votive depositions in wet places and bog bodies.

The earliest evidence of votive depositions in wetlands in European prehistory comes from Denmark. Here, during the Early Neolithic, *c.* 3950–2900 cal BC, whole pots of the Funnelbeaker culture, stone axes and animal remains, especially skulls, were placed in shallow water, at some distance from the bank. Subsequent peat growth has turned these wetlands into mires or bogs and these finds were thus initially noted as bog finds. Many are closely associated with human skeletons or bones, which were deposited in the same wetland locations (Koch 1998; 1999). Comparable evidence from Britain dates from the later Neolithic onwards and notable concentrations of such depositions can be found on the margins of the Fens of East Anglia and in the Thames basin (Bradley 1990). The evidence from the Thames is associated with the deposition of human remains, although the deposition or burial of human remains may have taken place on distinct stretches of the river (Bradley and Gordon 1988).

Over time, the practice of depositing goods in wetlands changed. During the Bronze Age, bronze artefacts and especially weapons appear to have been favoured. This practice continued in the Iron Age, the Roman period and beyond, and research in the Netherlands and Ireland has found that whole pots and metal objects including weapons were still deposited in bogs as late as the sixteenth and seventeenth centuries AD (Van der Sanden 1996). The principal religious motivation for this practice is the belief that ancestral or natural spirits or gods resided in undomesticated places, ranging from mountain tops in some societies to certain wetlands in others (Koch 1999; cf. Bradley

2000). Rituals, including the votive depositions of material goods, were a medium for communicating with or placating these spirits. In socio-political terms, this practice is explained through the concept of 'Gifts to the Gods', whereby the individual or group that is involved in the votive depositions derives status and prestige from the ritual, as an intermediary between people and the supernatural (Gregory 1980). The ritual itself acts as a counter-

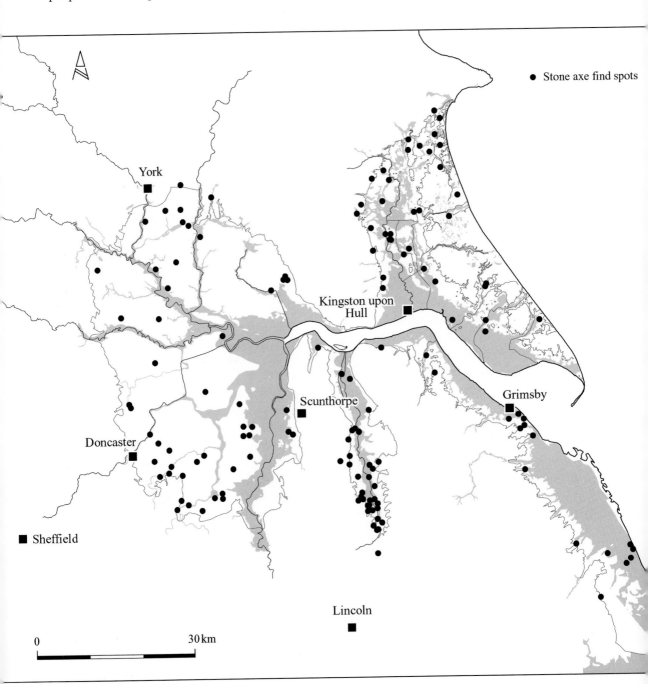

inflationary mechanism by removing prestige objects from the social system more effectively than by melting them down (Bradley 1990).

Were there votive depositions in the Humber Wetlands? The archaeological evidence is not as clear as it is in the East Anglian Fens and the Thames basin, but the sum of finds from wet places in the Humber basin amounts to a considerable corpus of what can only be described as votive depositions in wet places. Unfortunately, the majority of objects that fall into this category were found some time ago, and the context of these discoveries was only accurately recorded in a few instances. This chapter discusses these finds and the contemporary environmental context. It also looks at human remains in and adjacent to the wetlands, providing additional insights into the perception of wetlands as 'special places'.

Votive depositions in the Humber Wetlands

The earliest archaeological evidence for votive depositions in wet places in the Humber Wetlands is from the Neolithic period. Suspected concentrations of stone and flint axes suggesting such a practice have been found, for example, from the upper Ancholme floodplain, the eastern fringe of the lower Trent, the western flanks of the Isle of Axholme in the Humberhead Levels and the northern half of Holderness (Figure 42). However, the exact provenance and contemporary context of a majority of these finds remains unclear. Finds from the Ancholme valley upstream from Brigg, for example, include 44 stone and flint axes, including 18 polished axes, but it remains unclear whether their context at the time of deposition were wet places or the woodlands predating the wetland expansion (Van de Noort and Davies 1993; see also Chapter 2). Objects of Neolithic date include some fine individual examples, such as the jadeite axe from Wroot (Figure 43). Jadeite comes from the Alpine region. It is not a particularly suitable material for a functional axe and axes with a jadeite axehead are more likely to have performed ceremonial roles. This example was found in a workman's chest in Wroot, but had allegedly been discovered in the wetlands of nearby Haxey Carr during drain digging (Campbell-Smith 1963).

For the Bronze Age, the situation is somewhat more distinct. The total number of find spots comprising metalwork of Bronze Age date in the Humber Wetlands is 138 (Van de Noort and Davies 1993). These finds date overwhelmingly to the Middle and Late Bronze Age, or the period between 1500 and 600 BC (Figure 22). These include a large number of axes, chisels and tools, but also spearheads, rapiers, dirks, shields, bowls and, additionally, a golden torc (Figure 44). Despite difficulties with provenancing many of these finds, at least 50 find spots can be associated with wet places or contemporary wetlands. For example, finds from the Ancholme floodplain include at least 18 bronze axes and spearheads from near Redbourne, Brigg and Winteringham and a rapier from near Glentham. The clearest evidence for votive depositions in the Ancholme valley comes from Appleby Carrs, where three or four spearheads, eight rapiers and one cast-hilted sword have been found. Several

FIGURE 42.
Map of the Humber
Wetlands, showing all
locations of stone axes.

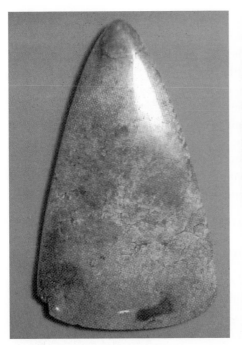

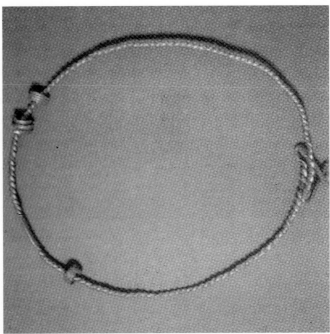

weapons had been broken before deposition, and it has been suggested that the bronzes were not thrown in the water, but laid out on the ground as a structural deposit, possibly in shallow waters (Davey and Knowles 1972).

From the floodplain of the River Hull, eight bronze axes have been recorded, as well as two spearheads of which one was broken in antiquity, two swords from near Nafferton and Leven Carrs and a bronze dirk from near Wawne. A second dirk, dated to *c.* 1200 BC, was discovered in the 1970s during dyke clearing of the Watton Beck (Trump 1985). Bronze tools have been found in a wetland context from near Wawne and Watton Abbey, but a collection of 12 axes and two parts of a sword from near Fox Hill by Nafferton have been described as a possible founders' hoard, rather than votive deposit. Finally, in the 1240s, nine metal bowls and a bronze axe were found on Eske Moor and are now believed to have been deliberately placed there (English and Miller 1991). The lower Trent valley has also contributed a significant number of bronze objects, including the Burringham shield, although the middle reaches of the Trent have produced greater amounts of material (Scurfield 1977). The material in the lower Trent valley appears to have been found in somewhat greater concentrations than elsewhere in the Humber Wetlands, with bronze hoards recorded from near Messingham, Bottesford, and Burringham. The latter included 22 socketed axes, 8 socketed spearheads, one chisel and six strengthening plates from the base of bronze buckets.

Elsewhere in the Humber Wetlands, ample evidence for the practice of depositing objects in wet places exists. Haxey Carrs, in the Humberhead Levels, was not only the findspot of the polished jadeite axe, but also of a golden multiple-ribbon torc, with rings attached and dated to the Middle Bronze

FIGURE 43 (*left*). Jadeite axe from Wroot, Humberhead Levels.

NORTH LINCOLNSHIRE MUSEUM

FIGURE 44 (*right*) Gold torc from Haxey Carrs, Humberhead Levels.

THE BRITISH MUSEUM

Age. From the vicinity of the Iron Age site of Sutton Common in the Humberhead Levels come the remains of several Bronze Age finds including a bronze dirk blade and several axes, one of which had been deliberately snapped in half in antiquity (Parker Pearson and Sydes 1997).

It appears that deposition of valuable metal objects in the Humber Wetlands during the Iron Age was not a regular custom. Against the 138 find locations in the Humber Wetlands of metal artefacts dated to the Bronze Age, the Iron Age contributes only 24 find spots. These include 16 finds of coins, often staters of late Iron Age date, and 2 small coin hoards from the till outcrop of Grimsby. The remaining examples include an Iron Age La Tène II sword from Hull (Evans 2000), and several finds not closely associated with wetlands.

One of the most enigmatic finds from the Humber Wetlands is the Roos Carr model of figurines and boat (Figure 45). The find originally comprised

FIGURE 45.
The Roos Carr model of figurines and boat, found in 1836 in southern Holderness.

HULL AND EAST RIDING MUSEUM, KINGSTON UPON HULL MUSEUMS AND ART GALLERY

eight wooden figurines and a 'boat', with a stern that appears to be an animal-head. Three figurines have been lost since their discovery in 1836 (Poulson 1840). Four pairs of hourglass perforations show that a maximum of four figures could stand in the boat. Several figurines carried shields, and may have held spears as well. Both boat and figurines were made of yew, and the eyes of quartzite pebbles. A recent radiocarbon assay of a loose fragment of wood has dated the model to 606–509 cal BC, in the Early Iron Age, but this date may be too early for the carving of the figurines, as yew is a particularly slow growing tree. Compared to other anthropomorphic wooden figures from Britain and Ireland, the Roos Carr figurines are rather small and less stylised in design (Coles 1990). The question of the gender of the figurines has caused considerable debate in the archaeological world, but during a recent refurbishment of the prehistoric displays in Hull and East Riding Museum, the male organs from the figures were restored to their rightful owners, having been considered too shocking for the museum's visitors in the Victorian period! The function of the model remains ambiguous. Its location on the edge of Roos Carr, which in the Early Iron Age was an expanding eutrophic wetland, suggests it was a votive deposition.

The environmental context of those artefacts that are incontrovertibly votive depositions in wet places requires further thought. Despite the lack of contextual information, it is clear that the majority of bronzes were not deposited in rivers as these objects were not discovered during the deepening or clearing of the old river channels. Furthermore, votive depositions in minerogenic wetlands, such as riparian meadows or saltmarshes, are rare for the Bronze Age both in the Humber Wetlands and elsewhere. Research in the Humber estuary has only produced a single bronze object from such a context, an axe from North Ferriby. Rather, the majority of bronzes appear to have been found during the digging of drains on the floodplain margins in the seventeenth century AD and later. The jadeite axe and gold torc from Haxey Carrs in the Humberhead Levels, the Burringham shield in the Trent valley, the Level Carr hoard in the Hull valley and the Appleby hoard in the Ancholme valley are all examples of finds from the floodplain margins. Moreover, the weapons in the Appleby hoard could not have been deposited in deep water.

The prehistoric context of these bronzes is clear from palaeoenvironmental work. This shows that in later prehistory the floodplain margins were predominantly 'eutrophic' in character. Pollen analysis of the peat deposits has furthermore conclusively shown that in the Humber Wetlands these landscapes were dominated by dense alder carr. As discussed in Chapter 2, during periods of sea-level rise, such alder carrs are wet and over time expanded laterally onto what was previously drier land. This process resulted in a belt of uncultivable and near-impassable land, forming a physical barrier between the higher ground and the rivers. The selection of this type of wetland for the deposition of bronzes and other valuable goods was no coincidence. Its 'otherworldly' nature allowed for the development of beliefs that ancestral or natural spirits or gods resided in such undomesticated places and that votive deposition of valuable goods were gifts to the gods or spirits.

Outside the Humber Wetlands, votive deposition in wet places predating the Iron Age also appears to be correlated with the onset of mire development, rather than wetlands as a broader category. In her evaluation of the finds from the Wissey Embayment in the southeastern parts of the East Anglian Fens, Frances Healy (1996) time and again concludes that many of the best finds such as complete pots and metal objects were found within the peat, but resting on the pre-peat surface. This shows that these ritual depositions were associated with the expansion of the peatlands following rising water tables. In addition, the construction of the large post-alignment and the associated metal finds in the Flag Fen area broadly correlate with the increased inundation of the area as a result of marine transgression, and the onset of mire development in this area (Pryor 1991; Hall and Coles 1994). Elsewhere, the best examples of votive depositions in peatlands are from the bogs at Almosen and Nydam in Denmark, and the raised mires in Ireland (Bloch Jørgenson *et al.* 1999; Rieck 1999; Eogan 1994). In essence, it appears that the dynamic nature of the expanding mires may have triggered the selection of these landscapes for ritualised behaviour (see also Chapter 10).

In the Iron Age, the practice of depositing valuable objects in wet places has been noted for the middle reaches of the Trent, the Fens, the Thames basin, and for large parts of western Europe, but not for the Humber Wetlands. Indeed, apart from the Late Iron Age staters and La Tène II sword from the lower reaches of the River Hull and, somewhat tenuously, the Roos Carr model, no examples of this practice in the Iron Age exist for the Humber Wetlands. It is tempting to relate the decline of this practice to the rapid coastal change of the first millennium BC and the disappearance of the extensive riverside alder carrs. During this period marine transgression overtopped many of these eutrophic riverside wetlands, depositing clays and silts, thus creating landscapes that were readily exploitable from an agricultural point of view. In addition, on the Yorkshire side of the Humber Wetlands, the emergence of the Arras culture offered an alternative method of expressing status, whilst preventing the accumulation of prestige goods through the inclusion of weapons and other valuables as grave goods (Stead 1979).

Bog bodies

In some areas in Britain, notably the Thames basin, votive depositions in wet places have been associated with burials, but such a relationship has not been established for the Humber Wetlands. The dearth of burials is generally well understood. Throughout our past, people were buried in free-draining soils where the body would be cleansed through a natural process of putrefaction. The concentration of Neolithic long barrows on the Lincolnshire Wolds, the distribution of barrows on both sides of the Humber estuary on higher grounds, the distribution of the square-ditched burial mound cemeteries of the Arras culture in East Yorkshire, and the location of the few Roman cemeteries and the many medieval churchyards in the region underpin this point. This does not mean that human remains have not been found from the Humber Wetlands, rather they constitute a very small proportion of the area's funerary archaeology.

In all, six bog bodies are known from the Humber Wetlands, all from the area around Thorne and Hatfield Moors in the Humberhead Levels. Recent research on the Moors has been very limited. Only one significant archaeological find has been reported from within the peat this century — a short trackway linking areas of dryer land across a hollow where early peat developed, dated to 1510–910 cal BC (Buckland 1979). Compared to other extensive peat workings in England and abroad, such a dearth of archaeological finds may appear surprising, but the modern method of peat extraction, using the milling method, offers limited visibility and therefore few opportunities for the recovery of archaeological remains. Our own survey did not add any new sites or finds (Van de Noort *et al.* 1997a). Nevertheless, the dividend is greater when we explore antiquarian reports of discoveries from Thorne and Hatfield Moors. These discoveries are without exception associated with drainage activities, peat cutting and excavation of buried trees, the latter used for firewood, fence staves and ships' masts (Stovin Ms).

Archaeological discoveries from what was Thorne Moors include at least two bog-bodies. Stovin reported in 1747 in a letter to the Royal Society the discovery 60 or 70 years previously of 'an arm cutt from a bog body', and also of an entire body of a man 'with his teeth firm in his head; the hair of his head firm and fast on, and of a yellowish collour, either naturally so or dyed by the water of this moor', and with his 'skin like a peece of tanned leather' (cf. Turner and Scaife 1995). Bog bodies from the Hatfield Chase have been reported by de la Pryme (1699), who describes a bog body whose skin had been tanned, but most of the flesh and bones consumed. Hunter (1828) reported a pair of 'bog feet' with sandals from Amcotts, in the lower Trent valley and these were recently dated to the late third to fourth centuries AD on stylistic grounds (Turner and Rhodes 1992). Finally Bakewell (1833) reported a bog body 'in ancient Saxon costume', discovered before 1720.

In his European-wide study of the bog body phenomenon, Wijnand van der Sanden (1996) concludes that the majority of prehistoric bog bodies date from the later Bronze Age, the Iron Age and the Roman period. The only dated body from the Humber Wetlands, at Amcotts, falls within this period. The other bodies, which have all been lost since their discovery, remain undated. More recent bog body discoveries elsewhere have been subjected to extensive analysis allowing a detailed reconstruction of their death and burial, concluding that many were the result of sacrifices. Bog bodies have been found with evidence of violent deaths including garrotting. A relatively large number show evidence of physical disability or abnormality. Where the hands of bog bodies were preserved, it appears that these had not been involved in manual labour and the associated grave-goods suggest a relatively high status of the dead. These aspects can be explained by a special status of the victims, and Parker Pearson (1999) has raised the possibility that these people were somehow imperfect (physically or mentally), allowed to live a life of leisure in preparation for their sacrifice. In the wider context, bog bodies were treated as votive depositions, similar to the metal objects discussed earlier, and were placed specifically in mires rather than other wetlands. Their sacrifices served to communicate with the spiritual world in a manner not dissimilar to the votive depositions of metal objects in wetlands. The black waters and pools in mires may well have been seen as places that were in direct contact with the underworld, and these places were therefore selected for communication with the ancestors, natural spirits or gods who resided there (Van der Sanden 1996).

Barrows and burials

Not all human remains from the Humber Wetlands are bog bodies. At West Furze in Holderness, one of the sites that was identified by Thomas Boynton as a lake-dwelling, several human skulls were found (Smith 1911). In reinterpreting this site, we have suggested that this site was not a crannog but a causeway or trackway (see Chapter 4). Dated to the Neolithic or Early Bronze Age, it crossed the 5 km long, but narrow, former mere complex of Bail and Low Mere at its narrowest point. By the later Neolithic, this mere complex had become a peatland through hydroseral succession. In the original report, Reginald Smith reports the presence of a wicket, or doorway, formed by two standing timbers at the eastern end of the structure, where the human skulls were uncovered. Our reassessment proposed several alternative explanations for the doorway and the associated human skulls (Van de Noort 1995). One of these was that the wetlands formed a boundary, real or symbolic, delineating the landscape for ritual, territorial or other reasons. It is conceivable that the wetlands formed a liminal zone separating the world of the living and the dead by placing the latter on the other side of running water, a concept that is well attested in both archaeological and ethnographical studies (cf. Parker Pearson 1993). The remains of two burial mounds on the east side of Low Mere support such an interpretation but, alternatively, these wetlands could have been a communal or territorial boundary, symbolically reinforced by the remains of ancestors (see also Chapter 10).

In all, nearly 100 burial mounds or ring ditches, considered to be the ploughed-out circular ditches surrounding barrows, are recorded from the Humber Wetlands. Over half this number can be found in Holderness and the Hull valley and a smaller number on the eastern edge of the Vale of York, where these lowland landscapes adjoin the monument-rich areas of the Yorkshire Wolds. Elsewhere, barrows survive in the Ancholme valley and in the Lincolnshire Marsh. The majority of these sites are situated on the margins of the higher grounds, close to the 10 m OD contour. As the wetlands themselves rarely occur above the 3 m OD contour, few of these barrows can be said to be closely associated with the wetlands (Van de Noort and Davies

1993). These burial mounds are better understood within the context of the
Yorkshire and Lincolnshire Wolds. We must remember, however, that the
concentration of known burial mounds on the higher and free-draining
grounds of the Yorkshire and Lincolnshire Wolds is at least in part the result

FIGURE 46.
Overview of the
part-surviving remains
of the circular
monument, measuring
c. 30 m in diameter,
on Easington beach,
Holderness.

of the effectiveness of aerial photography here. Aerial reconnaissance is much less effective on the saturated soils of the lowlands (cf. Chapman 1997).

Several Bronze Age barrows are known from the Kilnsea and Easington area in southern Holderness. These are too far apart to be called a barrow cemetery, but the group of four to eight burial mounds is significant in this part of Holderness, where few other Bronze Age burial monuments are known. One of the barrows, on Easington Beach, has been threatened by coastal erosion, and following its initial excavation in the 1960s, was re-excavated in the late 1990s by the East Riding Archaeological Society (Mackey 1998). The Bronze Age barrow included a central grave with a jet button, and the mound was found to overlie a small Neolithic house and hearth. Another barrow, some 200 m northeast from the excavated example, was eroded by the sea during storms in 1999. A Beaker was retrieved from the surface alongside human bones. These dated the burial mound to *c.* 2000 cal BC.

Intriguingly, just to the north of this barrow a larger circular site was exposed by the sea at the same time (Figure 46). Excavations undertaken by the team of the Humber Wetlands Project revealed the partial remains of a bank-and-ditch arrangement akin to a small henge, with the bank positioned outside the ditch. One entrance was found, facing due north, but a flood or the marine transgression of the first millennium BC destroyed about two-thirds of the monument and we do not know whether this was a real, albeit small, henge or another type of site. The remnants of a cremation of a young man had been placed in the ditch, which provides a *terminus post quem* for this little monument of *c.* 2500–2000 cal BC. This group of barrows is somewhat surprising, as the burial mounds in the Holderness region are mainly concentrated in the north, where it abuts the Yorkshire Wolds. However, the long-term interest in this area coincides with major changes in the landscape due to sea-level rise, including the development of the estuarine wetlands of the Kilnsea Fleet (see Chapters 2 and 5).

The most important prehistoric burial site within the limits of the Humber Wetlands is the barrow cemetery of Butterbump, near Willoughby in the Lincolnshire Marsh (Willoughby–13; Chapman *et al.* 2001). This cemetery comprises at least seven, but probably 11 burial mounds, all located on a glaciofluvial gravel promontory rising to 5.5 m OD. In the Bronze Age, this promontory would have been surrounded to the north, east and south by coastal wetlands that developed following the Holocene sea-level rise. Between 1972 and 1975, one of these barrows was excavated and a central cremation pit was dated to 2590–1640 cal BC in the Early Bronze Age. This pit had been covered by planks, initially interpreted as a bier but more probably the remains of a coffin or cyst. Remarkably, a bronze dagger of the Wessex type, with an ogival blade and three rivets, survived in its wooden sheath in the damp and anoxic conditions beneath the barrow. Apart from the central cremation, seven further interments of human remains, five cremations and two inhumations, took place during the Bronze Age and into the Early Iron Age.

Additional work by the Humber Wetlands Project included some small-scale excavations of a small elongated wetland on the promontory, probably a kettlehole or other feature created by glacial activity. Five worked roundwood stakes were identified here (Figure 47). Subsequent dating of four stakes showed that these are broadly contemporary and may derive from a structure of Middle Bronze Age date. We do not know anything about the form or function of this structure, but we do know it was placed in the peat. This raises the question whether this elongated wetland, in the centre of the barrow cemetery, was seen as special in the way other mires were seen as sacred or spiritual places and whether the barrow cemetery can only be understood within this context. Only further research can elucidate this matter, and in view of the rapid desiccation of the peat, such research should be undertaken without delay.

Apart from burial mounds, past research in the Humber Wetlands has resulted in a number of finds of beakers and cinerary urns (vessel for keeping the ashes of the dead after cremation), again with a bias in favour of the Holderness region. Here, a remarkable cremation cemetery has been excavated at Catfoss, near Seaton, which contained 17 cremations within a penannular ditch or earlier small henge. The majority of cremations were contained within bucket-shape urns and dated to the middle or later parts of the Bronze Age. At Cadney in the Lincolnshire Marsh, another cremation cemetery of Late Bronze Age or Iron Age date has been recorded. Four more Bronze Age barrows are known from Skipwith Common in the Vale of York, where excavations by the Yorkshire Antiquaries Club excavated a Middle Bronze Age urn from one of these.

Iron Age burials are similarly atypical in the wetlands of the region, but on Skipwith Common, over 35 square-ditched barrows form the Danes Hills

FIGURE 47.
Some of the Middle Bronze Age wooden stakes found within the small wetland at the centre of the Butterbump barrow cemetery, in the Lincolnshire Marsh in 1999.

© THE HUMBER WETLANDS PROJECT, UNIVERSITY OF HULL

complex (Finney 1994). The cemetery occupies an area that is relatively high within the Humber Wetlands, around the 9 m OD. The Common is on a spur of glacially deposited material overlain by aeolian sands. It is now an important lowland heath nature reserve, with some small isolated mires. These burials within square-ditched mounds have been attributed to the 'Arras culture', the distinctive funerary practice of the Parisi on the Yorkshire Wolds where square-ditched barrows are the norm (Chapter 4). This association is not necessarily correct. The location of Danes Hills, some 40 km from the nearest square-ditched barrow cemetery, could indicate that the builders knew about the practice and adopted it, but were not necessarily themselves 'Parisi'. The fact that calcinated bones were found during nineteenth-century excavations, rather than the standard inhumated skeletons from the square-ditched barrows on the Wolds, once more indicates that the form of the monuments is the result of acculturation, rather than a colonisation of this area by people living on the Yorkshire Wolds.

Conclusion

The analysis of votive deposition of the Humber Wetlands has suggested that this practice was concentrated in the expanding wet alder carrs that developed on the margins of the river floodplains from the Neolithic to the Late Bronze Age or Early Iron Age. The earliest such votive depositions included exotic objects such as the jadite axehead from Wroot, but in the Bronze Age a variety of bronze tools, weapons and ornaments found their way into the mires. The religious beliefs that lay behind this practice included the concept that these uncultivable lands were inhabited by gods, spirits or ancestors. In socio-economic terms this practice provided status to the person or groups that presented the valuable objects to the gods or ancestors, whilst acting as a 'counter-inflationary' method preventing the value of bronze tools and weapons from becoming debased through an increase in availability.

As many as six bog bodies have been found in the Humber Wetlands, but apart from the third century AD example from Amcotts in the lower Trent valley, most have been lost and remain undated. For an understanding of this practice, we must therefore look at the phenomenon at large. Bog bodies in Europe are predominantly of late prehistoric and Roman date. A significant number of these bodies bear witness to violent or ritualised deaths, for example showing evidence of garrotting and multiple stab wounds, indicating that bog bodies represent sacrifices. The evidence tentatively suggests that the individuals subjected to these sacrifices had been specifically selected. Wijnand van der Sanden entitled his overview of the bog bodies in Europe *Through nature to eternity* (1996). With this, he expressed the view that the natural pools in bogs were perceived as gateways to the realm of eternity and the after life, and that the sacrifices connected individuals and communities to the gods or ancestral or natural spirits who inhabited this realm.

A limited number of burial mounds existed in the Humber Wetlands, discounting here the *c.* 100 such barrows and ring ditches identified just below the 10 m OD contour and which are better understood in the context of the monument-rich areas of the Yorkshire and Lincolnshire Wolds. The barrow cemetery at Butterbump in the Lincolnshire Marsh, the group of barrows in the Kilnsea area in southern Holderness and the barrows at the West Furze site in northern Holderness are all spatially associated with wetlands, although the burial mounds themselves were built on till or glaciofluvial deposits. For each example, different interpretations have been proposed. The plan of the barrow cemetery at Butterbump could be considered as customary for its period, were it not for the activities that took place in the small wetland that formed the centre of the cemetery. The burial mounds at Kilnsea may be related to long-term landscape change in the region. Finally, the West Furze barrows appear to have been separated from the settlement by the elongated wetlands of Bail and Low Meres, and whilst a trackway enabled the crossing of this wetland, a wicket or doorway may have formed a symbolic boundary separating the living and the dead. The location of Danes Hills, the square-ditched barrow cemetery on Skipwith Common, at around 9 m OD, reinforces the concept that for 'normal' funerary practices the wetlands themselves were avoided.

The archaeological evidence suggests that wetlands were foci of ritualised activities but, more to the point, the wetland locales chosen for ritualised activities were predominantly mires, or peat-producing wetlands, rather than the minerogenic wetlands or the waterbodies themselves. These mires included the raised mires of Thorne and Hatfield Moors, smaller wetlands such as at Butterbump or the Low and Bail Meres complex at West Furze, and the wet alder carrs that dominated the floodplain margins between *c.* 5000 cal BC and the marine transgression of the first millennium BC (see Chapter 2). Before artificial drainage, these mires formed uncultivable and intractable landscapes, unsuited for agriculture and difficult to travel through. The association of such landscapes with the realm of gods or spirits contrasts with the association of the minerogenic wetlands with farming and industrial activities.

CHAPTER SEVEN

Roman Wetland Colonisation and Exploitation

With the arrival of the Romans, the way in which wetlands in the Humber basin were exploited and perceived changed profoundly, in line with what happened all over Britain. That is not to say that there was a complete discontinuity from later prehistory. Some Roman period activities in the wetlands, notably the salt production in the Lincolnshire Marsh and the industrial activity in the Holme-on-Spalding Moor area in the Vale of York, were clearly based on their prehistoric antecedents. Nevertheless, the Roman period brought significant changes and in the archaeological record this is signified by the construction of new roads and bridges, and the extensive expansion of settlements into the wetlands (Figure 48). These changes in the Humber Wetlands must be set against the background of regional sea-level change.

The Roman marine regression and transgressions

The debate on sea-level change in the period from 500 cal BC to cal AD 500 has a long history, although this period has been completely ignored in recent studies (e.g. Shennan and Andrews 2000). Research around the North Sea basin has shown that a phase of marine regression occurred during the Roman period with coastal wetlands being extensively occupied. Towards the end of the Roman period a new phase of marine transgression buried many of these sites (see Rippon 2000 for an up-to-date summary of research in England and the Continent). It is widely appreciated that these phases are not exactly synchronous in the various regions around the North Sea and that periods of marine regression may be partly the result of changes in the deposition regimes of the various rivers, estuaries and the North Sea, rather than an actual fall in the level of the sea. One cannot, however, escape the conclusion that significant environmental changes did occur in the Roman period.

In the Humber Wetlands, these significant environmental changes that eventually enabled the Roman colonisation and exploitation of the lowlands were set in motion some time in the first millennium BC. In Chapter 2 the development of the riparian wetlands was discussed. These 'eutrophic' wetlands – alder dominated carrs on the floodplain margins – were overtopped by a rapidly rising sea some time after 1000 cal BC and buried beneath minerogenic

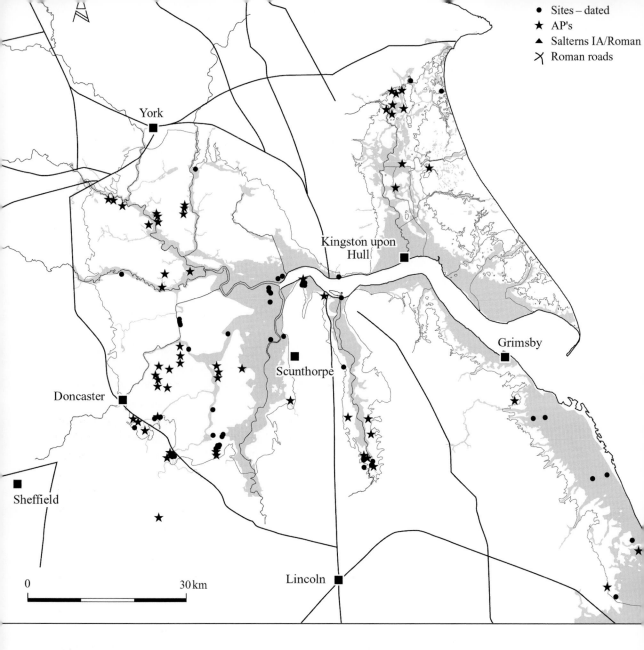

● Sites – dated
★ AP's
▲ Salterns IA/Roman
✕ Roman roads

York

Kingston upon
Hull

Grimsby

Scunthorpe

Doncaster

Sheffield

0   30 km

Lincoln

sediments. The dating of this sea-level rise is thwarted by the lack of organic source material and the very broad date ranges obtained in radiocarbon assays for this period. The process was probably time-transgressive, affecting some areas earlier than others. In coastal areas, the sea deposited considerable amounts of silts and clay containing shell fragments of the *Scrobicularia plana* mollusc, burying the peat of the eutrophic wetlands and greatly increasing the height of the land surface. This process was recognised for the Humber Wetlands as far back as the 1930s, in Swinnerton's (1936) natural history of the Lincolnshire Marsh. This is the deposit in which a large number of Roman period sites have been found, and which buried many prehistoric sites.

The surface levels of Roman settlements vary within the regions in the

Humber Wetlands. The lowest levels come from Kingston upon Hull, where remains of field systems have been excavated as low as −3.8 m OD (Didsbury 1990). This is 1.8 m below the Roman regional sea-level for the Humber, and nearly 5 m below the Roman period MHWST, as recently reconstructed by the LOIS programme (Metcalfe *et al.* 2000; see also Chapter 2). Other sites studied by the Humber Wetlands Project, such as the Roman road at South Ferriby, provide a further range of heights. The road surface was measured emerging from the eroding cliff at 1.2 m OD, but over the 40 m stretch surviving on the foreshore in 1996, the surface dropped some 1.5 m as it extended to the west. Against the most up-to-date sea-level curve for the Roman period, the road's surface would be above relative sea-level, but well below MHWST. Finally, the surface of the first phase of the settlement at Adlingfleet is at *c.* 1.6 m OD, just above MHWST on the recent sea-level curve. However, the site was entirely constructed on alluvial clays and silts, suggesting that MHWST before its foundation had been considerably higher than in the second century AD, when these clays and silt were considered suitable for permanent settlement.

We know that many sites were flooded during their existence. The date for this event is to be sought sometime between AD 150 and AD 250. Elsewhere, similar flood events during the Roman period have been noted, for example at Littleborough-on-Trent, to the south of Gainsborough, where alluviation occurred broadly at the same time as at Adlingfleet (Riley *et al.* 1995). Buckland and Sadler (1985) have suggested that in the Late Roman period much of the minerogenic alluviation in the Humberhead Levels could have been derived from eroding topsoil, linked to changes in the agricultural regime and the over-exploitation of the landscape. As this material has not been observed on archaeological sites on the southern margins of the wetlands, it is likely that the source of the eroding topsoil is the Humberhead Levels rather than the surrounding drylands. It appears that the Roman colonisation of the Humber Wetlands itself contributed to the environmental changes that in time caused its agricultural exploitation to end.

Evidence for a late and possibly post-Roman marine transgression and sea-level rise in the Humber Wetlands is extensive. Settlement sites at Adlingfleet, Faxfleet, South Ferriby and Hull, described in greater detail below, were buried beneath a metre or more of estuarine alluvium, probably all in the second half of the fourth century AD (Fenwick *et al.* 1998; Sitch 1989; Evans 2000). The mounds of waste from the salterns in the Lincolnshire Marsh were all concealed by up to a metre of marine alluvium, despite their elevated nature at the time of use, but clear evidence for the date of this event or process is not available. A layer of organic alluvium sealed the Roman road at South Ferriby, but the radiocarbon date of cal AD 20–340 is too wide to determine the date for the marine transgression in the Humber (Neumann 1998).

FIGURE 48.
Map of the Humber Wetlands, showing all Roman sites and the main Roman roads in the region.

Roman roads and bridges

The significance of the Roman road system in the conquest of Britain is beyond doubt. Ermine Street formed one of the most important contemporary routes in Britain. This road linked London with Lincoln, which had a military settlement by AD 50, and the strategically important Humber at Winteringham. However, military access to the area north and west of the Rivers Idle and Don, including the Humberhead Levels and the Vale of York, appears to have been an important objective by the AD 50s, as illustrated in the construction of the vexillation fortress at Rossington, on the banks of the River Torne to the south of Doncaster (Buckland 1986). A road, diverting from Ermine Street *c.* 5 km north of Lincoln, was constructed in the second half of the first century AD. It crossed the River Trent near the fort at Littleborough-on-Trent and travelled westwards over a Mercia Mudstone ridge before it reached the River Idle at Scaftworth (Figure 49).

This road, numbered as *Iter V* in the Antonine Initiary (Margary 1957), was to play an important role in the conquest of the territory of the Brigantes. It

FIGURE 49.
Aerial photograph of the late Roman-period 'fortlet' Scaftworth–10 on the Idle River, in the Humberhead Levels.

NATIONAL MONUMENTS RECORD

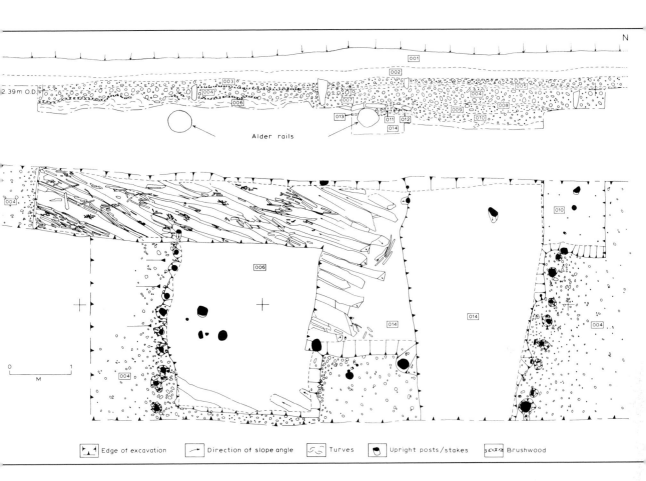

◣◢ Edge of excavation	⌐→ Direction of slope angle	∽∽ Turves	▮ Upright posts/stakes	⌾⌾⌾ Brushwood

FIGURE 50.
Section and plan of
the Roman roads
traversing the Idle
floodplain at
Scaftworth-Bawtry
(Scaftworth–5; Van de
Noort *et al.* 1997b,
413).

is currently unclear whether this road was built in the AD 50s servicing the vexillation fortress at Rossington, or in the AD 70s forming part of the grander strategy to control the Brigantes that involved the construction of forts at Doncaster, Castleford and possibly Burghwallis (Breeze and Dobson 1985). What is clear, however, is the ingenuity and engineering prowess of the Romans in constructing such roads, including the crossing of wetlands and rivers.

Prior to its discovery on the Idle floodplain in 1982, the route of the Roman road between Scaftworth and Bawtry was presumed to have followed the line of the modern A631, a conjecture initially supported by the discovery of eight *Antoniniani* in 1840 during construction of the stone bridge. The road would therefore have passed the fourth-century AD triple-ditched enclosure, sometimes also referred to as a Roman fort or 'fortlet', on its south side. Between Scaftworth and Bawtry, pre-Holocene deposits to the east and west constrict the floodplain of the Idle. To the north and south of this constriction, the floodplain widens considerably. Remains of a Roman road on the floodplain of the River Idle were first identified in 1982, when a 'crescent' of coarse gravel embedded in peat and timbers were found during drainage work, establishing the position of the Roman road to the north of the triple-ditched enclosure. Small-scale excavations in 1985 confirmed the existence of the road (Kennedy 1984).

In 1995, the Humber Wetlands Project undertook further excavations, exposing the full width of the road (Figures 50, 51 Scaftworth–5; Van de Noort *et al.* 1995). During the excavations it became apparent that our trench was located on the site of two different roads, each with slightly different orientations. The older road comprised a corduroy structure of three parallel alder

FIGURE 51.
Overview of the Roman roads crossing the River Idle at Scaftworth-Bawtry, in the Humberhead Levels.

© THE HUMBER WETLANDS PROJECT, UNIVERSITY OF HULL

FIGURE 52.
Excavations in the
Idle floodplain,
showing the posts
forming the basis of
the Roman bridge
over the earlier road
and in the
background the gravel
body of the second
Roman road is clearly
visible.

trunks on which smaller alder stems were laid transversely. The felled ends of the trees were positioned on the outside of the road. Branches had been removed, but the bark remained intact. On top of this structure was placed a concave surface of cut turves, presumably obtained from the nearby dryland. This 'floating road' was apparently constructed in some haste, using primarily local materials that were unlikely to last for decades. In 1997, an additional trench positioned nearer to the River Idle showed that the 'floating road' became a long bridge, founded on three parallel rows of oak stakes (Figure 52). These oak stakes had been carefully sharpened and this led to the contention that the road could have been built as part of a military campaign, using local resources where available, but using prefabricated components for the crossing of the river.

After some time, this floating road and its bridge were replaced by a second road, comprising a gravel body that had been compartmentalised using oak piles, and flanked by further piles and pegs, and by a new bridge for which we currently have no archaeological evidence. This would have provided a long-term solution for crossing the Idle floodplain at Scaftworth. Once the river and floodplain had been crossed, this road turned northwards to Rossington, passing the vexillation fortress and across another bridge over the River Torne. This was also exposed during excavations in 1995, and the piles were found to be in a poor state of preservation (Rossington–10; Head *et al.* 1997a; Van de Noort *et al.* 1997). Onwards, the road would have bridged the River Don at Doncaster, continuing along the 10 m OD contour through Adwick Le Street to Tadcaster, where the floodplain of the River Wharfe was crossed, possibly on a construction similar to that found at Scaftworth.

Whilst this road skirted the Humberhead Levels and the Vale of York on the west, an extension of Ermine Street was constructed from the Humber to York, along the eastern margins of the Vale of York following the conquest of the territory of the Parisi in the AD 70s. The route started at Brough on Humber via Shiptonthorpe and the early fort at Hayton before reaching York. Where this continuation of Ermine Street crossed the River Derwent, no Roman bridge has as yet been found. Additional roads existed, including one linking Brough directly with the Roman fort at Malton, another travelling eastwards from Brough to Melton, and several 'fragments' or sections identified on the wetland margins (e.g. Jones 1998b). The importance of Brough as the main trading place on the north bank of the Humber is beyond dispute (e.g. Creighton 1990). The town had supplanted the Redcliff settlement as the major trading post north of the Humber (see Chapter 5). Its political importance as the *civitas* capital of the *Petuaria Parisorum*, or alternatively as the civilian *vicus Petuariensis*, is clearly illustrated by its position in the regional road network.

The importance of cross-Humber trade, however, is maybe too easily overstated, as the crossing of the River Humber would have been far from straightforward. Archaeological evidence from the military but undefended Roman settlement of Winteringham at the *terminus* of Ermine Street on the south bank of the Humber suggests that this settlement was initially used as a military supply base until *c.* AD 70, after which it declined before becoming a small town in the AD 80s. The section of Ermine Street north of Lincoln may have lost much of its importance after the completion of the conquest of the Parisi in the early AD 70s (see below; Stead 1976; Ken Steedman in Chapman *et al.* 1998).

In 1996, another Roman road was excavated (Figure 53; South Ferriby–2; Chapman *et al.* 1998). This road, discovered by Ray Carey at South Ferriby on the foreshore of the Humber, was dated to cal AD 44–130. It is presumed that this road crossed the floodplain of the River Ancholme connecting the

FIGURE 53.
Excavating the Roman
Road on the Humber
foreshore South
Ferriby–2, in the
Ancholme valley.
© THE HUMBER WETLANDS
PROJECT, UNIVERSITY OF
HULL

Roman settlement at South Ferriby with the trading post at Winteringham. The road had been constructed as a raised causeway built on till, comprising layers of brushwood and limestone. The northern edge of the road comprised a wattle structure.

The role of Roman roads in military and political terms is acknowledged. In terms of this study, however, perhaps more interesting is the way in which the ability and ingenuity of the Romans to overcome the natural hurdles created by the wetlands must have contributed to a radical change in people's perception of these areas. As we have already seen, this perception was changing in the Iron Age, with the development of industrial activities and settlements in the Vale of York and the Lincolnshire Marsh (see Chapter 4). This changing view of the Humber Wetlands region may have been further reinforced by the period of marine regression that coincided largely with the Roman period. Nevertheless, the capability to travel across wetlands that had previously been impenetrable helped to open up the Humber Wetlands for a new phase of exploitation not seen before in the region.

Military sites

Several military forts constructed on the margins of the Humber Wetlands form the earliest phase of settlement activity. The vexillation fortress at Rossington, constructed to keep a close eye on the Brigantes, may well have been the very first military establishment in the Humber Wetlands (Rossington–8; Head *et al.* 1997a). The fortress was initially identified through aerial photography in the 1960s (St. Joseph 1969) and a range of metal-detected finds from the area suggests Roman presence in the early AD 50s (Buckland 1986). A geophysical survey undertaken by English Heritage of the northern corner of the fortress and surrounding area as part of the Humber Wetlands Project identified a second pair of double ditches, similar to those that formed its perimeter. If these features represent a second fort, then it would be located alongside the road from Lincoln to Doncaster crossing the River Torne at Rossington. This may represent a shift in location and emphasis from the River Torne to the road, immediately to the south of the bridge across the River Idle (Rossington–10; Head *et al.* 1997). Unfortunately, no additional evidence for its existence or date exists.

A second military site in the Humber Wetlands identified through aerial reconnaissance is the Roman fort at Roall overlooking Marsh Drain, a palaeochannel of the River Aire (Bewley and MacLeod 1993; Hensall–1; Head *et al.* 1997b). In terms of its location, it resembles the Rossington fortress in that it appears to control river traffic, but the Roall fort is a much smaller military site. On the basis of its morphology, it has been tentatively assigned to the reign of the Roman general Agricola, governor of Britain between *c.* AD 78 and AD 85. Just outside the Humberhead Levels and the Vale of York, additional first-century AD forts were constructed at Doncaster, Castleford and possibly Burghwallis to the west, alongside those at Brough on Humber, Hayton, Malton and Stamford Bridge in the east. Around AD 70, the fort at York was established (Breeze and Dobson 1985), enclosing the lowlands.

At York, Doncaster and probably Brough on Humber, civilian towns developed alongside or instead of the military foundations, and a series of Roman small towns developed on the margins of the Humber Wetlands – at Shiptonthorpe on the Yorkshire Wolds, at Winteringham, Dragonby and Owmby on the Lincoln Edge, and at Kirmington, Hibaldstow and Caistor on the Lincolnshire Wolds (Millett 1990).

Two Roman sites in the Humber Wetlands have been thought to belong to the Roman army. These sites are the triple-ditched enclosed site at Scaftworth and the double-ditched enclosed site at Sandtoft, both in the Humberhead Levels. The Scaftworth site, measuring c. 55 by 60 m internally, is located on the east bank of the River Idle, where the road linking Ermine Street via Doncaster to York crosses the Idle floodplain (see above; Scaftworth–10; Van de Noort *et al.* 1997). It was initially identified through aerial photography and an early assessment of the site dated it to the late fourth century AD (Bartlett and Riley 1958). The Sandtoft site, measuring approximately 160 by 160 m internally, was also discovered through aerial photography and was partly assessed in advance of the construction of the M180 road. It is located in a bend of the palaeochannel of the River Idle near its confluence with the Old River Don (Samuels and Buckland 1978). This site, too, is dated to the late fourth century AD on the basis of its pottery assemblage.

These sites have been assumed to be military in character, guarding strategic points in the road and river network during this period of increased raids from the Continent. Alternatively, these sites, and in particularly the smaller one at Scaftworth, may be examples of 'Romanised' behaviour, where status and ownership was emphasised by adopting Roman military features, but which were set within the much longer tradition of the field systems in this area (see Chapter 3). The fact that the ditches at Scaftworth were in profile shown to be a shallow 'U' rather than steep 'V' shaped, as would be expected from military constructions, and the character of the pottery assemblage that resembles many other late Roman sites in the region, may be taken as support for this alternative explanation.

Villas and estates

Rippon (2000) has argued for a relationship between the existence of villa or estate structures and the ways in which wetlands were exploited. He shows that where such estate structures existed, for example in the Somerset Levels, wetlands were transformed through reclamation, but where such estate structures were absent, wetlands were simply directly exploited or only marginally modified. In the Humber Wetlands, the villas are predominantly situated on the higher grounds, and the surrounding wetland margins would have been readily exploited as part of their estates. However, few villas are known within the extensive lowland area, indicating that the core area of the Humber Wetlands did not form part of larger estate structures, although low lying areas fringing higher areas with villas may have been part of these estates. The possible villa sites within the Humber Wetlands are at Drax and Cawood, both in the Vale of York. Neither has been excavated. Villa sites on the fringe or just outside the Humber Wetlands are at Brantingham and Kirkby Wharfe, respectively on the east and west of the Vale of York, at Horkstow and Cadney overlooking the Ancholme valley, and at Wadworth Carr, to the south of the Humberhead Levels. To what extent small settlements were part of the estate structures that belonged to these villas, and to what degree wetlands were transformed through reclamation, remains unclear.

'Romano-British' settlements

The total number of non-military or 'Romano-British' settlement sites dated to the Roman period recorded in the Sites and Monuments Records in 1992 was 89, including the sites from Hull. The Humber Wetlands Project found no fewer than 123 new sites designated, in some cases tentatively, as 'settlements'. These sites include scatters of Roman pottery and sites identified through the analysis of aerial photographs and geophysical survey. In all the regions apart from Holderness, we noted a clear correlation between these settlements and rivers. In some cases settlements were situated on the riverbanks, for example at Crowle in the Humberhead levels, where the pottery scatters follow the banks of the Old River Don for a very long distance. In other examples, it showed up as a distribution pattern that fell off with increased distance from the river, for example in the floodplain of the River Idle around Misterton. A small number of these sites were studied in greater detail, through excavation and geophysical survey.

The most enigmatic of the Roman period sites is at Adlingfleet, in the lower Trent valley (Figure 54; Adlingfleet–2 to –6; Fenwick *et al.* 1998). The site was identified as a pottery scatter during field walking, in an area that had previously produced not a single sherd of pottery or any other indication of the presence of a Roman period settlement. The landscape is flat and without undulation, and we considered our chances of finding anything worthwhile here as rather slim. Nevertheless, our persistence paid off, and a number of scatters of Roman pottery were found. The discovery was followed by a geophysical survey of a part of the site (Adlingfleet–2). This revealed the outline of a number of linear 'anomalies', interpreted as ditches and enclosures, and a pair of broad linear ditches. Subsequently, we excavated three trenches across the anomalies confirming the interpretations, with additional evidence for pits and stake holes, all forming part of a settlement that was located either on the banks of the former River Don, or on a palaeochannel of the River Trent.

Our small-scale excavations established two phases of occupation. Phase 1 has been dated to *c.* AD 100–230 and phase 2 to *c.* AD 230–370 on the basis of the pottery from the site. These were separated by a period of flooding,

FIGURE 54.
Examples of Roman pottery from Adlingfleet in the Lower Trent valley, A: calcareous tempered ware jar; B: grey ware bowl (scale 1:2) (Adlingfleet–2; Fenwick *et al.* 1998, 180).

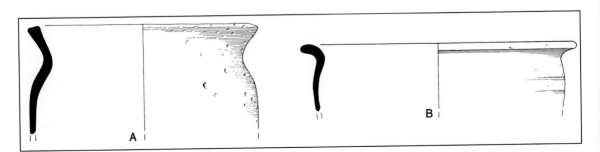

with the second phase occupation shifting slightly westwards, away from the River Trent floodplain. The earlier of these phases included evidence for post-in-trench constructions, considered by some to be principally used for structures with a military function (Riley *et al.* 1995). On the basis of our research, we estimate that Roman period occupation here extended over an area of at least 12 ha, and possibly over 20 ha, a formidable size for lowland Britain. The strategic location of this site, at the confluence of the Rivers Ouse, Don and Trent, may help to explain the importance and size of this settlement. It would have direct access to Yorkshire, the Midlands and parts of Lincolnshire and through the River Humber to England's east coast and continental Europe. Our excavations retrieved some evidence of industrial activities, in the form of burnt clay fragments reminiscent of pottery wasters and briquetage from saltern sites, but without further research it is not possible to determine the full range of functions of the Adlingfleet Roman site.

In the lower Hull valley, in the area now covered by Kingston upon Hull, the evidence for Roman period occupation has been accumulating over several decades and the existence of a substantial riverside settlement is now widely recognised (Didsbury 1990; Evans 2000). Occupation in the lower Hull valley resembles that at Adlingfleet in many ways. The pottery assemblages retrieved during watching briefs, assessments and excavations, range from the early second to the late fourth century in date, with limited evidence for activity in the late first century. The settlement is situated on the banks of the braiding River Hull, rather than the till outcrops to the east, and the density of Roman 'sites' in the lower Hull valley is comparable to the site density on the southern part of the Yorkshire Wolds (Evans 2000). As was the case at Adlingfleet, the archaeological material from Hull suggests industrial activities and a certain degree of 'Romanised' behaviour, adopting selected Roman practices and elements of Roman material culture, exemplified in the presence of building materials such as tiles, and parts required for hypocausts. This material is now so extensive that the Roman period site resembles a small town, rather than a rural settlement.

Whilst the research at Adlingfleet was severely hampered by the overburden of alluvial sediments that had accumulated here after the Roman period, research in the Vale of York produced an example of a Roman period riverside or 'ladder' settlement without such constraints. At Sutton upon Derwent, the existence of an archaeological site on the banks of an old course of the River Derwent had been known to local people for some time and during field walking we identified an area with Roman pottery measuring *c.* 400 × 200 m (Wheldrake–2; Chapman *et al.* 1999). The subsequent geophysical survey of the site produced the near-complete street plan of the settlement (Figure 55). It comprised a central road varying in width from 8 to 12 m and running east to west and parallel to the palaeo-Derwent for 370 m, and extending beyond the limits of the survey area. On either side of this central road were a series of variable-sized rectilinear enclosures. Several localities within the settlement produced intense magnetic anomalies, suggesting the presence of hearths or kilns.

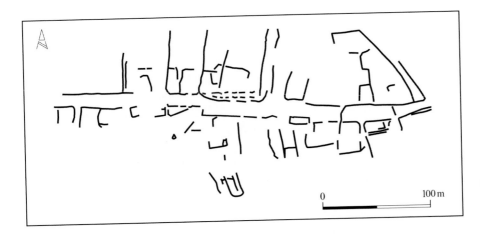

FIGURE 55.
Plan of the Roman period 'ladder' settlement at Sutton upon Derwent (Weldrake–2), in the Vale of York, based on geophysical survey and excavations by the Humber Wetlands Project.

We excavated two trenches, one across the road and adjacent enclosure, the other across enclosure ditches. On this occasion, no waterlogged deposits were found. Such remains may exist nearer to the palaeo-Derwent, but at the time of excavation in April 1998, the River Derwent had inundated this area. The Dales Ware pottery from the excavations allowed the site to be dated to *c.* AD 230–370. Other finds, including fine glassware, suggest that this riverside settlement, or some individuals within the village, had achieved a certain status, adopted Roman customs and techniques in their domestic lives and were to some degree part of a trade system than extended well beyond the Humber Wetlands. The most exciting find was that of a gold and glass earring. The earring comprises a rectangular box of twisted gold containing emerald green glass, in which the gold wire had been soldered to the centre of the base of the box. The earring has been dated to the later part of the second or third century AD (cf. Allason-Jones 1989).

Elsewhere in the Humber Wetlands, similar but smaller settlements have been found. The best example is the site near Whitton, alongside the Winterton Beck (Whitton–9; Fenwick *et al.* 1998), where aerial photography shows a linear ladder settlement of 300 m long and 100 wide. Similar to the Sutton upon Derwent site, enclosures are arranged on either side of a double-ditched droveway. The pottery found during field walking here includes some wares from outside the region, including a single sherd of Samian. Another Roman riverside settlement was found at Marshchapel in the Lincolnshire Marsh (Marshchapel–1; Fenwick *et al.* 2001b). The geophysical survey identified a palaeochannel alongside which a linear settlement developed. Ceramics from this site, collected by the landowner Ian Burgess and during the Humber Wetlands Project, comprise mainly regionally produced pottery, but also some sherds from imported wares such as Samian and Dales ware, and fragments of roof tile, box-flue tile and material associated with an hypocaust, or Roman underground heating system. Even within these smaller settlements, we can identify aspects of Roman technology.

Most of the remaining sites, often identified as scatters of Roman pottery covering an area less than 1 ha, presumably represent single farmsteads. This

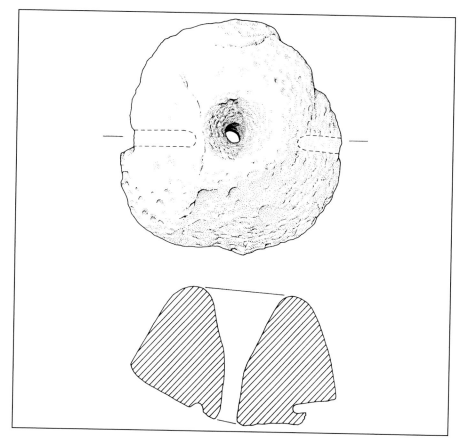

FIGURE 56.
The upper stone of a
beehive quern from a
small Roman period
settlement,
Moorends–2, in the
Humberhead Levels
(scale 1:4) (Head *et al.*
1997b, 254).

type of site has been recovered from all regions in the Humber Wetlands. Somewhat surprisingly, none of these sites has been excavated, but the complete quernstones and associated Roman pottery found at several such sites in the Humberhead Levels (Figure 56; Moorends–1 and 2 near the River Went; Head *et al.* 1997a; Rossington–1 near the River Torne and Hatfield Woodhouse–4 near the River Don; Head *et al.* 1997b) suggest that these farmsteads were settled permanently, rather than seasonally. In terms of their distribution, these sites have been found alongside and up to 2 km from rivers and along the coast. Their principal function was as farms, with the surplus from stock-breeding traded to settlements higher up the hierarchy.

It is possible that some of these Roman farms succeeded late Iron Age predecessors, but that Iron Age pottery has not survived in the modern ploughsoil. We do know, however, that the Roman period settlements in the Holme-on-Spalding Moor area had Iron Age forerunners. It appears that the Roman settlements here did not benefit from the market economy to the same degree as many other farmsteads, illustrated by a near-total lack of material brought into the region. Martin Millett described the area in the Roman period as a 'rural backwater' (Halkon and Millett 1999: 228). However, as the pottery produced here found its way to many Roman sites in East Yorkshire, we can only assume that the market economy did not work for the people in this area, as it did elsewhere in the Humber Wetlands. This suggests that where land ownership or territoriality existed by the time the Romans arrived, the socio-economic structures survived into the Roman period and local elite groups retained their control of the land and its produce.

Extensive geophysical survey of such a small settlement or farmstead in the East Halton Skitter area of the Lincolnshire Marsh, combined with trial-trench excavations, revealed evidence of a settlement centred on a double-ditched droveway (Neal 2001). A substantial enclosure ditch defined the main area of occupation, some 60 by 60 m in extent, and additional 'satellite' enclosures were located alongside the droveway. However, pottery analysis has shown a shift in settlement during the Roman period, and such information indicates that at any one time only parts of this area were occupied. The pottery varies in date from the mid-first to the end of the second century for the northern part of the site, and to the third and fourth centuries AD for the southwestern corner. Intriguingly, the geophysical survey shows two smaller droveways diverting from the main droveway towards lower ground that was probably a saltmarsh in the Roman period. Considering the use of double-ditched droveways in managing stock, these smaller droveways can be seen as evidence for the use of saltmarshes in the Roman period as feeding grounds for cattle or sheep.

Some of the smallest settlement sites may also have been occupied for a limited period only and this is almost certainly the case for the late Iron Age and Roman saltern sites in the southern parts of the Lincolnshire Marsh (Ingolldmells-3 to -12 and -15; Fenwick *et al.* 2001b; Thomas and Fletcher 2001). We also recognise that many more Roman period sites remain buried beneath marine alluvium of late or post-Roman date.

The relative sea-level fall in the late pre-Roman Iron Age and the early Roman period did not only affect the occupation of the Humber Wetlands, but coastal wetlands around the whole North Sea basin, as these were also settled in the first and second centuries AD (e.g. Rippon 2000). This has been observed in the Severn Estuary on the Welsh and English side, the south coast of England, the Thames basin, the East Anglian Fens and the Humber estuary and across the North Sea in Frisia, the Netherlands, Belgium and northern France. Roman-period settlement took a range of forms. In the Severn Estuary, coastal wetlands were transformed through the construction of sea walls. Elsewhere the settlements occupied higher grounds from where the surrounding landscape was exploited, with drainage ditches modifying the natural environment or, as in the case in Frisia, where *terpen* – artificial settlement mounds – were built to enable specialised wetland exploitation. In other places, the wetland resources were used as seasonal grazing ground, for salt making, providing clay for pottery industries, fuel in the form of wood and peat and a wide array of other natural resources, including fish, shellfish and reed, without significantly altering the landscape.

A settlement structure

From the evidence available to us, it is possible to reconstruct a settlement hierarchy for the Humber Wetlands, based on size and the nature of the archaeological remains. That it is at all possible to propose a settlement hierarchy suggests that market forces or high levels of military organisation existed to optimise production, trade and exchange, which resulted in a model that is predicated on the theory known as 'central place theory'. There is little doubt that markets and trade were active in the Roman period, but to what extent this was created or enabled by the Roman army remains a matter of debate.

The lowest level in this settlement hierarchy is formed by the large number of sites that are interpreted as single farmsteads, and the specialised production sites, notably the salt production site in Lincolnshire. The single farmsteads were presumably engaged in mixed farming, but with any surplus stock being sold or traded in local markets. The salt production sites may have been seasonal in nature, relying on the sun during the summer months to assist the evaporation process. Alternatively, these may have been permanent farms principally engaged in stockbreeding with salt making a seasonal activity.

Next up in the settlement hierarchy are sites such as the riverside ladder settlements at Sutton upon Derwent, at Crowle on the Old River Don, at Whitton in the Winterton Beck (Whitton–9; Fenwick *et al.* 1998), and at Marshchapel in the Lincolnshire Marsh (Marshchapel–1; Fenwick *et al.* 2001b). All these sites control access to rivers from areas of higher and dryer land, or *vice versa*, suggesting that trade and exchange played a role here. Their material culture typically includes imported pottery and occasionally more exotic items, such as the gold earring from Sutton upon Derwent. Nevertheless, the settlement plan indicates that these were rural villages with the villagers principally engaged in farming.

The largest riverside settlements such as Hull and Adlingfleet, the riverside settlement at South Ferriby in the lower Ancholme floodplain (Sheppard 1926), and possibly the Roman period 'harbour' at Faxfleet on the north bank of the River Ouse at its confluence with the River Trent (Sitch 1989) formed the next layer in the settlement hierarchy. When compared to their counterparts on the higher grounds, such as Shiptonthorpe on the Yorkshire Wolds, these settlements should be termed 'small towns'. These settlements occupied strategic positions at the confluence of rivers, with direct access to the Humber estuary and thus, one may speculate, played important roles in regional and possibly even supra-regional trade.

Military control, or at least presence, seems likely for these small wetland towns. The excavated evidence clearly shows that the inhabitants in such settlements were engaged in crafts and industrial activities alongside stockbreeding, small-scale arable farming and possibly fishing. A range of additional roles associated with trade and transport can be postulated for the small wetland towns, ranging from markets and storage to boat building or repair. However, only large-scale archaeological excavations will be able to inform us about the true range and scale of activities of these settlements.

We may assume that the top of any settlement hierarchy was formed by the large towns outside the Humber Wetlands, notably York, and Lincoln, and to a lesser extent by the smaller military settlements and villas forming the next layer. The settlement hierarchy in the Humber Wetlands after the first century AD focused on the rivers and estuary and these provided the arterial routes for the transport of all produce, rather than the Roman roads that had been used in the conquest of the region during the first century AD. In this respect, it is unsurprising that the settlement at Winteringham, the *terminus* of Ermine Street at the Humber, has been described as a trading post rather than a major harbour (see above; Stead 1976). It did not partake in the trade of goods produced in the Humber Wetlands to the same degree as the small wetlands towns of Adlingfeet and Hull.

Roman period wetland exploitation

The function of the Roman period settlements and the nature of wetland exploitation is becoming increasingly clear, with evidence for a range of industrial activities. These include salt making in the Lincolnshire Marsh and possibly in the Humber estuary, as well as pottery production. The latter activity was not exclusive to the wetlands, but the relatively large-scale pottery production sites in the Holme-on-Spalding Moor area, where it replaced the large-scale iron production of the later Iron Age (Halkon and Millett 1999), and at Rossington Bridge (Buckland *et al.* 2001) were significant. Large-scale pottery production took place in other wetlands too – the Nene valley pottery from the Fenlands is the best known example (Hall and Coles 1994). However, it is likely that salt and pottery production formed part of a wider range of activities that was primarily based on agriculture, dominated by stockbreeding but with some evidence of arable activity (e.g. Smith 1985).

On the basis of archaeological evidence, we cannot determine the scale of the salt production and the extent of the markets it served. Conjecturally, markets such as the Roman town Horncastle used the North Sea salt, but as salt had become an essential part in food processing, it would have been available in major towns much further afield as well. The distribution of pottery produced in the Humber Wetlands is easier to determine. At Rossington Bridge, where the River Torne enters the Humberhead Levels, an important pottery industry developed in the second and early third centuries. The excavation of eight kilns and material from additional unexcavated structures has shown that a range of ceramics was produced here, including mortaria, grey wares, fine wares and black-burnished wares. In the mid-second century AD, stamps on the mortaria have identified the potter Sarrius as one of the main producers. The pottery from the Rossington Bridge site found its way as far as the military markets on the Northern frontier (Buckland *et al.* 2001).

The use of a range of wetlands for breeding cattle and sheep is well understood and, as argued in Chapter 3, the saltmarshes of the Humber estuary were exploited as pasture grounds from at least the Middle Bronze Age onwards. The presence of extensive eutrophic wetlands, especially alder carrs, on the floodplain edges, would have prevented their exploitation as pasture grounds (Chapters 2 and 3). However, sea-level rise and marine transgression in the first millennium BC drowned many of these eutrophic wetlands, with mineral deposition burying the alder carrs. These mineral deposits of clay and silt provided suitable environments for farming when the regional sea-level fell, possibly in the later Iron Age and certainly by the early Roman period, and the archaeology of the Humber Wetlands reflect this. The large number of pottery scatters on the riverbanks and aerial photographs showing settlement with field systems (e.g. Bishopbridge–10 in the Ancholme valley; Chapman *et al.* 1998) suggests that these were rural settlements; and the field systems, which often include droveways, suggest that their primary function was the management of livestock. It is possible, and in the case of Hull likely, that the low-lying pasture grounds were liable to seasonal flooding. This would have added nutrient-rich sediments, enhancing the biomass.

Whilst stockbreeding provided the main source of income, this labour extensive activity allowed for a range of small-scale industries and crafts to be developed. The inhabitants of the riverside settlements not only exploited the rich meadows for grazing and the fattening of animals, but also used the rivers to transport their produce to near and possibly even distant markets. The presence of a broad range of artefacts that were clearly imported into the region, varying from the golden earring found at Sutton upon Derwent to the *tegulae* and boxtiles found in Hull, indicate that these settlements were well-integrated into the Roman market economy (e.g. Evans 2000). Brough on Humber is assumed to have been a major port on the Humber, although archaeological evidence is limited (Wacher 1995).

Conclusion

The manner in which the wetlands in the Humber basin were exploited and perceived during the Roman period stands in stark contrast to the role of the wetlands in prehistory. But wetlands (and uplands) elsewhere were similarly affected by the changes brought by the Romans. Parts of the East Anglian Fens, for example, have been described as the most intensively occupied area in Britain, on par with the lower Thames valley (Jones and Mattingly 1990), with the large classical tower at Stonea, in Cambridgeshire, the possible centre of an imperial estate (Jackson and Potter 1996). Elsewhere, Roman occupation and exploitation of wetlands has been noted from the Severn estuary, the Pevensey Levels and Romney Marsh on the south coast, in the lower Thames estuary and in the Norfolk Broads, and also in the lowlands of the Netherlands, Belgium and northern France (Rippon 2000).

The inter-relationship of the Humber Wetlands with the surrounding higher ground in the Roman period developed along lines that were established in the later Iron Age – that is, that the wetlands were either exploited from settlements located on the higher grounds, or were producing goods for use outside the Humber lowlands. Estates surrounding villas on the periphery of the lowlands, such as at Brantingham and Horkstow, where the main building contained mosaic floors, would have readily exploited the wetland margins. Elsewhere in the Humber wetlands, most notably the Humberhead Levels and the Hull and Ancholme valleys, a settlement hierarchy developed apparently based on the rivers, from which the use of river-based transport forming part of a broader market economy has been inferred.

It cannot be ruled out that the Roman army played a significant role in the development of such an economy. This market was probably mainly based in the towns of York, Lincoln and Doncaster, but through the river systems, large parts of the Midlands and Yorkshire, as well as the east coast of England and the Continent could be reached. The nature of the commodities traded remains somewhat elusive. Palynology from samples taken on Thorne Moors indicate that cereals were grown regionally, but it seems more likely that cattle, alongside pottery and salt, formed the main components of the trade.

CHAPTER EIGHT

Medieval Wetland Exploitation

The Humber Wetlands Project was far less successful in identifying sites and settlements of medieval date than those of the Roman period. This is undoubtedly partly the result of the methodology of the project, which covered all areas under agricultural use that allowed systematic survey, but excluded villages and towns, many with origins dating back to the Middle Ages.

However, it also reflects the fact that wetland exploitation and utilisation in the Middle Ages was predominantly undertaken from the surrounding higher areas, leaving little in terms of material culture for archaeologists to discover. This does not mean that the wetlands were of little importance during the Middle Ages and, indeed, the combined information from historical written sources and archaeology shows a myriad ways in which the wetlands were put to good use. However, a reduction in the amount of settlement and of the intensity of exploitation of the wetlands in the early part of the medieval period may have been caused by two factors: firstly, the collapse of the broader settlement structure and the consequent disappearance of a market for specialised wetland produce, and secondly the impact of the Late Roman marine transgression.

The early Middle Ages: a deserted landscape?

The Late Roman marine transgression sealed many Roman period sites under a metre or more of alluvium, but for how long the wetlands were considered unsuitable for settlement is unknown. We know that in other regions of the North Sea basin, for example in the East Anglian Fens and Holland, the first tentative recolonisation of the wetlands is dated to the seventh and eighth centuries AD (Hall and Coles 1994; Rippon 2000). The various models that have been constructed for regional sea-levels offer no clues as to when marine transgression receded. However, the environmental conditions may have suited a recolonisation of the Humber Wetlands, or parts of them, before the eleventh century AD, when historical sources show that the estuarine wetlands of the southern Vale of York were inhabited (Sheppard 1966).

Increasingly, archaeologists find evidence for a degree of continuity in the agricultural use of the British countryside in the centuries after the withdrawal of the Roman army alongside evidence for continued use of the Roman towns and villas, albeit on a much reduced scale. For example, Loveluck (1999) has argued that, in the case of lowland East Yorkshire in the fifth and sixth centuries AD, rapid changes in mortuary practices reflect the migration of Anglian settlers from the Continent and the rapid adoption of a hybrid Anglo-Saxon and native British fashion in funerary customs. However, he also suggests that there is no evidence to indicate anything other than continuity in the capacity of the agricultural economy. This cannot be said to be true

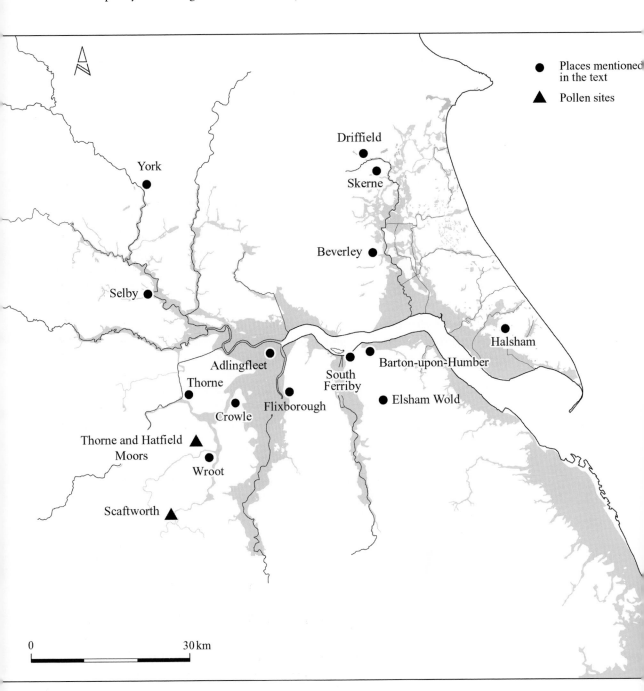

for the Humber Wetlands. Despite the reduced visibility of archaeological evidence as a result of the Late and post-Roman marine transgression, we have found a much reduced number of settlements and a near-deserted lowland countryside (Figure 57).

Environmental evidence for this period appears to support the suggestion that the population in the Humber Wetlands declined in the post-Roman period or, at least, that the population's impact on the landscape appears to have decreased. Brian Smith's (1985) analysis of the pollen record from Thorne and Hatfield Moors described his regional pollen zone HHL/D, radiocarbon dated to *c.* cal AD 440–1000, as a period that commenced with a marked decline in herb pollen in favour of tree and shrub pollen, with tree pollen accounting for nearly 65 per cent of the total pollen record. This evidence indicates woodland regeneration. Related results were found from our excavations of the Roman road crossing the River Idle floodplain at Scaftworth. Here, increased levels of alder pollen were interpreted as showing increased wetness, but the increase of oak pollen was seen as a possible indicator of woodland regeneration, with oak acting as the pioneer coloniser of abandoned farmland (Taylor and Kirby in Van de Noort *et al.* 1998).

Only on one occasion did we find pottery of early medieval date, in a field near the church of Halsham in southern Holderness. The material was retrieved from a semi-circular area enclosed by a ditch and bank, which partly survived under pasture in 1995 when we undertook the survey of Holderness. Pottery from the site included sherds of Torksey type ware, Charnwood pottery and two sherds of shell-tempered ware, providing a date range of AD 400–900, alongside material of later medieval date (Halsham–24; Head *et al.* 1995b). Halsham is situated on a spur of higher land overlooking the extensive wetlands of the Keyingham Drain, making it a settlement well-placed for exploiting both the wetlands and the higher ground. As such, it could well be typical for many other sites of this date, utilising the best of both landscapes rather than engaging in a specialised exploitation of the wetlands. The decline of the towns in the region following the collapse of the Roman empire, and the absence of new markets that could have taken the produce of wetland farming, especially the yield of specialised stockbreeding, prevented large-scale wetland exploitation. Instead, farming communities would have been largely self-sufficient and based on the drylands, near to their arable fields, but would have utilised the wetland margins as summer pasture and hunting grounds.

The natural resources from the Humber Wetlands that were exploited during the early Middle Ages are exemplified by the excavations of the Anglo-Saxon site at Flixborough by the Humberside Archaeology Unit (Loveluck forthcoming). This settlement, in use from the seventh to tenth centuries AD, was located on a wind-blown sand spur, overlooking the Trent floodplain. The excavations found evidence for more than 30 buildings, and the site is described as a high-status settlement and estate centre, or 'vill', which may have been used as a monastery from the mid-eighth to mid-ninth centuries AD. The unstable nature of the sands required that houses that were in need of

FIGURE 57.
Map of the Humber Wetlands, showing early medieval places mentioned in the text.

rebuilding were superimposed on earlier buildings, and the material that was dumped to create new platforms was rich in artefacts and animal bones.

The artefacts include Ipswich-type pottery ware from East Anglia, and pottery, glass vessels, coins and quern stones imported from continental Europe, stressing the importance of the rivers for connecting the elite groups at Flixborough with their English and European counterparts. Whilst the excavators found ample evidence for arable cultivation and grain processing, the presence of animal bones from geese, cattle and sheep, along with those of goat, pigs, and chicken, indicates that the wetland margins and meadows would have been a valuable resource. That the wetlands were readily exploited is further highlighted by the collection of bones of wild animals, which indicate both fishing and wildfowling. Evidence for fishing is also shown in the presence of net-sinkers. In addition, oyster shells and the bones of dolphin/porpoise and whale suggest that wetland exploitation was not restricted to the River Trent and its floodplain, but included the Humber estuary and the North Sea as well.

No other Anglo-Saxon site in the region can match the wealth in material culture of the Flixborough site, but the excavation of the site at Skerne, in the upper Hull valley, deserves some attention. The site was discovered in 1982, with the construction of fishponds alongside the River Hull. A series of large wooden stakes were discovered and a rescue excavation was organised by the Humberside Archaeology Unit under the direction of John Dent. Following additional work by the Humber Wetlands Project, an assessment of the work was published in 2000 (Dent *et al.* 2000). The site included two structures, the second more substantial than the first, and both dated to between the seventh and eleventh centuries AD. Both structures appear to have been part of a bridge or a jetty projecting into the River Hull. The structures are linked to a causeway on the river's east bank, while a causeway on the west bank has been identified from aerial photographs. Parallel to the causeway on the east bank was an artificial channel, which has been interpreted as the mouth of a possible leat of a watermill.

The range of finds was remarkable, and they have been attributed to different deposition activities. A Viking sword with scabbard found beneath the structure may have been a votive deposit in a wet place; the dress pins and metal buckles could similarly have been offered to the river, or were perhaps hidden there during a attack by Vikings or other foes; a selection of tools and bone points may well have been accidentally lost; and the large number of animal bones may have been simply dumped into the river as refuse. Nevertheless, the material culture indicates the presence of a nearby settlement, with an Anglo-Saxon or Anglo-Scandinavian ethnicity, that may have been part of the royal Northumbrian 'vill' at nearby Driffield. If this is the case, than the structures at Skerne, and the as yet unidentified settlement there, could have functioned as the port to Driffield, at the highest navigable point in the River Hull.

In general terms, early and middle Saxon settlements, ranging in date from the fifth to the middle of the ninth centuries, are few and far between in the

Humber Wetlands. Examples of such settlements include the modern towns of Barrow and Barton-upon-Humber in the Lincolnshire Marsh, Beverley in the Hull valley and Selby and York in the Vale of York. Many monastic sites were established in the early Middle Ages and, as was the case for the early settlements, their distribution is closely associated with the higher and drier grounds surrounding or occasionally within the Humber Wetlands. *Ad Barwe* was founded in the seventh century on the Lincolnshire Wolds-edge at or near Barrow upon Humber. Beverley was founded in the eighth century on the Yorkshire Wolds-edge. The early development of Howden, in Holderness, is also presumed to have had a Saxon ecclesiastical origin. The site of the eighth-century AD monastery *Donaemuthe* (Donmouth) is believed to have been located on the levees of the River Don, at or near Adlingfleet (Van de Noort *et al.* 1998).

Between the late ninth century and the Norman Conquest, the Humber Wetlands formed part of the Danelaw. This term defines the area that was ruled by Danish Vikings, as set out in a treaty between King Alfred and the Viking leader Guthrum. The Danelaw included most of eastern England and according to the Anglo-Saxon chronicle, its distinct administrative organisation was based on the Five Boroughs of Lincoln, Nottingham, Derby, Leicester and Stamford. Place names in this region, especially those ending with –by (e.g. Grimsby, Ferriby), are Danish in origin. These place names indicate a Danish presence, representing either a local elite within pre-existing villages or the founders of new settlements. Within the Viking-controlled area, a large number of stone carved crosses are thought to have been made by the christianised Vikings.

Despite the place-name evidence, archaeological research into the impact of the Danish settlement on the Anglo-Saxon population suggests that it was relatively limited. For example, the excavations at Flixborough could not identify any Viking influence, but found West Saxon coins issued by Alfred the Great, possibly minted at London. We must conclude that there was a considerable degree of continuity, or alternatively, that the Scandinavian elite quickly became anglicised through acculturation, leaving few material-culture clues as to their ethnic identity. The Viking sword deposited at the bridge or jetty at Skerne is unparalleled in this respect. It may have been a ritual deposit in a 'wet place', symptomatic of the belief that wetlands still had special meanings.

The settlement pattern of towns and villages in the Humber Wetlands, as recorded in the Domesday Book, probably has its origin – at least in terms of its main elements – in the Late Saxon period, from the second half of the ninth to the eleventh centuries AD, rather than in the Early or Middle Saxon period. Settlement clearly shows a continued preference for the higher and drier grounds (e.g. Fenwick 1997; 1999; 2001). Within the boundaries of the Humber Wetlands, such preferences are shown in the location of the settlements in the Humberhead Levels on dry 'islands' in the wetlands such as outcrops of glaciofluvial deposits, in the case of Thorne and Wroot, or of

Mercia Mudstones in the case of Crowle. Elsewhere, the levees of the rivers provided the slightly raised ground suitable for settlement, for example in the case of the village of Adlingfleet, founded on the levees of the River Don.

Throughout eastern England, a large number of cemeteries attributed to the Angles, Saxons and Jutes have illuminated the 'dark ages' where evidence for settlements is lacking. Unfortunately, with the exception of a possible cemetery at South Ferriby (Leahy 1992), no early medieval cemeteries are known from the Humber Wetlands, but we should not be too surprised about that. Throughout much of the prehistoric and historic past, a clear preference for deposition of the remains of the dead in free-draining soils existed, with only a few exceptions, notably the bog bodies (see Chapter 6). From the higher ground surrounding the Humber Wetlands, a number of these early medieval cemeteries have been excavated. At Elsham Wold on the Lincolnshire Wolds, *c.* 600 cremation burials accompanied by gravegoods were uncovered, dated to *c.* AD 450–600. A similar cemetery was discovered in the nineteenth century on the Yorkshire Wolds, containing over 500 burials of cremated remains (Lucy 1998; 2000). Finally, at Barton-upon-Humber, a small cemetery of inhumated remains furnished with weapons was excavated in the 1980s.

A phase of wetland abandonment in the later and post Roman period has been shown for all coastal wetlands in Europe. Marine transgression explains this in part, although the phase is broadly dated to the third century AD on the Continent (the 'Dunkirk II' marine transgression), and mainly to the fourth century AD in Britain. Alternatively, the lack of resettlement of many wetlands may principally have been the result of the decline of the Roman market economy and the absence of an organisation that could act as a catalyst in the rebuilding of such an economy. Nevertheless, most wetlands in Europe were recolonised at some point during the early medieval period. In Frisia and lower Saxony, the artificially enlarged mounds known as *terpen* were reoccupied by the late fifth and sixth centuries AD and formed the basis for the development of a wetland-based economy of stock breeding and trade, later exemplified in the Carolingian port of trade at Dorestad (Van Es and Verwers 1980). By the eighth and ninth centuries AD many wetlands both in Britain and on the Continent has been recolonised, including parts of the Fenlands and Romney Marsh in England, and Midden Delfland and the Assendelfder Polder in the Netherlands (Hall and Coles 1994, Allan and Gardiner 2000, Van den Broek and Van London 1995). In the latter case, it has been argued that settlement on peatlands was an attractive option for free farmers, as the distant king, formally the lord of such unused areas, had become ineffective in raising tax or rent (Besteman and Guiran 1987).

In this context, the near-complete absence of early medieval settlements in the Humber wetlands, and its exploitation solely from the surrounding higher grounds, is remarkable, and remains largely unexplained. The lack of *terpen* in the region has been a particular conundrum, as these artificial islands were very well known to the Anglo-Saxon settlers who had come from the Waddensea where these structures had been used so successfully. The only

FIGURE 58.
Luddington church
and cemetery, in the
lower Trent valley.
Could the small
'island' be artificial,
despite the
post-medieval date of
the church and
cemetery?

possible *terp* in the Humber Wetlands is at Luddington, in the lower Trent valley, where the now isolated church is located on an oval area of raised ground (Figure 58). Only further research can show whether this raised area is wholly natural or artificial.

How did early medieval people perceive the Humber Wetlands? The archaeological evidence indicates that a wide range of natural wetland resources were exploited. Apart from fishing and waterfowling, the wetland margins were important to the subsistence economy as summer pasture. The people of the towns, villages and monasteries that settled on the Wolds-edges and on the higher ground within the lowlands did not develop a specialised 'wetland economy' before the tenth and eleventh centuries AD, as has been suggested for the East Anglian Fens and the lowlands of Holland. Rather, the wetlands provided resources that complemented those found on the surrounding dry-lands.

The medieval recolonisation

The recolonisation of the Humber Wetlands during the high Middle Ages must be understood as forming part of a much broader intensification of agricultural activities and of settlement expansion into areas considered marginal across western Europe. This phenomenon has been attributed to a combination of increased political stability, economic prosperity and marine regressions or optimum climatic conditions (Duby 1968). This period, commencing in the tenth century AD, saw for example the growth of the wool trade with the Low Countries and the acceleration of urbanisation. At the time of the writing of Domesday Book, the recolonisation of the Humber Wetlands had already started as shown by the many references to settlements within its confines (Figure 59). Using historical accounts, we can see a recolonisation of the lowlands during

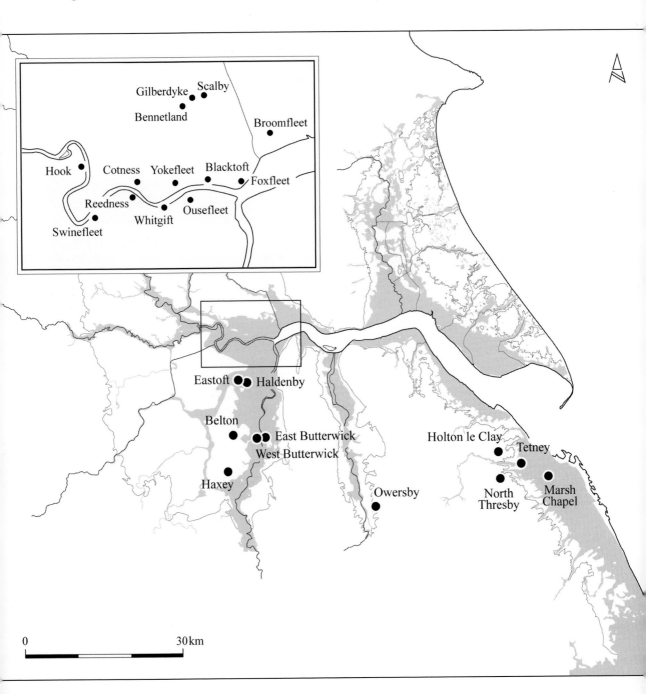

the following four centuries that went even beyond the intensity noted for the Roman period. Whereas the Romans and Romano- British settlers exploited the wetlands without making major changes to the landscape, during the high Middle Ages the Humber Wetlands were extensively transformed through the construction of seabanks and drainage channels. Both high and low status settlements were founded in the wetlands.

In her analysis of settlements mentioned in Domesday Book, Helen Fenwick (e.g. 1997; 1999) has shown that settlements were located either on the relatively higher ground (i.e. near the 10 m OD contour, beyond the limits of the contemporary floodplains or on the 'islands' of pre-Holocene deposits) or on riverbanks, most notably those of the Rivers Trent and Ouse. In the absence of natural riverbanks or levees here, this indicates that the building of banks or dykes may already had begun by this date, and therefore that the transformation and early reclamation of wetlands had started. Similarly, in the Humberhead Levels, the settlements of Reedness, Swinefleet, Whitgift and Hook on the banks of the tidal Rivers Aire and Ouse seem to have been possible only if embankments had provided essential protection during periods of spring high tides (Figures 60, 61; Dinnin 1997a). In the southern Vale of York, new settlements were founded in the estuarine wetlands, such as Yokefleet and Cotness, presumably to exploit more effectively the landscape as pasture land. Attempts to modify the landscape through the construction of drains are dated to the same period (Sheppard 1966).

In the Lincolnshire Marsh, the eleventh century AD also appears to have been a period for a renewed interest in salt production. Our own excavations of the site 'Burnt Hill' at Marshchapel found evidence of this (Marshchapel–2; Fenwick *et al.* 2001b; Fenwick 2001). Here, we excavated a saltern site comprising a channel for bringing seawater to the site, and storage tanks, found in association with pottery and other remains of tenth- or eleventh-century date. The evidence indicates that seawater was boiled in large open pans, supported on baked clay 'hand-bricks'. No fragments of the pans were found, but these may have been of lead and taken from the site when it was abandoned. The function of the clay bricks was similar to that of the Iron Age and Roman briquetage (Chapter 6), albeit of a different shape and superior quality.

The current landscape of the lower Trent valley and the Old River Don provides an illustration of medieval riverside settlements. The linear layouts of these settlements along the side of the bank resemble the Roman riverside settlements that were located on the rivers' levees (Chapter 7), or those of linear roadside developments. Some villages were paired, for example East and West Butterwick on the River Trent, and Haldenby and Eastoft on the River Don. These villages would have been in close contact by ferry, but remained administratively separated. In the southern Vale of York, new villages were founded during the twelfth and thirteenth centuries AD in the extensive alluvial plains, including Blacktoft, Faxfleet and Broomfleet in the twelfth century, and Bennetland, Gilberdike and Scalby in the thirteenth century AD. Long drains or 'dikes' were excavated to drain the land. In the upper parts of the

FIGURE 59.
Map of the Humber
Wetlands, showing
the places mentioned
in the text related to
the medieval
recolonisation.

FIGURE 60.
St Mary Magdalene at Whitgift on the River Ouse in the Humberhead Levels. The church was built on the inside of an early dike or embankment, with later dike improvements taking place on the riverside.

FIGURE 61.
A detail of the tower of St Mary Magdalene at Whitgift, showing the sloping nature of the underlying dike.

Humberhead Levels, the construction of a seabank along the tidal River Ouse appears to have been completed by the end of the eleventh century AD, and a series of settlements nestled on the land side of the seabank (Metcalfe 1960). The layouts of the villages of Whitgift and Ousefleet, for example, are still determined by the way they were originally formed.

Throughout the Humber Wetlands, settlement in the Middle Ages was characterised by a generally high proportion of nucleated villages, reflecting the dominance of the townfield system with its unified field system. Increasingly, discoveries of pottery and other finds from existing villages, including Holton le Clay, North Thoresby and Tetney in the Lincolnshire Marsh, suggest that their origin is to be sought in the Late, and occasionally Middle Saxon period (Fenwick *et al.* 2001a). A number of parishes comprise multiple townships at the time of Domesday Book, or as recorded in later manuscripts, indicating population growth and expansion onto the wetlands. For example Owersby, in the Ancholme valley, consisted of no fewer than six settlements on the valley floor (Everson *et al.* 1991). The most distinctive examples of multiple townships are those surviving on the Isle of Axholme, including Belton and Haxey. Whereas village nucleation and planning are frequently associated with the land-owing elite exercising their control and influence, the proliferation of townships is closely associated with the high proportion of freemen among the population. Keith Miller (in Head *et al.* 1998) has argued that the extensive wetland commons available to the freemen alongside good arable land, and the weakened power of the lord of the manor due to the isolated nature of the Isle, forestalled any attempts to consolidate the patterns of settlement.

On the Lincolnshire Marsh, new settlements were established on the lowlands as daughter settlements of the parishes named in Domesday Book, which were located near the 10 m OD contour. The eastward movement onto the marshland has been explained by the need to be close to the sea for salt production, and also by the creation of extensive saltern waste mounds, which were subsequently used as the location of settlements. This landscape development has left a number of isolated churches and abandoned villages in the Lincolnshire Marsh (Morris 1989; Fenwick 2001). The seawall post-dates the period of use of the Marshchapel–2 site, as this relied on an artificial channel bringing seawater to the site (see above). The majority of dispersed lowland settlements in the area originated at a much later date – at enclosure – when the townfield system made way for self-contained farms.

Following the Norman conquest, a number of important motte and bailey castles were built in the Humber Wetlands (Figure 62). In their location, these illustrate the importance of access to, or control of, major waterways. These motte and bailey castles formed part of a network of defensive sites from where the Normans ruled and controlled their new dominion, and they were built soon after the Conquest. The Norman baron Drogo de la Beuvriere, who had received extensive parts of Holderness and north Lincolnshire from William the Conqueror in 1071, was responsible for the construction of the motte and bailey castles at Skipsea Brough in Holderness and at Barrow upon Humber. Other barons too were granted extensive parts of the Humber Wetlands after the Norman Conquest which had been confiscated from Saxon nobles – a change of ownership imposed after sometimes violent conflict with the native population.

The motte and bailey castle at Barrow upon Humber controlled the Barrow

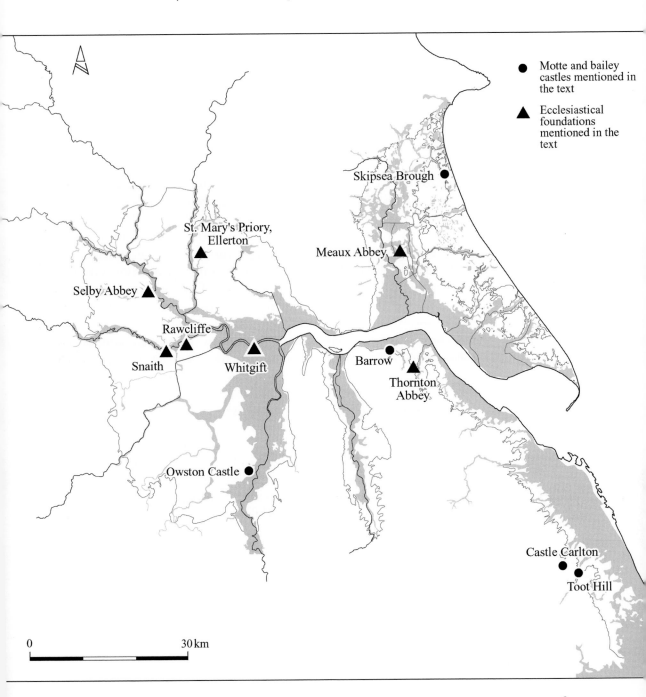

Beck, which provided access to the Humber estuary and was used as the southern landing of a ferry, operating by the later eleventh century AD. In the Lincolnshire Marsh, the motte and bailey castle at Toot Hill controlled the Great Eau and Castle Carlton the Long Eau. In the lower Trent valley, the lordship of Axholme was held in 1086 by Geoffrey de Wicre, who ordered the construction of strategically situated Owston castle, which controlled the cross-Trent ferry and thus access to the Isle of Axholme. Lastly, the motte and bailey castle at Skipsea in Holderness is located in the centre of the pre-Holocene Bail Mere (Chapter 2). The name 'Skipsea' means 'ship sea', and earlier writers suggest that this mere was used as a harbour. Modelling of the landscape around Skipsea, however, suggests that it is most unlikely that ships bigger than rowing boats could have been used on Bail Mere, as the depth of the elongated complex of Bail and Low Mere (which connects the site to the River Hull headwaters) was less than 1 m in places, and its width less than 3 m. At West Furze, the Neolithic or Early Bronze Age trackway and the Bronze Age logjam or beaver dam would have interfered with any waterborne traffic (see Chapter 4). It is more likely that the pre-Norman name Skipsea is derived from one of the meres that provided direct access to the sea, for example the Withow Gap, and the castle adopted the name.

As elsewhere in England, the Norman barons' lust for hunting can be observed in the Humber Wetlands. For example, in 1311, the then Lord of Axholme, John de Mowbray, retained the right of free chase in the manor and soke of Crowle in a grant to Selby Abbey (Miller in Head *et al.* 1998). Much of the Hatfield Chase in the Humberhead Levels fell under Forest Law, and after 1347 under Royal Forest Law, which refers to the punitive rules designed to preserve game for hunting purposes. Hunting, farming and woodland exploitation were restricted on the Chase (Dinnin 1997c). In all, 34 parks and hunting forests are recorded in the various Sites and Monuments Records in the Humber Wetlands (Van de Noort and Davies 1993).

The Norman nobility led the re-establishment of monasticism in what had been the Danelaw. The role of these ecclesiastical foundations in the wetland recolonisation in the Humber lowlands was remarkable. The earliest Norman ecclesiastical foundation in the area was Selby Abbey, established by William the Conqueror in 1069, and it played a significant role in the landscape change we can observe around this time. Its extensive holdings in the Humberhead Levels, including those at Snaith, Rawcliffe and Whitgift, were amongst the earliest areas where large-scale land conversion took place (Metcalfe 1960; Dinnin 1997c). The impact of Selby Abbey on the landscape includes the digging of drains, such as the Bishop's Drain in Selby as early as the eleventh or twelfth century (Blood and Taylor 1992). It is particularly well illustrated on the Inclesmoor Map, dated to *c.* 1405 (Beresford 1986), which shows a drain encircling 'Inclesmoor' (i.e. Thorne Moors). As part of the reclamation of its lands, drains were dug, roads built, bridges constructed, crosses erected, villages founded, and peat was extracted on a large scale for fuel, resulting in patterns of strip-like fields termed Moorland Allotments (Plate 5; Figure 63).

FIGURE 62 (*opposite*). Map of the Humber Wetlands, showing motte and bailey castles and ecclesiastical institutions mentioned in the text.

FIGURE 63. Detail from the Inclesmoor Map of Eastoft and Haldenby (redrawn by Keith Miller, in Van de Noort *et al.* 1998, 133).

These fields extended from the river embankments or levees deep into Thorne Moors. Remarkably, the Moorland Allotments between the River Ouse and Thorne Moors survive today as the principal landscape feature, although large-scale warping (Figure 64; see Chapter 9) has heightened the surface of the land considerably. Keith Miller's (1997) research into the medieval open strip fields in the Humberhead Levels and the Isle of Axholme has not only stressed the need to protect the last remains of the once extensive medieval open field systems here, but has also shown the interrelationship of the free farmers in the Humber Wetlands with their environment.

Following the foundation of Selby Abbey, a large number of monasteries were founded during the twelfth and thirteenth centuries AD by the Norman barons. At the time of the Dissolution, over 40 ecclesiastical foundations can be counted within the boundaries of the Humber Wetlands and extensive land was held here by abbeys and monasteries from outside the area. The large number of ecclesiastical foundations reflects the wider Norman practice of establishing abbeys, monasteries and priories in often remote areas. The improvement and reclamation of wastes, moors and wetlands not only contributed to economic development, and thus in the longer term to increased tax revenues, but from the point of view of the monasteries could also be seen as a 'conversion' of the land. After Selby, the two most prominent ecclesiastical foundations were Thornton Abbey in the Lincolnshire Marsh and Meaux Abbey in the lower Hull valley. Thornton priory was founded in 1139 by

FIGURE 64.
Aerial photograph of the post-medieval 'Moorland Allotments' in the area between Thorne Moors and the River Ouse; this type of land reclamation goes back to at least the fifteenth century.

PHOTOGRAPH BY KEITH MILLER

FIGURE 65.
The fourteenth-
century gatehouse of
Thornton Abbey in
the Lincolnshire
Marsh.

William LeGross, Count of Aumale, and raised to the status of abbey in 1148. It was to become one of the richest Augustinian houses in the country, exemplified in its magnificent fourteenth-century gatehouse (Figure 65). Meaux Abbey in the lower Hull valley was founded *c.* 1150. It survives as an extensive earthwork site, which includes ditches and drains dug by the monks for drainage and transport.

The wealth of these religious houses came, to a significant extent, directly from wetland exploitation, and the abbeys were the administrative centres of very large, usually dispersed domains. The estates were run remotely from monastic granges, often surviving as moated sites (see below). In the Hull valley, for example, the moated sites of Hayholme Grange, Barf Hill, Lockington, Fish Holme Barne and North Grange, near Wawne, all belonged to Meaux Abbey. Where excavations have taken place, it has been shown that the exploitation of the wetlands and surrounding lands included a range of activities, most notably farming. Fishponds are frequent features on ecclesiastical sites, both at the abbeys such as Thornton, and at granges, such as Woodhall Manor outside Beverley (Fenwick 2000). Palynological analysis from what was thought to be a fishpond from the St Mary's Gilbertine priory at Ellerton on the River Derwent in the Vale of York contained 98 per cent *Cannabis sativa* pollen, showing that hemp was grown here and ropes may have been made on site. The fishpond had, in fact, been used as a hemp-retting pond (Aughton–6; Chapman *et al.* 1999).

The study of the towns in the Humber Wetlands was not part of the remit of the project. Nevertheless, we recognise their importance in the history of the region and their key characteristics are summarised here (Figure 67). Historical sources, and to a more limited extent archaeology, tell us about the rise, and in some cases subsequent decline, of the towns in and around the

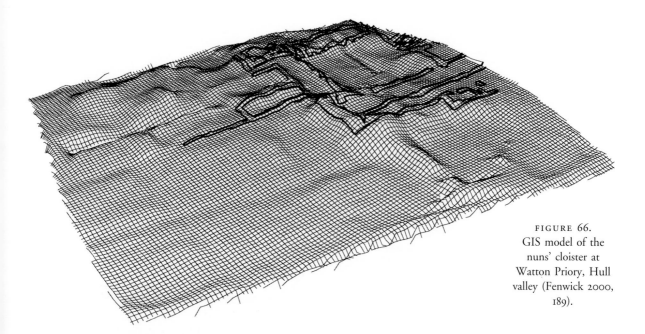

FIGURE 66.
GIS model of the
nuns' cloister at
Watton Priory, Hull
valley (Fenwick 2000,
189).

Humber Wetlands. The fortunes of the towns were in part dependent on the locations of markets, successful trade links, the silting up of harbours and the stimulus they received from ecclesiastical foundations or from royal patronage.

Only York, just outside the limits of the Humber Wetlands, remained an important administrative centre throughout the Middle Ages. Following the retreat of the Roman Army from Britain, little historical evidence exists for the continuation of urban life here, but excavations have shown that an Anglian population remained in the area of the Roman fortress and *colonia* in what was to become the town of York. In the early seventh century, King Edward of Northumbria reinstated York as a religious centre and a wooden church dedicated to St Peter was built. Furthermore, excavations beneath York Minster have shown that part of the Roman military headquarters, the basilica, survived and remained in good repair at least until the ninth century. Pope Gregory the Great determined that York was to become the seat of one of the two metropolitan bishops, and it regained its metropolitan status in AD 735.

The Scandinavians took control of York in AD 866 and York became the centre of a Viking 'kingdom' in the north of England. The famous excavations at Coppergate, which included four ninth-century houses, showed that York had once again become the centre of an extensive trade network, with the source of finds including the English hinterland, Ireland, Scandinavia, Byzantium and Arabia, and also a centre for crafts and small industries (Hall 1978; 1984). At the time of Domesday, the population of York was estimated at around 10,000. Throughout the Middle Ages, York remained by far the largest town in the region and retained the most important administrative functions, especially as the seat of the archbishop, alongside its role as a religious and

FIGURE 67 (*opposite*).
Map of the Humber
Wetlands, showing all
towns mentioned in
the text.

142

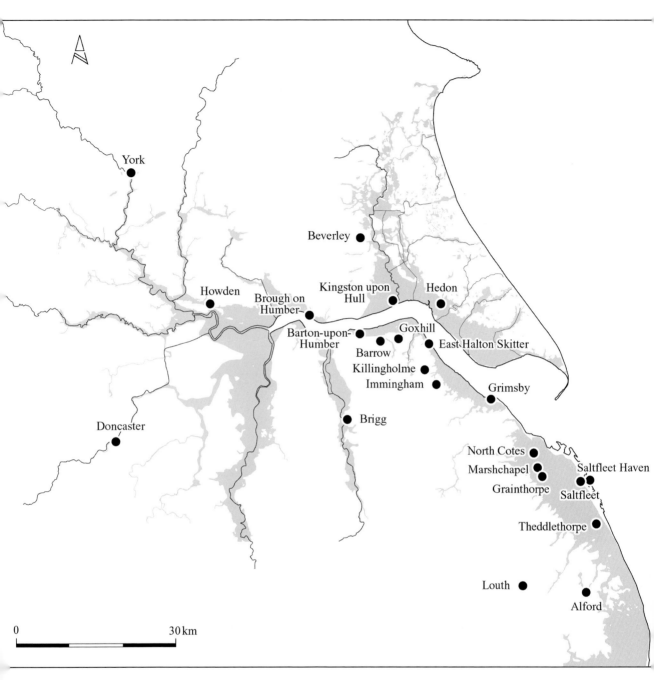

economic centre and its continued role in trade. The importance of York to
the Humber Wetlands is not easily determined, but what is certain is that
through its role in religious foundations such as Cawood in the Vale of York,
it contributed greatly to the recolonisation and transformation of extensive
areas within the region.

The history of the other Roman towns on the margins of the Humber
Wetlands, Doncaster and Brough on Humber, is altogether different. Despite

its strategic position on the River Don, no evidence exists for occupation in post-Roman Doncaster (Buckland *et al.* 1989). However, recent excavations by the South Yorkshire Archaeology Unit at Lower Fish Gate on the River Don have shown the existence of a riverside quay in the later eleventh and twelfth centuries, where it formed part of the renewal of Doncaster as an urban settlement. Its trade function in the Middle Ages relied on the ships reaching Doncaster from the Humber on the River Don, but by the middle of the fourteenth century the lower Don had silted up to the point that boats from the Humber could no longer reach Doncaster (Richardson 1981). The civilian settlement at Brough on Humber had been deserted in the fourth century in favour of reoccupation of the military fortifications. However, by that time the haven had already silted up, and Brough did not regain the status of a town in the Middle Ages (Wacher 1995).

Several towns in or near the Humber Wetlands can trace their origin to the Anglo-Saxon period, including Barton upon Humber and Grimsby in the Lincolnshire Marsh. Barton upon Humber in the Early Saxon period comprised an oval enclosed settlement, possible of elite status, at the head of a palaeo-creek off the Humber estuary (Figures 68, 69). Barton became part of the estate of the monastery at nearby Barrow and the Late Saxon church of

FIGURE 68 (*left*) Detail of the doorway of the Late Saxon tower of St Peter's, Barton upon Humber.

FIGURE 69 (*right*). St Peter's at Barton upon Humber, in the Lincolnshire Marsh; the central tower is of Late Saxon date.

St Peter's contained ninth-century graves. It enjoyed considerable success as a trading and market town on the Humber, and grew rapidly in the Late Saxon and Early Norman period, possibly even developing an artificial haven. In its heyday, Barton was the pre-eminent town on the Humber, but it lost its position and much of its trade to Hull in the late thirteenth and fourteenth centuries AD. Grimsby is first mentioned in AD 866. With its natural harbour, it enjoyed much success in the trade in fish and foodstuffs with the Low Countries, France and Scandinavia and reached its prime in the thirteenth and fourteenth centuries. Pressure in the fourteenth and fifteenth centuries from the Hanseatic League and competition from Hull and Boston caused its decline (Ambler 1990).

Beverley, on the margins of the Hull valley, may have had a Roman predecessor, but the present small town originated with the foundation of the monastery of *Inderawuda* by Bishop John of York in the early eighth century, as described by Bede. Beverley's growth has been attributed to the pilgrimage to Bishop John's tomb, one of the most important sanctuaries in northern England. By the twelfth century, Beverley was also an important market town and excavations at Eastgate and Hallgarth moat have shown a range of small-scale industries here in the Middle Ages, including smithing, pottery, brick and tile making, leather tanning and cloth fulling and dyeing (Miller in Fenwick *et al.* 1999).

The majority of 'new towns' in the Norman period were founded by ecclesiastical or seigneurial institutions or individuals, although archaeological evidence has suggested earlier phases of settlement for some of them. Hedon in southern Holderness was a new town founded in the early twelfth century by the William LeGross, Count of Aumale. It was established as a port with access to the Humber, serving the lordship of Holderness and receiving a royal charter as a borough in *c.* 1170. It flourished for a short period before its decline due to the silting of its haven, and increasing competition from nearby Kingston upon Hull. Two further new towns, Selby and Howden, developed around ecclesiastical foundations. Selby's origin is now thought to go back to the Late Saxon period, but it only became a town after the Abby was founded in 1069. It functioned as a market and riverside harbour on the Ouse. Howden, in the southern Vale of York, was granted to the bishops of Durham in 1086–7, and flourished under the bishops' patronage and periodical residence, reflected in the magnificent remains of St Peter's and the bishops' manor house (Figure 70).

Unlike many other towns in the Humber Wetlands, Hull's archaeology has been much advanced in the last decades. Hull has its origins in the settlement of Wyke, between 1180 and 1200, on land owned by Meaux Abbey. Excavations have shown that a regular town plan was already in place before the purchase of the settlement by Edward I from Meaux Abbey and the foundation of the King's Town or Kingston upon Hull in 1293. Hull was the most successful trading port on the Humber, exporting wool fleeces, other agricultural produce and manufactured goods to the Low Countries, the Baltic, France, the Iberian Peninsula and the Mediterranean. From there it imported foodstuffs, especially

fish, wine from France, luxury food and spices, and raw materials such as timber from the Baltic (Evans 2000). The growth of Hull as a trading port represents a reverse image of what happened on the farmed lands in the Hull and Ancholme valleys, where a significant depopulation of the countryside including the desertion of villages can be observed (see Chapter 9). Its growth also had a negative impact on the status and activity of the many smaller ports along the Humber and the coast. The list of small ports in the Lincolnshire Marsh illustrates how numerous these ports were. They included, from west to east, Barrow, Coxhill, East Halton Skitter, Killingholme, Immingham, Northcotes, Marshchapel, Grainthorpe, Saltfleet, Saltfleethaven and Wilgrip Haven at Theddlethorpe. These small ports exported locally produced grain, textiles and salt, and imported peat, timber, cloth, stockfish and wine (Miller in Fenwick *et al.* 2001a). Most of them had ceased trading by the late Middle Ages, either because their havens had silted up, or because the larger ships increasingly in use were not able to enter their ports, thus enhancing the maritime activity at Hull.

Numerous other settlements were granted markets and fairs in the Middle Ages. For example, no fewer than twenty settlements on the Lincolnshire Marsh alone received market charters, but only Barton, Grimsby, Louth and Alford developed into towns. In the Ancholme valley, Brigg is such a late-coming

146

'new town', founded in the twelfth or thirteenth century AD on the corner of four existing parishes, where it operated as a market and riverside port.

The impact of these towns, and urbanisation in general, on the surrounding countryside of the Humber Wetlands was manifold. The present landscape includes remnants of the extensive commons that served the needs of the towns, with those at Beverley largely surviving, and parks were established, such as Selby's hunting forest. Urbanisation contributed indirectly to the

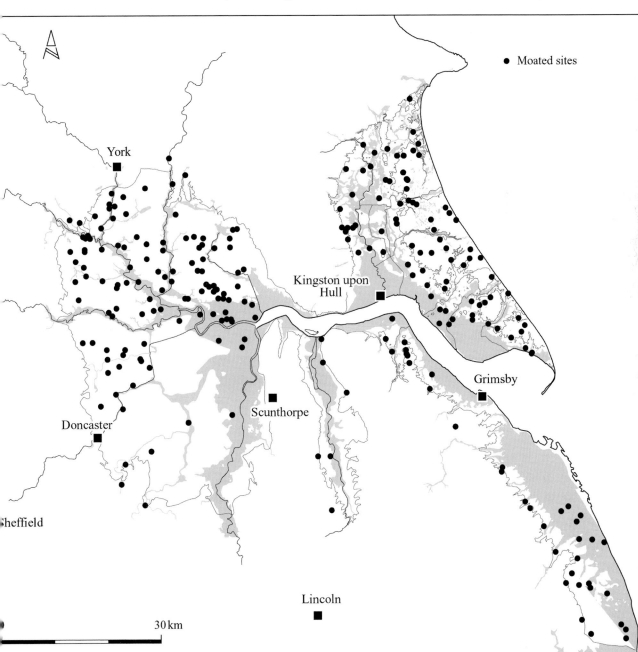

accelerated recolonisation and intensified exploitation of the Humber Wetlands. And, mainly through ecclesiastical institutions, it played a significant role in their transformation through drainage schemes and reclamation. The farming community had once again become part of a wider economic system as a result of its interrelationship with the towns within and surrounding the Humber Wetlands.

One particular form of wetland recolonisation requires further discussion – moated sites. Over 250 moated sites are recorded from the Humber Wetlands (Figure 71; Van de Noort and Davies 1993), and a majority of these are believed to have been constructed between 1250 and 1350 (Le Patourel 1973). Most moats surrounded manor houses, manorial complexes, monastic granges and farms or estate buildings (Figure 72). Many moated sites were owned by the numerous religious houses in the Humber Wetlands, although some moats were linked to the property of the nobility or, occasionally, of freeholders (Hey 1986). Analysis of the distribution of moated sites has shown that moats were located in areas not yet exploited from the surrounding villages, with

FIGURE 72.
Metham Hall moated site, near Yokefleet in the Vale of York, one of the few water filled moats in the Humber Wetlands.

the area between the Rivers Aire and Don in the Humberhead Levels providing a particular clear example (Fenwick 1997). This indicates that ecclesiastical institutions, and to a lesser extent the seigneurial classes, took an active lead in the process of recolonisation and intensification of the exploitation of the lower-lying areas in this part of the Humber Wetlands.

Despite being one of the most numerous types of site, relatively little archaeological research has been undertaken on moated sites. Important exceptions are the research at the Wood Hall moated site in the Humberhead Levels, which has shown the wealth and prestige of the people living here, where the moat produced a range of wet-preserved structures and artefacts (V. Metcalf pers. comm.), and at Cowick, also in the Humberhead Levels, where pottery wasters were found (Hayfield and Greig 1990 – see below). The function of the moats themselves continues to cause debate amongst archaeologists. While their role as status-enhancing features is widely recognised, their operation within the wetlands as a method of creating small areas of slightly higher and thus dryer ground remain a matter of dispute. Undoubtedly, the moats would have a 'drawing-down' effect on the watertable of the area enclosed by the moat, but it remains unclear whether this was the intention, or a fortunate consequence, of the creation of the moats.

Medieval wetland exploitation: a 'concave landscape'?

The concept of the 'concave landscape' has been used to illustrate the varied types of ecosystems that can be found in wetlands and the surrounding land. Although the Humber Wetlands contains considerably more diverse landscapes than many other wetlands, the 'concave landscape' can be used here as a model to describe the diverse resources and opportunities available in the Middle Ages and early post-medieval period.

The highest ground in this model was predominantly used as arable land. In the rule, this arable land was farmed in the townfield system, with open strip fields surrounding nucleated settlements, also found on these areas of higher ground. Open strip fields survive in a number of locations in the Humber Wetlands as ridge and furrow, most notably on the Isle of Axholme. Around Crowle in the Humberhead Levels, current landownership and the present-day field system appear to be directly descended from the open field system (Miller 1997; English and Miller 1991). This higher ground embraces most areas that were above HMWST. It includes the valley sides, and the lower extents of the Yorkshire and Lincolnshire Wolds, the Lincoln Edge and the Sherwood Sandstone and Magnesian Limestone on the southern and western limits of the Humber Wetlands. It also includes the many 'islands' in the region, varying in size from the Isle of Axholme to much smaller ones such as Holme-on-Spalding in the Vale of York and Wroot in the Humberhead Levels. Additionally, higher ground could be found on the levees of the major rivers, such as the Trent, Ouse and Hull. The surface geology of these areas, either of pre-Holocene origin or alluvial bank material, frequently reworked

by the wind, created free-draining soils, which were well-suited to the cultivation of cereals.

No palaeoenvironmental source material was identified by the Humber
Wetlands Survey that provides new insights into the environment and agriculture of the last millennium, but such information was provided by Smith's
(1985) palynological study on Thorne and Hatfield Moors. His regional pollen
zone HHL/E, radiocarbon dated to the period after *c.* AD 1100, shows a marked
decrease in the value of tree and shrub pollen, with a concomitant rise in
herbs to 80 per cent of the total land pollen. The most frequently encountered
pollen are Gramineae (grasses), Cyperaceae (sedge family) and *Calluna vulgaris*
(heather), but also includes *Cannabis* (hemp), *Plantago* (Plantain family), *Urtica*
(nettles) and *Secale cereale* (rye). This indicates that the landscape beyond the
Moors was increasingly cleared of shrub and woodland, and that agricultural
activity intensified, with an increased emphasis on arable rather than pastoral
farming. The pollen evidence from Thorne Moors, and also from the moated
site at Cowick (Hayfield and Greig 1989) and a 'fishpond' from St Mary's
Gilbertine priory at Ellerton in the Vale of York (see above), show the extensive
presence of *Cannabis sativa* pollen, showing that hemp was grown and worked
here. The use of hemp in the production of ropes, often associated with the
demand by the navy, is also shown in the many hemp-retting pits on the Isle
of Axholme (e.g. Scotter–4; Chapman 1998).

Further down the valley were the meadows and ings, these terms being used
here to define the floodplains predominantly made up of minerogenic sediments. For the farmers and the economy of the Humber Wetlands in the
Middle Ages and early post-medieval period, these lands were valued above
all others, and for much of the medieval period, these ings were farmed as
common lands within the townfield system. The ings and meadows were used
both for grazing stock and as hay land, providing the main source of food
for livestock and plough animals. The richness of the commons, especially
where it benefited from regular floods that brought new nutrients on the land,
was widely recognised. This type of landscape was widespread throughout the
Humber Wetlands, especially in the Hull and Ancholme valleys, in the
northern parts of the Humberhead Levels, the lower Trent valleys and the
Lincolnshire Marsh, but was more restricted in Holderness and the Vale of
York.

The lowest terrestrial areas in the concave landscape were the carrs, moors
and wastes, lands where persistent high water tables had resulted in extensive
peat formation. The carrs and moors were extensively exploited as seasonal
pastures and as such formed an essential part of the rural economy, enabling
the use of some of the higher ings as hay lands. The use of these low-lying
lands was increasingly regulated, in order to prevent over-grazing. In the Hull
valley, this process of 'stinting' is shown in the Meaux Abbey Chronicle, which
describes the regulations concerning how the villagers of Wawne and Sutton
should use their lands in the thirteenth century. It is also shown in a survey
of Eske in the Hull valley, dated to AD 1278, which stipulates the use of its

North Carr by the village tenants, listing cattle, draught oxen, horses, sheep, pigs and geese (Miller in Fenwick *et al.* 2000). Where these lands were particularly extensive, they were organised as common land, such as around the Isle of Axholme.

These low-lying lands provided more than just seasonal grazing, and historical sources show that peat cutting, for both fuel and as building materials ('turves'), was an important activity by the thirteenth and fourteenth century. The Inclesmoor map shows an advanced stage of peat cutting on Thorne Moors by the early fifteenth century, with arterial drainage, roads, bridges and turbaries (the areas where peat was cut) clearly indicated. Here, as elsewhere, ecclesiastical institutions appear to have taken a lead-role in the exploitation of the turbaries, with peat not only being used as a domestic fuel, but also providing the essential energy in a range of industrial processes, such as pottery, tile and brick manufacture (Dinnin 1997a). One of the most surprising resources harvested from these low-lying areas in the Humber Wetlands were the wooden trees dug from the peat at Hatfield Moors and sold as ships' masts (Stovin Ms).

Further down the concave landscape were the intertidal areas. In the Lincolnshire Marsh, salt production during the Middle Ages and early post-medieval period was an expanding industry. Rather than boiling seawater, as was the practice during the Roman period and presumably also during the Late Saxon period as indicated by our work at Marschape–2 (Fenwick *et al.* 2001b), the filtering of salt-laden sand and subsequent boiling of the brine became the customary method. The filtered sand was deposited to form huge mounds, the so-called 'red hills' (e.g. Healey 1999). These 'red hills' formed the foci for further seaward settlement expansion, and provided suitable ground for arable agriculture (Fenwick 2001), with the areas of the 'red hills' currently classified as Grade 1 agricultural land (Ellis 2001). Apart from saltmaking, the intertidal areas, both on the Lincolnshire coast and in the Humber estuary, continued to be used for seasonal grazing throughout the Middle Ages and the post-medieval period. One farmer working the north bank of the Humber recalled that his family continued to use the saltmarshes in the estuary as a winter grazing ground for cattle up to the early twentieth century (cf. Van de Noort and Fletcher 2000). We may assume that this obvious use of saltmarshes was practised throughout the Middle Ages, and may even be of much greater antiquity than that (see Chapter 3).

The lowest lying landscapes in the model are formed by the waterbodies – the rivers, estuary and sea. Their margins provided reeds for building, thatching and basket making, but of considerably greater importance were fishing and fowling. The importance of fishing is widely recognised. Fishing was undertaken in all wetlands. The meres of Holderness were renowned for their eel (Sheppard 1957), fishing rights were held by the towns on the Isle of Axholme covering the pools surrounding the Isle and the Rivers Trent, Idle and the Old River Don (Platts 1985), and tidal fishweirs survive in the Humber estuary, for example at West Clough (Melton–2; Fletcher *et al.* 1999) and at Grimsby

(Grimsby–3; Fenwick *et al.* 2001b). The importance of fishing is also reflected in historical accounts. For example, at Tudworth in the Humberhead Levels, Domesday Book mentions 20 fisheries rendering 20,000 eels annually (Dinnin 1997a). Here, as elsewhere in the region, fish were habitually used as gifts or payments to ecclesiastical institutions with eels being particularly favoured, supplementing the yield from the numerous fishponds that can be found near most monasteries, manors and towns.

Wild fowling was undoubtedly also extensively practiced, but this has left few tangible medieval remains. Duck decoys are a post-medieval innovation for maximising the catch of fowl, and in the Hull valley such decoy sites are known from Meaux (Figure 73; cf. Weel–4; Chapman *et al.* 2000), Brandesburton, Leconfield, Leven and Watton, and in the Humberhead Levels from the parishes of Crowle, Rawcliffe, Snaith and Cowick (Van de Noort and Davies 1993). Records from Leconfield Castle in the Hull valley show that a broad range of birds were caught and eaten, including mallards, snipes, curlews, redshanks, plover and swans, reflecting the wetland habitats of this region (cf. Miller in Fenwick *et al.* 2000).

FIGURE 73.
The duck decoy at Meaux, in the Hull valley.

© NEIL MITCHELL APS/UK BEVERLEY

Conclusion

The importance of the Humber Wetlands in the Middle Ages must be understood in the context of changes in sea-level in the region. These may be characterised as follows. A major marine transgression has been dated to the Late Roman period, followed by a prolonged phase of marine regression or sea-level equilibrium. Historical sources have documented a period of higher sea-levels or increased storminess for the period after AD 1250. This phase of marine transgression may have lasted for two centuries. Its impact on the lowest lying lands in the Humber Wetlands is discussed further in Chapter 9.

Against this background, the significant reduction of occupation activity in the Humber Wetlands between the fifth and the ninth centuries seems understandable. However, wetlands elsewhere in England and further afield include ample archaeological evidence for local adaptations to the new environmental conditions, enabling the continued exploitation of, and habitation in, a range of wetland landscapes. The lack of such activity in the Humber Wetlands requires alternative explanations. It has been argued here that the lack of any kind of market that could have taken the produce of specialised wetland farming, especially stock breeding, resulted in farming activity becoming more or less self-sufficient. The resources in the region were undoubtedly exploited, and the wetlands were unquestionably perceived as rich resources. These resources were not, in the first instance, exploited from farms and settlements located within the wetlands, but from the surrounding drylands and from the larger 'islands'. The example of Flixborough has shown this most clearly. These farms and settlements were recipients of long-distance traded goods, but it remains unclear how this trade was organised and who exactly was responsible for carrying it out.

From the ninth century onwards, during the Late Saxon period, we can detect a recolonisation of the wetlands, at first occupying the 'islands' within the Humber Wetlands, but from as early as the eleventh century also occupying the sides of rivers, presumably on constructed riverbanks. This recolonisation is part of an economic upturn, which had a profound impact on much of western Europe. The role of ecclesiastical institutions in this process has been highlighted, and the larger-scale reclamation projects of the high Middle Ages were always undertaken under the supervision of these institutions. Many of the estimated 250 moated sites in the Humber Wetlands, occupying some of the lowest lying land, were monastic granges. The settlements were organised in the townfield system, but the frequent multiple townships on the Isle of Axholme, the Ancholme valley and elsewhere have led to the suggestion that seigneurial control on the local population was not as strong in these remote parts as it was elsewhere in eastern England. Urbanisation changed the landscape from the twelfth century onwards, but the development of towns, trade and wool production eventually contributed to the decline of many villages.

CHAPTER NINE

The Drainage of
the Humber Wetlands

Although the drainage of the Humberhead Levels by Cornelius Vermuyden in the first half of the seventeenth century symbolises – as no other undertaking – the transformation of the Humber Wetlands, their drainage work should be considered within the wider context of attempts to control the water level, and the sea, that may have started with the Romans and continue today. This chapter looks at the reasons and history of drainage in the Humber Wetlands and the creation of the modern landscape.

Early drainage ventures

The Roman colonisation of the East Anglian Fenlands not only involved a large number of settlements and roads, including the Fen Causeway, but also a number of canals (Hall and Coles 1994). While some of these canals may have been primarily dug as part of wetland drainage and reclamation, the majority of canals were used for transport, linking active rivers and other sites of particular importance. Several authors have argued that the north branch of the River Don in the Humber Wetlands, or Turnbridge Dike, was a similar artificial waterway (Gaunt 1975), which could have only been built by the Romans (Jones 1995). Although such a proposition would complement what we know of the intensity of the colonisation and exploitation of the Humberhead Levels in the Roman period, it does not as yet stand up to scrutiny.

As part of the Humber Wetlands Project, Malcolm Lillie (1997) cored the palaeochannel of the north branch of the River Don near Turnbridge – the only part of the proposed canal that was not reused in the drainage works of the seventeenth century. Pollen analysis of samples from the palaeo-channel suggest that river aggradation (see Chapter 2) commenced at the boundary of pollen zones VIIa and VIIb, or c. 4000 cal BC. Although this date is not wholly unambiguous, with some evidence of reworking of older deposits, it suggests that the Don's north branch existed by the later Neolithic or the Early Bronze Age. Of course, this evidence does not indicate that the Romans were not involved in the straightening of rivers. Apart from the Don's north branch, both the Bycarrs Dike, linking the Rivers Idle and Trent to the south of the Isle of Axholme, and the lower reaches of the River Derwent in the

Vale of York have been mentioned as possible canals or canalised rivers. Only further archaeological or palaeoenvironmental research can provide proof for these suggestions.

In the Middle Ages, drainage undertakings were mainly instigated by religious houses, although the laity played a role as well. We have already discussed the role of Selby Abbey in the transformation of the northern parts of the Humberhead Levels, in particular through the drains dug around Thorne Moors to enable peat extraction to take place on a much larger scale, and through the settlement of the southern parts of the Vale of York (see Chapter 8). Selby Abbey has also been implicated in the construction of the Don's north branch or Turnbridge Dike, but unambiguous evidence for its involvement here is lacking. It is possible that, like the Romans, Selby Abbey was involved in straightening the Don's north branch, but the palaeoenvironmental evidence from our survey indicates a natural origin for this channel.

The drainage schemes were instigated by the ecclesiastical and seigneurial authorities. Among them was Hugh de Pudsey who, as Bishop of Durham, was also Lord of Howdenshire and responsible for the resettlement of the southern Vale of York. Others involved in the drainage activities were the Knights Templars at Faxfleet, naming the new dam Temple Dam, the Canons of Thornton at Thornton Land, with the new Thornton Dam and Gilbert Hansard at Blacktoft, with the new Hansardam (Sheppard 1966). Probably the best known engineering venture was the construction of the Ashdyke in the 1160s by Meaux Abbey, in the southern part of the Hull valley. Although this was primarily used for transport, it is likely that other ditches were dug to alleviate the problems of waterlogging (Sheppard 1956).

Recent work around Kingswood immediately north of Kingston upon Hull, has shown the intensity of wetland exploitation in this area, including the construction of the Foredyke in the thirteenth century and its possible use in the management of fishponds, and the existence of a possible fish house, part of the Meaux estate (Steedman in Evans 2000). In the Ancholme valley, the earliest attempts to alleviate flooding problems commenced in the thirteenth century, when the course of the river between Bishopsbridge and the Humber was straightened. Siltation was always a problem here and dredging began as early as 1312 (Straw 1955).

Precursors to drainage: the early enclosures

Whereas the establishment of new villages in the Humber Wetlands provides the clearest evidence for the scale of recolonisation of the lowlands, not all settlements succeeded, and towards the end of the Middle Ages and in the early post-medieval period a degree of depopulation can be observed. This is clear from the shrunken and deserted villages, which show that from the middle of the fifteenth century many villages in the region were in decline. The reasons for this development are diverse, and include the impact of the Black Death from the middle of the fourteenth century, poor crops and rising water tables. However, the main reason for depopulation appears to have been an economic one. In the case of the village of Eske in the Hull valley, English and Miller (1991) suggest that local elite groups, in this case the Grimston family, were buying up land for conversion to pasture, resulting in the widespread practice of land enclosure. This was used for sheep and the profitable wool trade – but sheep breeding is a labour extensive occupation, and the lack of labour resulted in farmers moving to the towns.

The Hull valley alone includes nineteen settlements with evidence of desertion, settlement shift or shrinkage (Loughlin and Miller 1979). The Ancholme valley appears to have witnessed a similar degree of depopulation associated principally with the conversion of arable into pasture, enclosure and emparking by the major landowners, who had 'grown rich on the spoils of the Dissolution of the monasteries' (Miller in Van de Noort *et al.* 1998: 137). Deserted and shrunken villages here include Owersby, Somerby, Searby, Horkstow, Kettleby, Kettleby Thorpe and Castlethorpe, and their demise coincides with the rapid growth of the town of Brigg. Similar developments, albeit on a smaller scale, have been observed in the lower Trent valley, where villages such as Haldenby and Waterton all but disappeared in the fifteenth and sixteenth centuries whilst others, notably Adlingfleet, shrank considerably. However, settlement desertion was much less common further west and, if we discount the moated sites, no large-scale desertions of settlements are known from the Humberhead Levels and only one example is known from the Vale of York, namely the riverside settlement at Kirby Wharfe (Chapman 1999). The settlement shifts in the Lincolnshire Marsh further east, where the coastline was regressing, have already been described in Chapter 8, and the many isolated churches there can be assigned to this process.

Insufficient research has taken place, either as part of the Humber Wetlands Project or elsewhere, for us to have unambiguous answers to this geographical riddle. However, it is apparent that the farmers working the lower-lying lands on the Hull and Ancholme floodplains and in the lower parts of the Trent valley suffered from increased problems with water. This predicament was apparently not shared by farmers in the Vale of York and the Humberhead Levels, where floodplains comprise only a small part of the total landsurface. These increased problems with water can be attributed to a period of cooler and wetter weather, dated to the 200 years after 1250, and to a relative regional sea-level rise. The former affected the whole of the Humber Wetlands, but the latter had a disproportionate impact on the floodplains, most notably those of the Rivers Hull and Ancholme, and on the Lincolnshire Marsh. The Chronicle of Meaux Abbey, in the lower Hull valley, reported extensive flooding in 1253 and the Hull valley was flooded again in 1265. Historical evidence, including the appointment of commissioners who were to survey the riverbanks and sea defences in 1285, shows continued problems throughout the thirteenth, fourteenth and much of the fifteenth century (summarised in Miller in Fenwick *et al.* 2000). Palaeoenvironmental research has similarly shown the existence of a period of increased wetness (see Chapter 2).

Archaeological evidence of floods in the lower Hull valley is indirect, such as the construction of the monastic 'cattle ledges' on a clay platform at Kingswood and the completion of Foredyke, which could be interpreted as 'a concerted programme by the Meaux Abbey estate to restore the land to economic use following the catastrophe' of 1253 (Steedman in Evans 2000: 212). In the Ancholme valley, the grounds of Thornholme Priory were raised behind a precinct wall after 1260, presumably in response to rising water levels (Coppack 1989). These sea-level changes may not have been directly responsible for settlement desertion and depopulation, but would certainly have reduced the viability of arable farming in these low-lying areas. The resulting conversion to pasture, either by the farmers themselves or under the direction of the principal landowners, would have contributed to unemployment and depopulation and thus to settlement desertion.

The process described here included the enclosure of land, normally referred to as 'early enclosure', distinguishing this from the Parliamentary enclosures of the late eighteenth and nineteenth centuries. The early enclosure of large tracts of the Humber Wetlands affected particularly, as we have already seen, the valleys of the Hull and Ancholme and the Holderness region. This piecemeal process, usually undertaken by the major landowners, has created irregular field patterns contrasting with the larger regular field systems of the parliamentary enclosures (Harris 1961; Miller in Fenwick *et al.* 2000). These changes, and the accruing of extensive landholdings in the hands of relatively few landowners, created the necessary setting for the large-scale drainage of the Humber Wetlands.

The large-scale drainage ventures of the post-medieval period

The accumulation of extensive tracts of land by major landowners and the economic opportunities provided by the wool trade set the stage for the large-scale drainage ventures of the seventeenth century. The first drainage scheme took place on the Hatfield Chase in the Humberhead Levels.

In the middle of the fourteenth century, the Hatfield Chase returned to the Crown, and came under Royal Forest Law – underlining its importance as a hunting reserve rather than the existence of an actual forest. Nevertheless, by 1608, a survey of the Royal Forest and Chases described Hatfield Chase as utterly wasted. In 1600, an *Act for the recovery and inning of drowned and surrounded grounds and the draining dry of watery marshes, fens, bogs, moors and other grounds of like nature* was passed by Parliament. Although intended for the East Anglian Fenlands, it was first used in the Humberhead Levels. After years of debate and negotiations, the newly crowned king, Charles I, signed a contract with the Dutch drainage engineer Cornelius Vermuyden in 1626.

The drainage history of the Humberhead Levels has been recorded and described in some detail (e.g. Stonehouse 1839; Tomlinson 1882; Dunston 1909; cf. Dinnin 1997a), and in essence involved the drainage of 24,280 ha in the areas of the Hatfield Chase, Dikes Marsh, the manors and lordships of Wroot

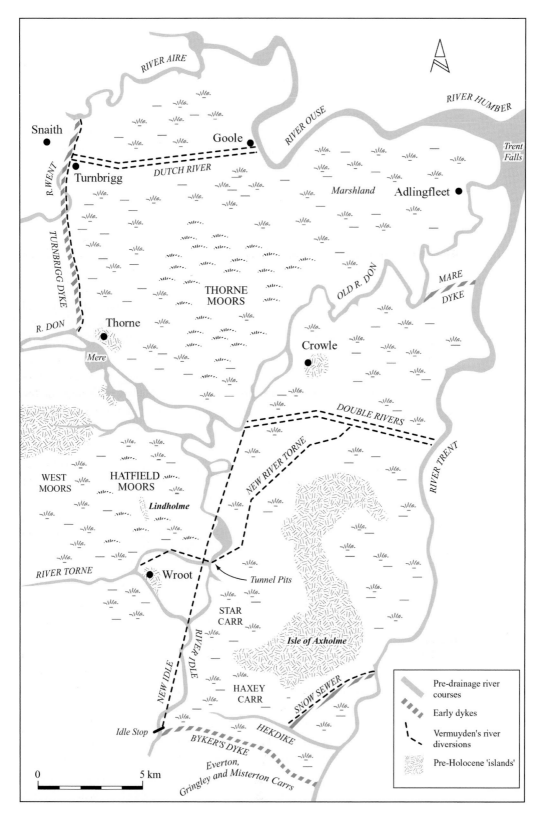

and Finningley and the Isle of Axholme, and the areas alongside the River Idle (Figure 74). The project was to result in land being made suitable for tillage and pasture. Only the modern Thorne and Hatfield Moors were to remain as undrained mires. The newly reclaimed land was to be split three ways – one third for the Crown, one third for Cornelius Vermuyden and his supporters, and one third for the tenants – the commoners living in neighbouring villages – who had land in the reclaimed areas. Cornelius Vermuyden received financial backing from the 'Participants', mostly Dutch and French financiers and landowners, some of them actively participating in the venture. The responsibility for the maintenance of the drainage system rested with Vermuyden and the Participants. A Crown commission was set up to settle disputes resulting from the loss of common lands to the venture.

The central component of the drainage scheme was the diversion of the River Don into the Turnbridge Dike, cutting off the eastern branch of the Don or the 'Old River Don'. It can be recognised today on aerial photographs as a palaoechannel. The drainage of the southern parts of the Humberhead Levels involved the blockage of the River Idle at Idle Stop and its partial diversion into the Bykers Dike. The New Idle was cut, taking water in a direct line first northwards to Dirtness and then eastwards to Althorpe on the River Trent. The New Torne followed a similar route, passing beneath the New Idle at Tunnel Pits. Elsewhere, existing streams were straightened and deepened, for example the Snow Sewer, draining Haxey Carr. The drainage of the Levels was not accomplished without its problems and in the late 1630s the Participants were forced to construct Dutch River to alleviate the shrinking land from flooding. By that time, Cornelius Vermuyden had sold his entitlement and was no longer a party in the drainage venture. Additional drainage work was required throughout the seventeenth, eighteenth and nineteenth centuries, as floods were frequent, resulting in several new drains being cut. For example, the Mother Drain was excavated between 1769 and 1803. Running alongside the Bykers Dike, it received the waters from Everton, Gringley and Misterton Carrs. Not until the introduction of steam pumps in the 1820s was the fundamental problem of drainage of the Humberhead Levels overcome – the problem being that the surface of much of the Levels lies below the high tide levels in the Rivers Ouse and Trent. The first steam pump was installed on the Mother Drain at Misterton Sluice, following major flood problems in the area.

The drainage of the Humberhead Levels is undoubtedly a major feat of seventeenth-century engineering, although its success was not achieved without considerable problems. Apart from the problems with the efficacy of Vermuyden's drainage venture, a number of conflicts arose from the loss of resources by the commoners. The external perception of the Humberhead Levels was that of an 'utter waste', but not even the moors and marshes were *tabula rasa* in the 1620s. Large tracts of both previously reclaimed and unreclaimed wetlands were exploited for a wide variety of functions, and the drainage of the Humberhead Levels resulted in the partial or wholesale loss

FIGURE 74 (*opposite*).
The large-scale
drainage of the
Humberhead Levels,
after Dinnin (1997a:
20).

of these resources. These losses were most clearly felt by the commoners, and their grievances included the loss of common land, the impoverishment of the ancient pasture lands that were no longer enriched by floodwater, the flooding of arable lands that had been dry before the 1620s, and the loss of income due to a reduced return from fishing and fowling. Unsurprisingly, during the Civil War the commoners of Isle of Axholme, who were on the Parliamentarian side, sabotaged drainage works and attacked the settlement of the Participants, who sided with the Royalists, near Sandtoft. Nevertheless, the engineering activities continued, along with legal disputes and occasional sabotage, for many years following the Civil War. In 1862, an Act of Parliament was obtained incorporating the Participants, as specified in Vermuyden's contract with Charles I (Dinnin 1997a).

Outside the Humberhead Levels, drainage projects were undertaken in all regions, although these have not received the same level of attention in past research. The drainage of the Ancholme valley was given new impetus in 1637, with the construction of a new cut from the River Ancholme from Bishops-bridge to the Humber (summarised in Neumann 1998; Figure 75). At South Ferriby, a tidal sluice was constructed in 1635 about 1.5 km to the south of the present tidal sluice. The new cut and the sluice served to improve navigation and drainage, but as in the Humberhead Levels, the drainage was only partially successful and flooding remained a problem. The drainage of the Hull valley has been studied by Sheppard (1966; and summarised in Miller in Fenwick *et al.* 2000). After the Middle Ages, the southernmost carrlands of Wawne, Routh and Swine were successfully drained in the seventeenth and eighteenth centuries, but the floodplain further north remained liable to flooding. Only in the nineteenth century was this land fully reclaimed, following the construction of the Beverley-Barmston Drain and the Holderness Drain, and the dredging of the River Hull from Driffield to Hull. In Holderness, a large number of meres survived into the medieval period, with historical records indicating their value as a resource for fishing and waterfowling. It appears that many smaller and several larger meres, including Lambwath Mere, disappeared in the thirteenth or fourteenth centuries, but the main period of drainage is the sixteenth and seventeenth centuries (Sheppard 1956, Flenley 1987; summarised in Dinnin and Lillie 1995a), and the first edition 1 inch Ordnance Survey map of 1858 shows Hornsea Mere as the only surviving mere. In the southern Vale of York, Walling Fen remained undrained until the cutting of the Market Weighton Canal in the later eighteenth century. Various attempts to drain the Derwent valley have been made, but the Derwent remains an extensive washland that is annually flooded. The Lincolnshire Marsh did not require extensive artificial drainage schemes, thanks to continuing alluviation and marine sediment accretion, aided by the formation of extensive storm beaches and the construction of the seabank (Fenwick 2001).

The land reclamation of the area around Sunk Island in Southern Holderness has been particularly well documented. Spurn Point, a natural spit of sand and shingle extending into the Humber estuary from Holderness, has aggregated

FIGURE 75.
The New River
Ancholme at
Bishopsbridge. This
drain was initially
constructed in 1637.

and eroded on possibly five occasions, according to research by De Boer (1964). Historical references suggest that towards the later part of the sixteenth century, the predecessor of the current Spurn Point evolved resulting in diminished storminess in the lower estuary. Towards the end of the seventeenth century, Sunk Island had begun to reform. Natural sedimentation resulted in an enlarged Sunk Island, and the saltmarshes were enclosed and embanked between 1762 and 1965 (Berridge and Pattison 1994). Similar reclamations in the Humber estuary were successfully completed in the area south of Broom-fleet in the southern Vale of York.

The movement of enclosing land previously organised as commonland from the fifteenth century onwards has been associated with a range of factors, particularly with the extensive conversion of arable to pasture land. This new regime required far less labour and thus resulted in an extensive depopulation of the wetlands, most notably in the lower areas of the Hull, Ancholme and lower Trent valleys. In the subsequent centuries, considerably more land was enclosed here and elsewhere, and a further major impetus to this development was provided by the Parliamentary Enclosures of the late eighteenth and early nineteenth centuries (e.g. Miller in Fenwick *et al.* 2001a). The Enclosure Movement brought about major landscape changes, which included further drainage projects, warping (see below), additional land divisions and the construction of large dispersed farms, replacing the townfield system of open fields and commons. This new settlement pattern, comprising both the new dispersed farms and the old nucleated villages, remains visible throughout the Humber Wetlands today.

Warping as a method of wetland reclamation appears to be unique to the Humber Wetlands, at least in the scale of its application (cf. Cook and Williamson 1999). Warping, or floodwarping, involves the embankment of fields and the deposition of minerogenic sediments carried by tidal floodwater onto the enclosed land over a period of several years. It was used extensively during the nineteenth and the first half of the twentieth centuries. The purpose of warping is to bury unproductive peat soils beneath mineral-rich silts and clays and to heighten the level of the land, thereby preventing frequent flooding and waterlogging of the soils. The alternative method of cartwarping, where silts and clays were transported by cart, has only been practised on a small-scale in the Humberhead Levels (Creyke 1845; Gaunt 1976). Warping was applied extensively in the lower Trent valley, to the peatlands forming the northern parts of Thorne Moors and to a smaller extent in the southern parts of the Vale of York. Malcolm Lillie (1997b; 1998b; 1999) has investigated the warp deposits in these regions. This work showed the variable depth of the warp deposits, the extent to which they masked older wetland landscapes and their potential for preserving archaeological and palaeoenvironmental deposits in the underlying peat.

To an extent, the history of the drainage of the Humberhead Levels reflects the drainage of the Humber Wetlands as a whole and wetlands elsewhere as well. The conflict between people living in the wetlands, who benefited from a range of resources and had access to the commonlands and wastes, and the often distant landowners with capital available for investment, has been acted out in many wetlands, for example the Fenlands of East Anglia (Darby 1983). The reclamation of the wetlands forms part of a more general capitalisation of the wider countryside, with the replacement of open field systems and commonland by enclosure. In the Humber Wetlands, as elsewhere, the onset of this process can be traced back to the eleventh century, with the planned recolonisation and transformation of areas alongside the lower reaches of the River Ouse. It was given further impetus in the fifteenth century, with the conversion of arable land into pasture by larger landowners when the revenue from wool traded on the international market was greater than the rent from tenants.

Conclusion

The history of drainage in the Humber Wetlands may go back to the Roman period, but pending further archaeological and palaeoenvironmental research this can not be confirmed. The impact of the ecclesiastical institutions on the reclamation and drainage of the parts of the region is undeniable, but not until the early seventeenth century did the engineering know-how exist to tackle the wetlands on a large scale.

The fact that drainage projects were promoted and sometimes financed by outsiders, whilst frequently facing opposition from those living from the wetlands, comes as no surprise. The economic value of these wetlands was made up of a myriad of resources – salt, fish, waterfowl, peat, reed, hemp, wood and seasonal grazing and hay grounds, to name only the most important. This diversity provided a first-rate basis for farmers who were largely self-sufficient and offered many opportunities for small-scale production of goods that could be traded on local markets. Such labour-intensive economic activities provided a healthy basis for the commoners' way of life, but for the landlords they created insufficient produce that could be taxed or traded for profit. This division illustrates the often contrary perceptions of wetlands held by insiders and outsiders.

CHAPTER TEN

The Archaeology of a Dynamic Landscape

Over a period of more than 10,000 years, the context of people's daily life in the Humber Wetlands was one of a continually changing environment. Rather than treating this environmental change as little more than the backdrop to social change or, conversely, identifying this environmental change as the prime mover of social adjustments, this book has shown many examples of inter-relationships between environmental and social changes. This has been illustrated from the Mesolithic period through to the post-medieval era. In the Early Mesolithic, hunting strategies were not only altered to cope with the dense forests, but lake-side vegetation was repeatedly burned to create local environments where the hunting of larger mammals could be undertaken with higher success rates (see Chapter 3). In the post-medieval period, large-scale drainage schemes significantly altered the wetlands of the Humberhead Levels and elsewhere, contributing significantly to the concentration of landownership and the gradual disappearance of the township system with common lands (Chapter 9). Similar examples have been provided for other archaeological periods elsewhere in this book.

All environments alter over several millennia. Even so, landscape change in the Humber Wetlands has been particularly dynamic. In summary, natural changes in the Late-glacial include the retreat of the icesheets from the north of England, the creation and disappearance of Lake Humber, and rapid climatic amelioration, which contributed to the swift afforestation of the lowlands. The rapid sea-level rise of the early Holocene inundated the extensive plains of the North Sea basin. The character of rivers changed in response to sea-level change and, from *c.* 5000 cal BC, river floodplains were characterised by extensive carr woodlands on their margins. From *c.* 3200 cal BC, low-lying wetlands in the Humberhead Levels developed to become the extensive raised mires of Thorne and Hatfield Moors. Sometime during the first millennium BC, marine transgression buried most of the riparian wetlands, and a new scenery dominated by claylands and siltlands dominated the Humber Wetlands. This surface was flooded for some time between AD 150 and 250, and marine transgression in the Late Roman period flooded extensive parts of the lowlands. At the end of the Middle Ages, a further period of marine transgression flooded the Hull and Ancholme valleys. Climatic change, vegetation change and, indeed, the impact of people on the environment, all contributed further to the dynamic landscape of the Humber Wetlands (see Chapter 2).

This chapter provides the conclusions of the Humber Wetlands Project. It will do so by exploring three aspects of our research. First, it considers the paradox that wetlands were both extensively exploited for resources and also used for ritualised activities. Second, it looks at the contribution of the Project to our understanding of past human behaviour. Thirdly, it considers the future of the Humber Wetlands and their archaeological remains.

The wetland paradox

In Chapter 1, it was noted that the Humber Wetlands present us with a paradox. This paradox, which has been noted for wetlands across the world, is that these wet landscapes were both economically valuable and also seen as natural places linked to ancestor cults and spiritual activity. Sacred and profane are usually geographically separated. This separation exists on a range of levels. Within a family unit, for example, a particular object within the household may be dedicated to the sacred. On the community level, this separation may involve a distinctive structure or space within or on the edge of the village. The dynamic nature of the landscape – and how people understood it in the past – hold the key to explaining why this separation seems not to have existed in the Humber Wetlands.

From a palaeoenvironmental point of view, the range of wetland types is boundless, but in terms of past exploitation, the principal differences were between alluvial or minerogenic (i.e. silt and clay) wetlands on the one hand, and mires or peat-producing ecosystems on the other. The alluvial or minerogenic wetlands include former and active saltmarshes and river floodplain meadows – in the Humber Wetlands usually called sands, levels and ings. These were nutrient-rich and fertile landscapes with high biomass and biodiversity, sometimes on a par with rainforests (cf. Dinnin and Van de Noort 1999). At present, minerogenic wetlands comprise over 95 per cent of the landscape defined as the Humber Wetlands. In terms of their contribution to food subsistence strategies, these minerogenic wetlands provided returns from hunting, gathering and agriculture that were, in the main, higher than those from the free-draining drylands.

The organic peatlands principally include raised mires and floodplain mires – called moors, wastes, carrs and fens, although the latter term was not often used in the Humber Wetlands (cf. Mitsch and Gosselink 1993). The raised mires of Thorne and Hatfield Moors survive as badly damaged landscapes, but silts and clay largely buried the floodplain mires during the first millennium BC (see Chapters 2 and 7). Mires are nutrient-poor and unfruitful landscapes, with low biomass and biodiversity. The yields from organic peatlands were significantly lower than those from the free-draining drylands. These landscapes were inaccessible and often dangerous. Raised mires can be particularly treacherous, but the alder-dominated carrs, when flooded, were similarly perilous. In North America, such wetlands are called 'riparian forested swamps' (Nicholas 2001).

These differences can be translated into people's perceptions. The alluvial lands were seen as extensive and open 'flatlands'. Especially where the sea or river had retreated in the recent past, the vegetation was dominated by grasses and shrubs, and with stands of trees rather than extensive woodlands. This relative openness offered ample opportunities for hunting and farming. Such landscapes were also readily accessible, either by foot or by boat. As 'new lands', minerogenic wetlands were free from ancestral associations and were not owned by individuals or groups of people, at least not until the later part of prehistory. On the silts and clays in the Humber Wetlands, we found few sites that could be considered monuments or that were associated with death and burial. The types of sites found frequently during our survey included hunting camps and flint production sites, and for the later prehistoric period the trackways on the Humber foreshore, field systems, settlements and sites of industrial activities, including salt winning and metal production (Chapters 3 and 4). These sorts of energetic activities undertaken by commoners dominate other wetlands too (cf. Coles 2001). Monuments and other remains relating to elite activity in prehistory are uncharacteristic of these landscapes.

The peatlands, on the other hand, were often perceived as boundaries or as marginal and sometimes liminal places. In the Humber Wetlands, evidence for this perception in the archaeological record includes the dearth of settlements and field systems, and a lack of finds of flint or pottery. However, the antiquarian finds of bog bodies from Thorne and Hatfield Moors in the Humberhead Levels, and a large number of bronze objects ritually deposited in the moors and floodplain mires (see Chapter 6), testify to a perception of these areas that is strikingly different from the perception of the minerogenic wetlands.

This perception varied, to a degree, over time. For example, the value of peat as fuel was recognised probably in the Roman period, as suggested from the palaeoenvironmental research at Askham Bog (Chapter 2), and was certainly considered of great importance from the twelfth century AD onwards (Chapter 8). Although the archaeological evidence for the Humber Wetlands is absent, peatlands such as raised mires could be burned during extended dry periods, thus releasing nutrients for plant growth, and creating areas suitable for short-term pasture. Such a practice may have occurred during later prehistory. This perception varied too with the points of view of 'insiders' and 'outsiders'. The farmers living in or on the edge of the peatlands recognised the value of the peat, and of alder and willow trees, as building material and fuel, and made use of the yield from coppiced and pollarded trees for basket making. Such small-scale exploitation would not have impressed distant elite groups or landowners. The title of the 1600 *Act for the recovery of inning and drowned and surrounded grounds and the drainage dry of watery marshes, fens, bogs, moors and other ground of like nature* illustrates the disparaging perception of wetlands from the point of view of London parliamentarians and distant landowners (see Chapter 9).

Nevertheless, as a rule it is true to say that the minerogenic wetlands were exploitable and exploited throughout prehistory and the historic period, whilst the mires were at best sporadically exploited for relative small gains. As such, the dichotomy between the fertile clay and silt wetlands and the uncultivable peatlands remains one of the most striking characteristics of the archaeology of the Humber Wetlands. It has also been highlighted in research elsewhere, most notably in the Fenland Project where settlement and exploitation are consistently associated with the silts and clay rather than the peat. Peter Hayes (1988), for example, discussed the emptiness of the East Anglian peat fen in the pre-Roman to Saxon period, showing a clear correlation between landscape change and occupation. Similarly, in a summary of the evidence for the Netherlands, the general absence of settlements on peatlands from the end of the Early Bronze Age to the start of the late medieval period has been noted (Louwe Kooijmans 1993). In coastal wetlands throughout western Europe preference has been given to silt and clay deposits over peatlands for the location of settlements, notwithstanding the fact that a number of relict raised mires were settled for the exploitation of intertidal landscapes (e.g. Goldcliff in the Severn estuary; Bell *et al.* 2000).

This dichotomy has been developed furthest by Rob Giblett (1996) who, in his *Postmodern Wetlands*, proposes post-structuralist oppositions. He connects the 'white waters' (i.e. rivers and the minerogenic wetlands) with masculinity, culture, progress and development, the latter often under the direction of distant owners, authority and capital. The 'dark pools' (i.e. peatlands) signify femininity in Giblett's scheme, as well as nature and wilderness, stagnancy, disease and opposition to progress and development. Although English literature forms the basis of his arguments, the archaeology and history of the Humber Wetlands contain certain elements that support aspects of this post-structuralist description, notably the association of peatlands with spiritual space (see Chapter 6 and below) and the opposition of the Isle of Axholmers to the externally imposed and financed drainage of the Humberhead Levels (see Chapter 9). The material culture from the Humber Wetlands does not, however, support the connotation of landscape types with gender.

The economic marginality of the peatlands cannot be directly translated into their role in ritualised behaviour. However, peatlands were not only marginal zones but were also uncultivable and often dangerous places. In this context, the term 'wilderness' seems more appropriate than the concept 'natural places' to describe how people perceived peatlands in prehistory (cf. Bradley 2000). Wilderness is not nature untainted by humans and human action, but a landscape-construct formed by human perception and imagination (Cosgrove 1984). In many societies across the world, wilderness is the perceived place of origin of distant ancestors, or is sensed as that part of the landscape where natural or social rebirth and regeneration takes place (e.g. Oelschlaeger 1991;

Cosgrove 1993). This is also plainly expressed in the title of Van der Sanden's (1996) book on bog bodies *Through nature to eternity*. Mires are therefore frequently associated with supernatural powers, a notion that was reinforced by their constantly changing geography. Thus, the dynamic landscape itself had become an active element in people's perception of wetlands in the past.

Archaeologically, this is demonstrated by the context of the votive deposition of bronze artefacts, which appear to have been laid down near the peat's edge in shallow water or on waterlogged soils, and were subsequently buried beneath the expanding mire (see Chapter 6; Evans 2002). Our research has shown that on average the floodplain mires grew annually, upwards, by 1.5 mm, or over a 50 year period by 75 mm (see Chapter 2). On the very flat-bottomed river floodplains, this translates into a lateral expansion of the peatlands measuring tens of metres within the lifespan of individuals. These mires may have been viewed as being alive.

Our research has also shown that peat accumulation accelerated after *c.* 2000 cal BC. This acceleration could have been brought about by the people who had settled on the floodplain margins. One consequence of the extensive forest clearance was a reduction in the evapo-transpiration of vegetation, producing higher groundwater tables and accelerated peat growth. Moreover, the widespread introduction of farming in this period increased the run-off of mineral rich water into the floodplain mires, again contributing to an acceleration of the expansion of these fen peats. The irony of the situation, that the enculturation of the landscape resulted in an accelerated expansion of the wilderness, no doubt escaped the people who lived there at the time.

Within this wilderness, selected locales may have acted as liminal zones. Liminality is the concept that certain areas or zones were 'thresholds' which need to be traversed as part of a rite of passage, such as becoming an adult or marriage (Van Gennep 1908). If the votive deposition of bronze artefacts formed part of such rites of passage, we can conclude that these locales correlate with specific points in the peatlands, rather than the peatlands themselves. Analysis of the distribution of votive deposits in the Humber Wetlands indicates that concentrations of bronze artefacts have been found at places where rivers and wetlands could be crossed. For example, such a concentration was found at Brigg where a natural constriction in the Ancholme valley floodplain created an obvious place to cross the river and its riparian wetlands (e.g. Davey 1973; see Chapter 6). Whether the 'oversized' trackway at Brigg, or its 'raft' or logboat could have played a part in such rituals is a matter of speculative debate.

Liminal areas may have existed elsewhere, for example at Bail and Low Mere in Holderness. Hydroseral succession had transformed these meres into mires, which may have been seen as a boundary between the world of the living and the world of the dead (Chapter 4). The trackway at West Furze that crossed these wetlands included several features that could have symbolised this liminal space, such as the wicket or doorway, the bronze spearhead and the skulls. Similarly, the small elongated peatland at the centre of the barrow

FIGURE 76 (*opposite*). Model of a riverside landscape in the Humber Wetlands. Boats are likely to have been used throughout prehistory, but the archaeological evidence for their existence is restricted to the period after *c.* 2000 cal BC. Around 6000 cal BC, the wetlands are confined to the river channels, and archaeological evidence shows clearances and the use of fires. At *c.* 1500 cal BC, the 'eutrophic' wetlands form boundaries between 'drylands' and rivers. Archaeological evidence for human activity includes large trackways and votive deposition in the

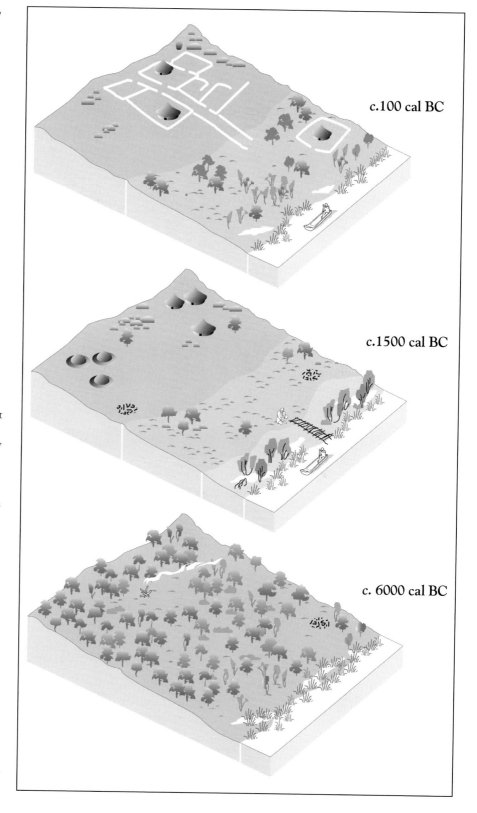

c.100 cal BC

c.1500 cal BC

c. 6000 cal BC

'eutrophic' wetlands.
Flint scatters, both
adjacent and further
from the river, suggest
continued hunting,
gathering and possibly
fishing activities.
Several barrow
cemeteries and
settlements are known
to have existed just
below the 10 m OD.
Around 100 cal BC,
the 'eutrophic'
wetlands had been
overtopped by silts
and clays, and human
activity include
specialised settlements
in the minerogenic
wetlands (e.g. iron
making). On the
higher grounds,
settlements within
field systems indicate
mixed farming,
including the use of
the wetlands as pasture.

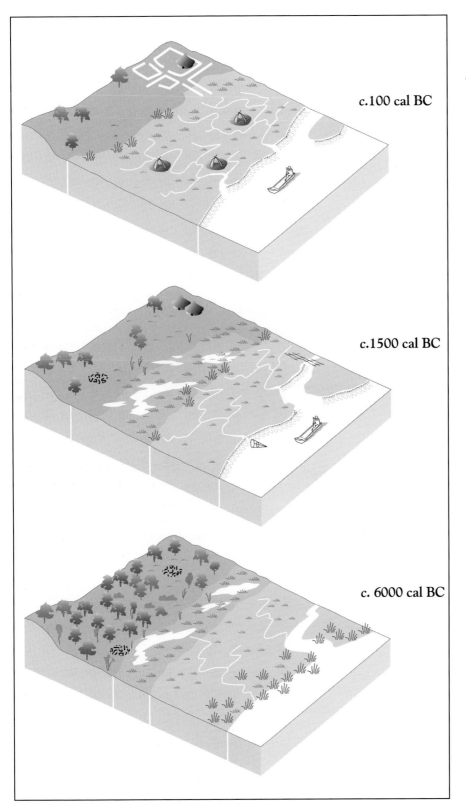

c.100 cal BC

c.1500 cal BC

c. 6000 cal BC

FIGURE 77.
Model of a coastal
landscape in the
Humber Wetlands.
Marine transgression
continues throughout
these stages. Boats are
likely to have been
used throughout
prehistory, but the
archaeological
evidence for their
existence is restricted
to the period after *c.*
2000 cal BC. At *c.*
6000 cal BC,
archaeological
evidence for human
activity of the coastal
zone is limited to flint
scatters. At *c.* 1500 cal
BC, the fishtrap and
hurdle trackways
indicate exploitation
of the saltmarsh – the
latter presumable used
to optimise the use of
the saltmarsh as
pasture – from
settlements on nearby
higher grounds.
Around 100 cal BC,
salt making is
undertaken in the
saltmarsh from
temporary settlements
on saltern mounds.
On the higher
grounds, settlements
and field systems
indicate mixed
farming.

cemetery at Butterbump on the Lincolnshire Marsh, rather than the extensive alluvial wetlands surrounding Butterbump 'island', could have been the liminal focus of the cemetery.

Historical sources clearly show that rivers and major streams frequently formed boundaries, and this is still true at present. However, in a prehistoric and early historic context where most transport took place using boats on these rivers, it is likely that the rivers themselves were not boundaries but neutral spaces. Territorial possession, or ownership of 'half' of the Humber estuary or River Trent was meaningless. The places where contact was made between people from different families, clans or tribes were the margins of the floodplains. These areas, or particular locations within these wetlands such as clearances, became social boundaries.

Hence, the wetland paradox can been clarified by gaining understanding of the perceptions of the different types of wetlands. The alluvial wetlands were exploitable and exploited and these landscapes were encultured through the activities of daily life, such as hunting, gathering, fishing, farming and through small-scale industrial activities such as salt, iron and pottery production. The peatlands were seen as an uncultivable and often dangerous wilderness or as boundaries, rather than as static natural places. Even so, the mires were encultured through ritualised activities such as the deposition of bodies in bog pools and of bronze artefacts at the edge of expanding peatlands – and, one might suggest, through the construction of trackways, beliefs and myths (e.g. Tilley 1994, 206–7). The dynamic nature of this landscape was an important factor in the development of how it was perceived.

In the Humber Wetlands, the floodplain mires were buried beneath silts and clays during a period of marine transgression in first millennium BC. Consequently, the archaeological evidence for the continuation of this perception of peatlands is slight, comprising mainly the poorly dated bog bodies from Thorne and Hatfield Moors and the lower Trent valley. If we turn to research elsewhere, it is clear that certain practices, such as the deposition of valuable objects, continued both in the peatlands of Drenthe in the Netherlands and in the Midlands of Ireland into the sixteenth and seventeenth centuries AD (Van der Sanden 1996). A recent study from the Witham valley in Lincolnshire provides a particular inspiring example. David Stocker and Paul Everson (2003) found a persuasive correlation between the location of Bronze Age barrow cemeteries, prehistoric votive depositions, Iron Age causeways and medieval monasteries on either side of the River Witham. They argued that the importance of particular locales, all associated with areas where the extensive floodplain mires could be crossed, had accumulated during later prehistory and the early historic period. Medieval monasteries were purposely located near these crossroads, in effect christianising pagan practices and beliefs that had survived well into the Middle Ages. For the Humber Wetlands, such a correlation has not been shown for any of the ecclesiastical foundations. Nevertheless, the reclamation of the wetlands such as Thorne Moors may well have been experienced as a 'converting' the pagan wilderness into a Christian landscape.

The contribution of the Humber Wetlands Project

So, what has the Humber Wetlands Project contributed to our understanding of past human behaviour? This is how I see it.

The palaeoenvironmental research undertaken as part of the Project has identified new aspects of the development of the landscape in the Late-glacial and the Early Holocene. It has offered a new hypothesis for the date of the onset of channel aggradation, suggesting that landscape development was considerably more dynamic than has previously been thought. The systematic study of 35 meres in Holderness provides an in-depth understanding of their diversity and natural development. For the Holocene period, the research into the wetlands in the valleys of the Rivers Hull and Ancholme, and in the Keyingham Drain in southern Holderness, are unparalleled in terms of spatial and dating resolution, and the results contribute significantly to our detailed understanding of riparian wetland development. These data have contributed significantly to ongoing debates about sea-level (e.g. Metcalfe *et al.* 2000). The extensive coring programmes involving all the rivers in the Humber lowlands provides an unequalled primary resource for future work and, in its own right, has added considerable detail to our appreciation of the natural history of these rivers, and how it differed both spatially and over time. Palynological research at Askham Bog, Routh Quarry and Butterbump has added new insights into vegetational change in the Humber Wetlands. For the late Holocene period, the study of warping must be mentioned as a significant contribution to the palaeoenvironmental history of the region.

In identifying over 400 new archaeological sites and artefact scatters, of which over 40 were waterlogged or had waterlogged components, and several thousand finds, the archaeological survey has addressed a long-standing bias towards the higher grounds surrounding the Humber Wetlands. Archaeological survey of the Humber estuary has identified its extensive archaeological heritage, which was previously scarcely known. The Project has also identified archaeological sites in areas where previously no archaeological sites had been known or were expected to be found, markedly the extensive Roman small town of Adlingfleet. The Humber Wetlands Project has also endeavoured to bring hitherto unpublished information from past excavations into the public domain and succeeded in a number of instances, most notably the Iron Age enclosure with evidence of bronze casting at Weelsby Avenue, Grimsby, and the Middle Saxon bridge or jetty at Skerne.

The Humber Wetlands Project has added great detail to our understanding of the activities of Mesolithic and Neolithic hunter-gatherers on these land-scapes and of their perceptions of them. For northeastern England, Star Carr in the Vale of Pickering remains the type-site, but the activities around Lake Pickering are not to be seen in isolation, and we have examined the focus of hunter-gatherers on wetlands and rivers. In terms of our understanding on the spread of Neolithic farming practices, the Project has shown the slow pace of this process and the persistence of particular hunting strategies into the

Bronze Age. Whether this reflects the parallel co-existence of farmers on the higher grounds and hunter-gatherers/pastoralists in the wetlands remains a matter of debate, but it is beyond doubt that the two groups, if they existed for so long, met and exchanged goods.

For the Bronze Age, the Project has provided new evidence, and new insights and understanding, notably for the exploitation of salt-marsh environments and for the absence of such regimes in the eutrophic wetlands, for the interaction between people and their environment, and for the nature of votive deposition in wet places – which, significantly, was connected to areas that must have been perceived as wilderness. Following the discovery of the Kilnsea boat, the Project reopened the debate on the function of sewn-plank boats and their role in exchange networks. For the Iron Age, the Project has raised new questions about the function and nature of some of the most important sites of this period, such as Sutton Common; it has found a rare instance of a site where bronze casts were produced, Kelk–6 in the Hull valley; and has added further detail to our understanding of the intensity of salt production in the Lincolnshire Marsh.

For the Roman period, the Humber Wetlands Project has provided significant new evidence for extensive wetland exploitation, and for wetland-specific road building techniques. For the Middle Ages and the post-medieval periods, new research and the regional syntheses have highlighted the importance of wetlands to those societies, and the discovery of the Late Saxon salt making site at Marshchapel should be mentioned as a special highlight.

Reclaiming the wetlands; a future for the Humber Wetlands?

A recent study for English Heritage on the Monuments at Risk in England's Wetlands (MAREW), concluded that at least 50 per cent of the original extent of lowland peatland has been lost in the last 50 years, that practically all alluviated lowlands are drained, and that upland peats suffer extensively from erosion. Consequently an estimated 10,450 wetland monuments have been destroyed or damaged during this period (Van de Noort *et al.* 2001). The causes of this widespread destruction are drainage, water abstraction, conversion of pasture into arable, peat wastage, peat erosion, peat extraction, and urban and industrial development.

These key causes of wetland destruction are closely interrelated. The direct consequence of drainage is the lowering of the shallow groundwater table through accelerated run-off, and water abstraction contributes further to this. Land was drained in order to increase agricultural capability, or to convert semi-natural or permanent pasture into more profitable arable land. Drainage and land conversion are the main cause of peat wastage, which occurs as a result of desiccation and coincident oxidation, in combination with much increased microbiological action (Burton and Hodgon 1987, Crowson *et al.* 2000). Industrial-scale peat extraction relies on effective drainage, as do urban and industrial developments on (former) wetlands.

Future threats to the wetlands and their heritage must also be considered. Climate change will be reflected in sea-level change, changes in weather patterns and hydrological cycles, and changes in (groundwater) temperatures (IPCC 1996). These will directly affect wetlands (Bergkamp and Orlando 1999), and the archaeological resources contained within them (Long and Roberts 1997).

Quantifying the impact of some of these changes on the archaeological and palaeoenvironmental resource on the Humber Wetlands provides some more tangible information. On average, the groundwater table has been lowered by 2 to 3 m over the last 50 years, bringing previously waterlogged resources within an oxidating environment. Since the 1930s, some 26,500 ha of pasture land have been converted to arable land, introducing ploughing as a threat, and 23,000 ha of pasture land has been lost to urban and industrial development, road building and other land uses (Middleton 1995, 1997, 1998, 1999, 2000 and 2001). The Soil Survey for England and Wales estimates the loss of peat under arable landuse at around 13.7 mm/year for eastern England. If the rate of peat 'growth' is 1 m/millennium (or 1 mm/year), then in the last 50 years an estimated 700 years of archaeology and palaeoenvironments have, in effect, been lost. Past and present peat extraction has affected *c.* 7000 ha of land, mainly on Thorne and Hatfield Moors, and archaeological monuments contained within these mires have been, or are likely to be, destroyed. The UK is now a major importer of peat for horticultural use, in effect exporting the destruction of wetland archaeological remains to other countries, especially Ireland (DETR 1998, 2000).

So where do we go from here? Following the MAREW project, English Heritage produced a Strategy for Wetlands (Olivier and Van de Noort 2002). The strategy comprises four principles. In terms of wetland management, we must promote practical mechanisms for conserving and protecting the cultural heritage by developing guidance, and a concept of best practice, for the integration of cultural heritage and nature conservation in wetland management. Continued programmes of survey and excavation are an essential precondition for the development of successful management policies. In terms of education, we must promote and disseminate an understanding of the cultural heritage of wetlands. Regarding policy, the promotion of the cultural heritage interests of wetlands in the work of local authorities, national, international, and intergovernmental agencies (e.g. the Ramsar Convention on wetlands) is of paramount importance, and must include appropriate legislation. Finally, applied research is needed to underpin and inform the management of wetlands.

Central to this strategy is the need to cooperate closely with other organizations that have specific or generic concerns for wetlands, for example for reasons of nature conservation, the preservation of the historic environment, or for recreation and tourism. These include English Nature, the Environment Agency, the Countryside Agency, the Countryside Trusts, the Royal Society for the Protection of Birds and other national, regional and local organizations already involved in wetland management. Wetlands also have a value as

FIGURE 78.
A deserted narrow
gauge railway truck,
used for the tranport
of peat from Thorne
Moors, at the
Swinefleet factory, in
the Humberhead
Levels.

washlands, alleviating the threat of flooding to areas outside the wetlands. This cooperation must include individuals and organizations whose economic existence depends on wetlands, and whose sustainable exploitation of wetlands and their resources contributes to the value of these places, for example through fishing, agriculture or the harvesting of reeds for thatching (Maltby 1986; Coles 1995; Coles and Olivier 2001). Only then can we hope that our wetlands will have a future.

In the Humber Wetlands, some important initiatives are underway. Peat extraction has completely halted on Thorne Moors, and has a limited future at Hatfield Moors (Figures 78, 79). An increasing number of wetland landscapes are managed as Ramsar sites – wetlands of international importance. Concerns for archaeology are increasingly taken into consideration by organisations responsible for wetland management. The Countryside Agency's 'Value in wetness' initiative explores the economic value of wetlands in the Humberhead Levels. Large-scale excavations at Sutton Common, possibly the most enigmatic site in the Humber Wetlands, are ongoing.

Of course, much more information could be obtained from further work, principally through excavation of a range of sites, including 'special' sites such as the Iron Age settlement with evidence for bronze casting in the Hull valley, but also of a number of more 'typical' sites, such as Mesolithic flint scatters and Roman farmsteads. It must also be stated that the Humber Wetlands Project undertook a systematic but selective survey, and the unsurveyed areas retain substantial archaeological potential.

It is no longer possible to wander through this '... wonderful conflux of great rivers, all pouring down into the Humber, which receiving the Aire, the Ouse, the Don and the Trent, becomes rather a sea than a river ...', as Daniel Defoe did (1726; Volume 3, letter 9). But glimpses of the greatness of the former wetlands and the people who lived here in the past 10,000 years are still to be seen by those with an eye for nuance. It can be awe-inspiring to experience the Humber estuary, preferably from a small boat. The internationally important Derwent Ings are best appreciated when fully flooded, and the emptiness of the mires of Thorne and Hatfield Moors cannot be equalled in this densely populated country. The enigmatic Iron Age site at Sutton Common near Askern, and the so-called Moorland Allotments and the colonising villages that originated in the eleventh and twelfth centuries AD, provide insights into the long history of man's interaction with this environment. Many landscape features date back to the Late Saxon and Norman period, and the remains of the monasteries such as Thornton Abbey in the Lincolnshire Marsh and its magnificent gatehouse are intrinsic parts of this landscape and its people. We must also recognize the drains and rivers constructed from the seventeenth century AD onwards as landscape features of considerable historic importance, alongside the many historically-rich place-names that survive, such as Dirtness and Saltfleetby. Through all this, the Humber Wetlands are, and one hopes they will long remain, a unique and important historic landscape.

FIGURE 79.
Reclaimed wetlands:
former peat extraction
site at Thorne Moors
conserved and rewet
by English Nature.

Bibliography

Allan, M. J. and Gardiner, J. (2000) *Our Changing Coast. A Survey of the Intertidal Archaeology of Langstone Harbour, Hampshire*, Council of British Archaeology Research Report 124, York.

Allason-Jones, L. (1989) *Ear-rings in Roman Britain*, British Archaeological Reports 201, Oxford.

Ambler, R. W. (1990) 'The small towns of South Humberside', in S. Ellis and D. Crowther (eds) *Humber Perspectives: a Region through the Ages*, Hull, 293–306.

Andersen, S. H. (1987) 'Mesolithic dug-outs and paddles from Tybrind Vig, Denmark', *Acta Archaeologica* 57, 87–106.

Armstrong, A. L. (1922) 'Two Yorkshire bone harpoons', *Man* 75, 130–2.

Armstrong, A. L. (1923) 'The Maglemose remains of Holderness and their Baltic counterparts', *Proceedings of the Prehistoric Society of East Anglia* 4, 57–70.

Atkinson, A. (1887) 'Notes on the ancient boat found at Brigg', *Archaeologia* 50, 361–70.

Baker, F. T. (1960) 'The Iron Age salt industry in Lincolnshire', *Lincolnshire Architectural and Archaeological Society Reports and Papers* 8, 26–34.

Bakewell, R. (1833) *An Introduction to Geology*, London.

Bartlett, J. E. and Riley, D. N. (1958) 'The Roman fort at Scaftworth, near Bawtry', *Transactions of the Thoroton Society of Nottinghamshire* 62, 24–35.

Bateman, M. D. (1995) 'Thermoluminescence dating of the British coversand deposits', *Quaternary Science Reviews* 14, 791–8.

Bateman, M. D., Murton, J. B. and Crowe, W. (2000) 'Late Devensian and Holocene depositional environments associated with the coversands around Caistor, north Lincolnshire, UK', *Boreas* 29, 1–15.

Bayliss, A., Bronk Ramsey, C., Cook, G., Gearey, B., Sparks, R. and Van de Noort, R. (1999) 'Radiocarbon dates', in R. Van de Noort and S. Ellis (eds) *Wetland Heritage of the Vale of York, an Archaeological Survey*, Hull, 289–96.

Beck, C. and Shennan, S. (1991) *Amber in Prehistoric Britain*, Oxford.

Beckett, S. C. (1975) *The Late Quaternary Vegetational History of Holderness, Yorkshire*. Unpublished PhD thesis, University of Hull.

Beckett, S. C. (1981) 'Pollen diagrams from Holderness, North Humberside', *Journal of Biogeography* 8, 177–98.

Bell, A., Gurbey, D. and Healey, F. (eds) (1999) *Lincolnshire Salterns: Excavations at Helpringham, Holbeach St Johns and Bicker Haven*, East Anglian Archaeology 89.

Bell, M., Caseldine, A. and Neumann, H. (2000) *Prehistoric Intertidal Archaeology in the Welsh Severn Estuary*, Council of British Archaeology Research Report 120, York.

Bennett, K. D. (1984) 'The Post-glacial history of Pinus sylvestris in the British Isles', *Quaternary Science Review* 3, 133–55.

Beresford, M. W. (1986) 'Inclesmoor, West Riding of Yorkshire', in R. A. Skelton and P. D. A. Harvey (eds) *Local Maps and Plans from Medieval England*, Oxford, 147–61.

Bergkamp, G. and Orlando, B. (1999) *Wetlands and Climate change, Exploring Collaboration between the Convention on Wetlands (Ramsar, Iran 1971) and the United Nations Framework Convention on Climate Change*, New York.

Berridge, N. G. and Pattison, J. (1994) *Geology of the Country around Grimsby and Patrington. Memoir for 1:50.000 sheets 90 and 91 and 81 and 82 (England and Wales)*, London.

Bibliography

Besteman, J. C. and Guiran, A. J. (1987) 'An early peat bog reclamation area in medieval Kennemerland', in R. W. Brandt, W. Groenman-van-Waateringe and S. E. van der Leeuw (eds) *Assendelvder Polder Papers* 1, Amsterdam, 297–332.

Bewley, R. H. (ed.) (1998) *Lincolnshire's Archaeology from the Air*. Occasional Papers in Lincolnshire History and Archaeology 11, Lincoln and Swindon.

Bewley, R. H. and Macleod, D. (1993) 'The discovery of a Roman fort at Roall Manor Farm, North Yorkshire', *Britannia* 24, 243–7.

Bidgood, S. (2002) *A Reconstruction of the Walton Heath Hurdle Trackway*. Unpublished MA thesis, University of Exeter.

Blood, N. K. and Taylor, C. C. (1992) 'Cawood: an archiepiscopal landscape', *Yorkshire Archaeological Journal* 64, 83–102.

Boutwood, Y. (1998) 'Prehistoric linear boundaries in Lincolnshire and its fringes', in R. H. Bewley (ed.) *Lincolnshire's Archaeology from the Air*, Lincoln, 29–46.

Bradley, R. (1990) *The Passage of Arms*, Cambridge.

Bradley, R. (1998) *The Significance of Monuments: on the Shaping of Human Experience in Neolithic and Bronze Age Europe*, London.

Bradley, R. (2000) *An Archaeology of Natural Places*, London.

Bradley, R. and Edmonds, M. (1993) *Interpreting the Axe Trade: Production and Exchange in Neolithic Britain*, Cambridge.

Bradley, R. and Gordon, K. (1988) 'Human skulls from the river Thames, their dating and significance', *Antiquity* 62, 503–9.

Brandt, R. W. and Van der Leeuw, S. E. (1987) 'Conclusions', in R. W. Brandt, W. Groenman-van-Waateringe and S. E van der Leeuw (eds) *Assendelvder Polder Papers* 1, Amsterdam, 339–52.

Breeze, D. J. and Dobson, B. (1985) 'Roman military deployment in North England', *Britannia* 16, 1–18.

Brinkkemper, O. (1991) *Wetland Farming in the Area to the South of the Meuse Estuary during the Iron Age and Roman Period. An Environmental and Palaeo-economic Reconstruction*, Analecta 24, Leiden.

Bronk Ramsey, C. (2000) *Oxcal 3.5*, http://www. rlaha. ox. ac. uk/calib. html.

Brown, A. G. (1988) 'The palaeoecology of *Alnus* (alder) and the Post-glacial history of floodplain vegetation. Pollen percentage and influx data from the West Midlands, United Kingdom', *New Phytologist* 110, 425–36.

Brown, A. G. and Bradley, C. (1995) 'Past and present alluvial wetlands and the eco-archaeological resource: implications from research in East Midland valleys, UK', in M. Cox, V. Straker and D. Taylor (eds) *Wetlands. Archaeology and Nature Conservation*, London, 189–203.

Buckland, P. C. (1973) 'Environment and archaeology in the Vale of York', *South Yorkshire Studies in Archaeology and Natural History* 1, 6–16.

Buckland, P. C. (1979) *Thorne Moors: a Palaeoecological Study of a Bronze Age Site*, Birmingham.

Buckland, P. C. (1986) *Roman South Yorkshire. A Source Book*, Sheffield.

Buckland, P. C. and Dinnin, M. H. (1997) 'The rise and fall of a wetland habitat: recent palaeoecological research on Thorne and Hatfield Moors', *Thorne and Hatfield Moors Papers* 4, 1–18.

Buckland, P. C. and Dolby, M. J. (1973) 'Mesolithic and later material from Misterton Carr, Nottinghamshire: an interim report', *Transactions of the Thoroton Society of Nottinghamshire* 17, 5–33.

Buckland, P. C. and Edwards, K. J. (1979) 'The longevity of pastoral episodes of clearance activity in pollen diagrams: the role of post-occupation grazing', *Journal of Biogeography* 11, 243–9.

Buckland, P. C. and Sadler, J. (1985) 'The nature of late Flandrian alluviation in the Humberhead Levels', *East Midlands Geographer* 8, 239–51.

Buckland, P. C., Hartley, K. F. and Rigby, V. (2001) *The Roman Pottery Kilns at Rossington Bridge. Excavations 1956–1961*, Journal of Roman Pottery Studies 9, Oxford.

Buckland, P. C., Magilton, J. R. and Hayfield, C. (1989) *Archaeology of Doncaster 2. The Medieval and later Town*, British Archaeological Reports 202, Oxford.

Burgess, C. (1990) *The Age of Stonehenge*, London.

Burton, R. G. O. and Hodgon, J. M. (1987) *Lowland Peat in England and Wales*, Harpenden.

Campbell-Smith, W. (1963) 'Jade axes from sites in the British Isles', *Proceedings of the Prehistoric Society* 29, 133–72.

Catt, J. A. (1990) 'Geology and relief', in S. Ellis and D. R. Crowther (eds) *Humber Perspectives: a Region through the Ages*, Hull, 13–28.

Chadwick, A. (1999) 'Digging ditches, but missing riches? Ways into the Iron Age and Romano-British cropmark landscapes of the north midlands', in B. Bevan (ed.) *Northern Exposure: Interpretative Devolution and the Iron Age in Britain*, Leicester Archaeology Monographs 4, Leicester, 149–71.

Chadwick, A. M. and Cumberpatch, C. G. (1995) 'Further work on the Iron Age and Roman landscape at Edenthorpe', *Archaeology in South Yorkshire 1994–95*, Sheffield, 69–74.

Challis, A. J. and Harding, D. W. (1975) *Later Prehistory from the Trent to the Tyne*, British Archaeological Report 20, Oxford.

Chambers, F. M. and Elliot, L. (1989) 'Spread and expansion of *Alnus* Mill in the British Isles: timing, agencies and possible vectors', *Journal of Biogeography* 16, 542–50.

Chapman, H. (1997) 'The Humberhead Levels from the air: a landscape in context', in R. Van de Noort and S. Ellis (eds) *Wetland Heritage of the Humberhead Levels, an Archaeological Survey*, Hull, 397–407.

Chapman, H. (1998) 'The Ancholme and lower Trent valleys from the air: a landscape in context', in R. Van de Noort and S. Ellis (eds) *Wetland Heritage of the Ancholme and lower Trent Valleys, an Archaeological Survey*, Hull, 249–64.

Chapman, H. (1999) 'The Vale of York from the air: a landscape in context', in R. Van de Noort and S. Ellis (eds) *Wetland Heritage of the Vale of York, an Archaeological Survey*, Hull, 254–53.

Chapman, H. (2000) 'The Hull valley from the air: a landscape in context', in R. Van de Noort and S. Ellis (eds) *Wetland Heritage of the Hull valley, an Archaeological Survey*, Hull, 175–81.

Chapman, H. (2001) 'The Lincolnshire Marsh from the air: a landscape in context', in S. Ellis, H. Fenwick, M. Lillie and R. Van de Noort (eds) *Wetland Heritage of the Lincolnshire Marsh, an Archaeological Survey*, Hull, 203–13.

Chapman, H., Head, R., Fenwick, H., Neumann H. and Van de Noort, R. (1998) 'The archaeological survey of the Ancholme valley', in R. Van de Noort and S. Ellis (eds) *Wetland Heritage of the Ancholme and lower Trent Valleys, an Archaeological Survey*, Hull, 199–248.

Chapman, H., Fenwick, H., Head, R., Fletcher, W. and Lillie, M. (1999) 'The archaeological survey of the Rivers Aire, Ouse, Wharfe and Derwent', in R. Van de Noort and S. Ellis (eds) *Wetland Heritage of the Vale of York, an Archaeological Survey*, Hull, 205–41.

Chapman, H., Fletcher, W., Fenwick, H., Lillie, M. and Thomas, G. (2000) 'The archaeological survey of the Hull valley', in R. Van de Noort and S. Ellis (eds) *Wetland Heritage of the Hull Valley, an Archaeological Survey*, Hull, 105–73.

Chapman, H. P. and Van de Noort, R. (2001) 'High-resolution wetland prospection, using GPS and GIS: landscape studies at Sutton Common (South Yorkshire), and Meare Village East (Somerset)', *Journal of Archaeological Science* 28, 365–75.

Chiverell, R. C. (1988) *Moorland Vegetation History and Climate Change on the North York Moors during the last 2000 years*. Unpublished PhD thesis, University of Leeds.

Christensen, C. (1990) 'Stone Age dug-out boats in Denmark: occurrence, age, form and reconstruction', in D. E. Robinson (ed.) *Symposia of the Association of Environmental Archaeology* 9, Oxford, 119–41.

Clark, J. G. D. (1954) *Excavations at Star Carr. An early Mesolithic Site at Seamer near Scarborough, Yorkshire*, Cambridge.

Clark, J. G. D. (1972) *Star Carr: a Case Study in Bioarchaeology*, New York.

Clark, J. G. D. and Godwin, H. (1956) 'A Maglemosian site at Brandesburton, Holderness, Yorkshire', *Proceedings of the Prehistoric Society* 22, 6–22.

Clark, P. (ed.) (forthcoming), *The Dover Bronze Age Boat*, London.

Clough, T. H. McK. and Cummins, W. A. (1979) *Stone Axe Studies. Volume 1*, Council for British Archaeology Research Report 23, London.

Coles, B. J. (1990) 'Anthropomorphic wooden figures from Britain and Ireland', *Proceedings of the Prehistoric Society* 56, 315–33.

Coles, B. J. (1995) *Wetland Management. A Survey for English Heritage*, London and Exeter.

Coles, B. J. (1998) 'Doggerland: a speculative survey', *Proceedings of the Prehistoric Society* 64, 45–82.

Coles, B. J. (1999) 'Doggerland's loss and the Neolithic', in B. Coles, J. Coles and M. Shou Jørgenson (eds) *Bog Bodies, Sacred Sites and Wetland Archaeology*, Exeter, 51–58.

Coles, B. J. and Coles, J. M. (1989) *People of the Wetlands. Bogs Bodies and Lake-dwellers*, London.

Coles, B. J. and Olivier, A. (2001) *The Heritage Management of Wetlands in Europe*, Brussels and Exeter.

Coles, J. M. (1984) *The Archaeology of Wetlands*, Edinburgh.

Coles, J. M. (2001) 'Energetic Activities of Commoners', *Proceedings of the Prehistoric Society* 67, 19–48.

Coles, J. M. and Coles, B. J. (1986) *Sweet Track to Glastonbury*, London.

Coles, J. M. and Coles, B. J. (1996) *Enlarging the Past. The Contribution of Wetland Archaeology*, Edinburgh and Exeter.

Coles, J. M. and Hall, D. (1997) 'The Fenland Project: from survey to management and beyond', *Antiquity* 71, 831–44.

Coles, J. M. and Minnett, S. (1995) *Industrious and Fairly Civilized: the Glastonbury Lake Village*, Taunton.

Cook, H. F. and Williamson, T. (eds) (1999) *Water Management in the English Landscape: Field, Marsh and Meadow*, Edinburgh.

Coppack, G. (1989) 'Thornholme Priory: the development of a monastic outer court', in R. Gilchrist and H. Mytum (eds) *The Archaeology of Rural Monasteries*, British Archaeological Reports 203, Oxford: 185–213.

Cory, V. (1985) *Hatfield and Axholme: an Historical Review*, Ely.

Cosgrove, D. E. (1984) *Social Formation and Symbolic Landscape*, Wisconsin.

Cosgrove, D. E. (1993) 'Landscapes and myths, gods and humans', in B. Bender (ed.) *Landscape: Politics and Perspectives*, Providence and Oxford, 281–305.

Cowell, R. W. and Innes, J. B. (1994) *The Wetlands of Merseyside. Northwest Wetlands Survey 1*, Lancaster Imprints 2, Lancaster.

Creighton, J. (1990) 'The Humber frontier in the first century AD', in S. Ellis and D. Crowther (eds) *Humber Perspectives: a Region through the Ages*, Hull, 182–98.

Creyke, R. (1845) 'Some accounts of the process of warping', *Journal of the Royal Agricultural Society, England* 5, 398–405.

Crowson, A., Lane, T. and Reeve, J. (eds) (2000) *Fenland Management Project Excavations 1991–1995*, Lincolnshire Archaeology and Heritage Report Series 3, Sleaford.

Cunliffe, B. (1991) *Iron Age Communities in Britain*, London.

Darby, H. C. (1983) *The Changing Fenland*, Cambridge.

Darby, H. C. and Maxwell, I. S. (1977) *The Domesday Geography of Northern England*, Cambridge.

Dark, P. (2000) *The Environment of Britain in the First Millennium AD*, London.

Davey, P. J. (1973) 'Bronze Age metalwork from Lincolnshire', *Archaeologia* 104, 51–127.

Davey, P. J. and Knowles, G. C. (1972) 'The Appleby hoard', *Archaeological Journal* 128, 154–61.

de Boer, G. (1964) 'Spurn Head: its history and evolution', *Transactions of the Institute of British Geographers* 34, 71–89.

de la Pryme, A. (1699) 'Letter of November 20, 1699', in: C. Jackson (ed.) (1870) *The Diary of Abraham de la Pryme, the Yorkshire Antiquary*, Durham.

Dent, J. S. (1982) 'Cemeteries and settlement patterns of the Iron Age on the Yorkshire Wolds', *Proceedings of the Prehistoric Society* 48, 437–57.

Dent, J. S. (1983) 'The impact of the Roman rule on native society in the territory of the Parisi', *Britannia* 14, 33–4.

Dent, J. S., Loveluck, C. and Fletcher, W. (2000) 'The Early Medieval site at Skerne', in R. Van de Noort and S. Ellis (eds) *Wetland Heritage of the Hull valley, an Archaeological Survey*, Hull, 217–42.

Department of the Environment, Transport and the Regions (1998) *Peatland issues: Report on the Working Group on Peat Extraction and Related Matters*, London.

Department of the Environment, Transport and the Regions (2000) *Monitoring and Assessment of Peat and Alternative Products for Growing Media and Soil Improvers in the UK (1996–1999)*, London.

Didsbury, P. (1990) 'Exploitation in the lower Hull valley in the Roman period', in S. Ellis and D. Crowther (eds) *Humber Perspectives: a Region through the Ages*, Hull, 199–210.

Dinnin, M. (1997a) 'The drainage history of the Humberhead Levels', in R. Van de Noort and S. Ellis (eds) *Wetland Heritage of the Humberhead Levels, an Archaeological Survey*, Hull, 19–30.

Dinnin, M. (1997b) 'Introduction to the palaeoenvironmental survey', in R. Van de Noort and S. Ellis (eds) *Wetland Heritage of the Humberhead Levels, an Archaeological Survey*, Hull, 31–46.

Dinnin, M. (1997c) 'The palaeoenvironmental survey of the Rivers Idle, Torne and Old River Don', in R. Van de Noort and S. Ellis (eds) *Wetland Heritage of the Humberhead Levels, an Archaeological Survey*, Hull, 81–155.

Dinnin, M. (1997d) 'The palaeoenvironmental survey of West, Thorne and Hatfield Moors', in R. Van de Noort and S. Ellis (eds) *Wetland Heritage of the Humberhead Levels, an Archaeological Survey*, Hull, 157–89.

Dinnin, M. and Lillie, M. (1995a) 'The palaeoenvironmental survey of the meres of Holderness', in R. Van de Noort and S. Ellis (eds) *Wetland Heritage of Holderness, an Archaeological Survey*, Hull, 49–85.

Dinnin, M. and Lillie, M. (1995b) 'The palaeoenvironmental survey of southern Holderness and evidence for sea-level change', in R. Van de Noort and S. Ellis (eds) *Wetland Heritage of the Humberhead Levels, an Archaeological Survey*, Hull, 87–120.

Dinnin, M. and Van de Noort, R. (1999) 'Wetland habitats, their resource potential and exploitation', in B. Coles, J. Coles and M. Schou Jørgensen (eds) *Bog Bodies, Sacred Sites and Wetland Archaeology*, Exeter, 69–78.

Duby, G. (1968) *Rural Economy and Country Life in the Medieval West*, London.

Dunston, G. (1909) *The Rivers of Axholme*, Hull.

Edmonds, M. (1995) *Stone Tools and Society. Working with Stone in Neolithic and Bronze Age Britain*, London.

Edmonds, M. (1999) *Ancestral Geographies of the Neolithic. Landscapes, Monuments and Memory*, London.

Ellis, S. (2001) 'Physical background to the Lincolnshire Marsh', in S. Ellis, H. Fenwick, M. Lillie and R. Van de Noort (eds) *Wetland Heritage of the Lincolnshire Marsh, an Archaeological Survey*, Hull, 7–12.

Ellis, S., Fenwick, H., Lillie, M. and Van de Noort, R. (eds) (2001) *Wetland Heritage of the Lincolnshire Marsh, an Archaeological Survey*, Hull.

English Heritage (1991) *Management of Archaeological Projects* (2nd edition), London.

English, B. and Miller, K. (1991) 'The deserted village of Eske, East Yorkshire', *Landscape History* 13, 5–32.

Eogan, G. (1994) *The Accomplished Art: Gold and Gold-working in Britain and Ireland during the Bronze Age*, Oxford.

Etté, J. and Van de Noort, R. (1997) ' Introducing the survey of the Humberhead Levels', in R. Van de Noort and S. Ellis (eds) *Wetland Heritage of the Humberhead Levels, an Archaeological Survey*, Hull, 1–5.

Evans, C. (2002) 'Metalwork and "Cold Claylands": Pre-Iron Age Occupation on the Isle of Ely', in T. Lane and J. Coles (eds) *Through Wet and Dry; Essays in Honour of David Hall*, Sleaford and Exeter, 33–53.

Evans, D. H. (2000) 'Archaeology in the modern city Kingston upon Hull, and recent research at Kingswood', in R. Van de Noort and S. Ellis (eds) *Wetland Heritage of the Hull Valley, an Archaeological Survey*, Hull, 193–216.

Everson, P., Taylor, C. C. and Dunn, C. J. (1991) *Change and Continuity: Rural Settlement in North-West Lincolnshire*, London.

Fenwick, H. (1997) 'The wetland potential of moated sites in the Humberhead Levels', in R. Van de Noort and S. Ellis (eds) *Wetland Heritage of the Humberhead Levels, an Archaeological Survey*, Hull, 429–38.

Fenwick, H. (1999) 'Medieval moated sites in the Vale of York: distribution, modelling and wetland potential', in R. Van de Noort and S. Ellis (eds) *Wetland Heritage of the Vale of York, an Archaeological Survey*, Hull, 255–67.

Fenwick, H. (2000) 'Medieval sites in the Hull valley: distribution and modelling', in R. Van de Noort and J. Ellis, *Wetland Heritage of the Hull Valley, An Archaeological Survey*, Hull, 183–91.

Fenwick, H. (2001) 'Medieval salt-production and landscape development in the Lincolnshire Marsh', in S. Ellis, H. Fenwick, M. Lillie and R. Van de Noort (eds) *Wetland Heritage of the Lincolnshire Marsh, an Archaeological Survey*, Hull, 231–41.

Fenwick, H., Chapman, H., Head, R. and Lillie, M. (1998) 'The archaeological survey of the lower Trent valley and Winterton Beck', in R. Van de Noort and S. Ellis (eds) *Wetland Heritage of the Ancholme and lower Trent valleys, an Archaeological Survey*, Hull, 143–97.

Fenwick, H., Thomas, G. and Van de Noort, R. (2000) 'Introduction to the archaeological survey', in R. Van de Noort and S. Ellis (eds) *Wetland Heritage of the Hull Valley, an Archaeological Survey*, Hull, 87–103.

Fenwick, H., Van de Noort, R., Fletcher, W. and Thomas, G. (2001a) 'Introduction to the archaeological survey', in S. Ellis, H. Fenwick, M. Lillie and R. Van de Noort (eds) *Wetland Heritage of the Lincolnshire Marsh, an Archaeological Survey*, Hull, 63–97.

Fenwick, H., Chapman, H., Fletcher, W., Thomas, G. and Lillie, M. (2001b) 'The archaeological survey of the Lincolnshire Marsh', in S. Ellis, H. Fenwick, M. Lillie and R. Van de Noort (eds) *Wetland Heritage of the Lincolnshire Marsh, an Archaeological Survey*, Hull, 99–202.

Fenwick, V. (1995) 'A paddle from the North Ferriby foreshore (Vale of York)', *First Annual Report Humber wetlands Survey (1994–95)*, Hull, 16–9.

Finney, A. (1994) *Presentation survey: Skipwith Common*. Unpublished Report MAP Archaeological Consultancy Ltd, Malton.

Fischer, A. and Myrhøj, H. M. (1995) 'Introduction', in A. Fischer (ed.) *Man and Sea in the Mesolithic. Coastal Settlement above and below Present Sea Level*, Oxford, 11–2.

Flenley, J. R. (1987) 'The meres of Holderness', in S. Ellis (ed.) *East Yorkshire Field Guide*, Cambridge, 73–81.

Fletcher, W., Chapman, H., Head, R., Fenwick, H., Van de Noort, R. and Lillie, M. (1999) 'The archaeological survey of the Humber estuary', in R. Van de Noort and S. Ellis (eds) *Wetland Heritage of the Vale of York, an Archaeological Survey*, Hull, 205–41.

Fowler, P. J. (1983) *The Farming of Prehistoric Britain*, Cambridge.

Gaunt, G. D. (1975) 'The artificial nature of the River Don north of Thorne, Yorkshire', *Yorkshire Archaeological Journal* 47, 15–21.

Gaunt, G. D. (1976) *The Quaternary Geology of the Southern Part of the Vale of York*. Unpublished PhD thesis, University of Leeds.

Gaunt, G. D. (1981) 'Quaternary history of the southern part of the Vale of York', in J. Neale and J. Flenley (eds) *The Quaternary in Britain*, Oxford, 82–97.

Gaunt, G. D. (1994) *Geology of the Country around Goole, Doncaster and the Isle of Axholme. Memoir for one-inch sheets 79 and 88 (England and Wales)*, London.

Gaunt, G. D. and Tooley, M. J. (1974) 'Evidence for Flandrian sea-level changes in the Humber estuary and adjacent areas', *Bulletin of the Geological Survey of Great Britain* 48, 25–41.

Gaunt, G. D., Jarvis, R. A. and Matthews, B. (1971) 'The late Weichselian sequence in the Vale of York', *Proceedings of the Yorkshire Geological Society* 38, 281–4.

Gaunt, G. D., Fletcher, T. P. and Wood, C. P. (1992) *Geology of the Country around Kingston upon Hull and Brigg. Memoir for the 1:50000 geological sheets 80 and 89* (England and Wales), London.

Gearey, B. and Lillie, M. (1999) 'Aspects of Holocene vegetational change in the Vale of York: palaeoenvironmental investigations at Askham Bog', in R. Van de Noort and S. Ellis (eds) *Wetland Heritage of the Vale of York, an Archaeological Survey*, Hull, 109–23.

Giblett, R. J. (1996) *Postmodern Wetlands. Culture, History, Ecology*, Edinburgh.

Gilbertson, D. D. (1984) *Late Quaternary Environments and Man in Holderness*, British Archaeological Reports 134, Oxford.

Godwin, H. (1940) 'Studies of the post-glacial history of British vegetation. III. Fenland pollen diagrams. IV. Post-glacial changes in relative land- and sea- level in the English Fenland', *Philosophical Transactions of the Royal Society of London* 230, 239.

Godwin, H. and Willis, E. H. (1960) 'Cambridge University natural radiocarbon measurements III', *Radiocarbon* 3, 60–76.

Grant, S. M. (1904) 'Ancient pottery kilns', *Lincolnshire Notes and Queries* 8, 33–8.

Gregory, C. (1980) 'Gifts to men and gifts to god: gift exchange and capital accumulation in contemporary Papua', *Man* 25, 628–52.

Greig, J. R. A. (1982) 'Past and present lime woods of Europe', in M. Bell and S. Limbrey (eds) *Archaeological aspects of Woodland Ecology*, British Archaeological Reports 146, Oxford, 23–56.

Gurney, D. (1999) 'A Romano-British salt-making site at Shell Bridge, Holbeach St Johns: excavations by Ernest Greenfield, 1961', in A. Bell, D. Gurney and H. Healey (eds) *Lincolnshire Salterns: Excavations at Helpringham, Holbeach St Johns and Bicker Haven*, East Anglian Archaeology 89, 21–69.

Halberstma, H. (2000) *Frieslands Oudheid. Het Rijk van de Friese Koningen, Opkomst en Ondergang*, Utrecht.

Halkon, P. (1997) *Aspects of Romano-British Landscape around Holme-on-Spalding Moor, East Yorkshire*. Unpublished MA thesis, University of Durham.

Halkon, P. and Millett, M. (eds) (1999) *Rural Settlement and Industry: Studies in the Iron Age and Roman Archaeology of Lowland East Yorkshire*, Yorkshire Archaeology Report 4, Leeds.

Hall, D. and Coles, J. (1994) *Fenland Survey. An Essay in Landscape and Persistence*, London.

Hall, R. (1984) *The Viking Dig. The Excavations at York*, London.

Hall, R. (ed.) (1978) *Viking age York and the North*, London.

Harding, A. and Lee, G. (1987) *Henge Monuments and Related Sites of Great Britain*, British Archaeological Reports 175, Oxford.

Harris, A. (1961) *The Rural Landscape of the East Riding of Yorkshire 1700–1850*, Oxford.

Hayes, P. (1988) 'Roman to Saxon in the south Lincolnshire fens', *Antiquity* 62, 321–6.

Hayfield, C. and Greig, J. (1989) 'Excavations and salvage work on a moated site at Cowick, South Humberside 1976, Part two: the Finds Assemblage', *Yorkshire Archaeological Journal* 62, 111–124.

Head, R. (1995) 'The use of lithic material in prehistoric Holderness', in R. Van de Noort and S. Ellis (eds) *Wetland Heritage of Holderness, an Archaeological Survey*, Hull, 311–22.

Head, R., Fenwick, H., Van de Noort, R., Dinnin, M. and Lillie, M. (1995a) 'The meres and coastal survey', in R. Van de Noort and S. Ellis (eds) *Wetland Heritage of Holderness, an Archaeological Survey*, Hull, 163–239.

Bibliography

Head, R., Fenwick, H., Van de Noort, R., Dinnin, M. and Lillie, M. (1995b) 'The survey of southern Holderness', in R. Van de Noort and S. Ellis (eds) *Wetland Heritage of Holderness, an Archaeological Survey*, Hull, 241–310.

Head, R., Chapman, H., Fenwick, H., Van de Noort, R. and Lillie, M. (1997a) 'The archaeological survey of the Rivers Aire, Went, former Turnbridge Dike (Don North Branch) and the Hampole Beck', in R. Van de Noort and S. Ellis (eds) *Wetland Heritage of the Humberhead Levels, an Archaeological Survey*, Hull, 229–64.

Head, R., Chapman, H., Fenwick, H., Van de Noort, R. and Dinnin, M. (1997b) 'The archaeological survey of the Rivers Idle, Torne and Old River Don', in R. Van de Noort and S. Ellis (eds) *Wetland Heritage of the Humberhead Levels, an Archaeological Survey*, Hull, 267–67.

Head, R., Chapman, H. and Fenwick, H. (1998) 'Sites and Finds from the Isle of Axholme', in R. Van de Noort and S. Ellis (eds) *Wetland Heritage of the Ancholme and lower Trent valleys, an Archaeological Survey*, Hull, 265–288.

Healy, F. (1996) *Fenland Project 11. Wissey Embayment. The Evidence for pre-Iron Age Occupation*, East Anglian Archaeology 78.

Healey, H. (1999) 'An Iron Age salt-making site at Helpringham Fen', in A. Bell, D. Gurney and H. Healey (eds) *Lincolnshire Salterns: Excavations at Helpringham, Holbeach St Johns and Bicker Haven*, East Anglian Archaeology 89, 1–19.

Hey, D. (1986) *Yorkshire from AD 1000*, London.

Hill, J. D. (1995) *Ritual and Rubbish in the Iron Age of Wessex. A study on the formation of a specific archaeological record*, British Archaeological Reports 242, Oxford.

Hodder, I. and Shand, P. (1988) 'The Haddenham long barrow: an interim statement', *Antiquity* 62, 349–53.

Hunter, J. (1828) *South Yorkshire: the History and Topography of the Deanery of Doncaster in the Diocese and Country of York, Volume*, London.

Intergovernmental Panel on Climate Change (1996) *Climate change 1995 – Impacts, Adaptations and Mitigation of Climate Change: Scientific Technical Analysis*, Cambridge.

Jackson, R. P. J. and Potter, T. W. (1996) *Excavations at Stonea, Cambridgeshire, 1980–85*, London.

Jacobi, R. M. (1978) 'Northern England in the eight millennium B.C.: an essay', in P. Mellars (ed.) *The Early Postglacial Settlement of Northern Europe*, London, 295–332.

Jones, B. and Mattingly, D. (1990) *An Atlas of Roman Britain*, Oxford.

Jones, D. (1998a) 'Long barrows and Neolithic elongated enclosures in Lincolnshire. An analysis of the air photographic evidence', *Proceedings of the Prehistoric Society* 64, 83–114.

Jones, D. (1998b) 'Romano-British settlement on the Lincolnshire Wolds', in R. Bewley (ed.) *Lincolnshire's Archaeology from the Air*, Lincoln, 69–80.

Jones, P. (1995) 'Two early Roman canals? The origin of the Turnbriggdike and Bycarrsdike', *Journal of the Railway and Canal Historical Society* 31, 522–31.

Jørgenson, A. B., Robinson, D. and Christensen, C. (1999) 'Almosen Denmark. A ritual bog site from the 1st millennium BC', in B. Coles, J. Coles and M. Shou Jørgenson (eds) *Bog Bodies, Sacred Sites and Wetland Archaeology*, Exeter, 121–25.

Kennedy, D. L. (1984) 'Floating road: timber rafted Roman causeway at Scaftworth', *Popular Archaeology* (March), 20–1.

Koch, E. (1998) *Neolithic bog pots from Zealand, Møn, Lolland and Falster*, Copenhagen.

Koch, E. (1999) 'Neolithic offerings from the wetlands of eastern Denmark', in B. Coles, J. Coles and M. Shou Jørgenson (eds) *Bog Bodies, Sacred Sites and Wetland Archaeology*, Exeter, 125–132.

Kristiansen, K. (1987) 'From Stone to Bronze. The Evolution of Social Complexity in Northern Europe 2300–1200 BC', in E. M. Brumfiel and T. K. Earle (eds) *Specialization, Exchange and Complex Societies*, Cambridge, 30–51.

Lamb, H. H. (1982) *Climate History and the Modern World*, London.

Lamb, H. H. (1988) *Weather, Climate and Human Affairs*, London.

Lane, T. and Morris, E. L. (eds) (2001) *A Millennium of Salt-making: Prehistoric and*

Romano-British Salt Production in the Fenland, Lincolnshire Archaeology and Heritage Reports Series 4, Sleaford.

Le Patourel, H. E. J. (1973) *The Moated Sites of Yorkshire*, London.

Leah, M. D., Wells, C. E., Appleby, C. and Huckerby, E. (1997) *The Wetlands of Cheshire*, Lancaster Imprints 4, Lancaster.

Leahy, K. (1992) 'The Anglo-Saxon settlement of Lindsey', in A. Vince (ed.) *Pre-Viking Lindsey*, Lincoln, 29–42.

Legge, A. J. and Rowley-Conwy, P. A. (1988) *Star Carr revisited: a Re-analysis of the Large Mammals*, London.

Lillie, M. (1997a) 'The palaeoenvironmental survey of the Rivers Aire, Went, former Turnbridge Dike (Don North Branch) and the Hampole Beck', in R. Van de Noort and S. Ellis (eds) *Wetland Heritage of the Humberhead Levels, an Archaeological Survey*, Hull, 47–78.

Lillie, M. (1997b) 'Alluvium and warping in the Humberhead Levels: the identification of factors obscuring palaeo-landsurfaces and the archaeological record', in R. Van de Noort and S. Ellis (eds) *Wetland Heritage of the Humberhead Levels, an Archaeological Survey*, Hull, 191–218.

Lillie, M. (1998a) 'The palaeoenvironmental survey of the lower Trent valley and Winterton Beck', in R. Van de Noort and S. Ellis (eds) *Wetland Heritage of the Ancholme and lower Trent valleys, an Archaeological Survey*, Hull, 33–72.

Lillie, M. (1998b) 'Alluvium and warping in the lower Trent valley', in R. Van de Noort and S. Ellis (eds) *Wetland Heritage of the Ancholme and lower Trent valleys, an Archaeological Survey*, Hull, 103–22.

Lillie, M. (1999) 'The Palaeoenvironmental survey of the Humber estuary, incorporating an investigation of the nature of warp deposition in the southern part of the Vale of York', in R. Van de Noort and S. Ellis (eds) *Wetland Heritage of the Vale of York, an Archaeological Survey*, Hull, 79–108.

Lillie, M. and Gearey, B. (1999) 'The palaeoenvironmental survey of the Rivers Aire, Ouse, Wharfe and Derwent', in R. Van de Noort and S. Ellis (eds) *Wetland Heritage of the Vale of York, an Archaeological Survey*, Hull, 35–77.

Lillie, M. and Gearey, B. (2000) 'The palaeoenvironmental survey of the Hull valley, and research at Routh Quarry', in R. Van de Noort and S. Ellis (eds) *Wetland Heritage of the Hull valley, an Archaeological Survey*, Hull, 31–82.

Long, A. J. and Robert D. H. (1997) 'Sea level change', in M. Fulford, T. Champion and A. Long (eds) *England's Coastal Heritage, a Survey for English Heritage and the Royal Commission on the Historical Monuments of England*, English Heritage Archaeological Report 15, London.

Long, A. J., Innes, J. B., Kirby, J. R., Lloyd, J. M., Rutherford, M. M., Shennan, I. and Tooley, M. J. (1998) 'Holocene sea-level change and coastal evolution in the Humber estuary, eastern England: an assessment of rapid coastal change', *The Holocene* 8, 229–247.

Loughlin, N. and Miller, K. R. (1979) *A Survey of Archaeological Sites in Humberside*, Hull.

Louwe Kooijmans, L. P. (1971) 'Mesolithic bone and antler implements from the North Sea and from the Netherlands', *Berichten van de Rijksdienst voor het Oudheidkundig Bodemonderzoek* 20–21, 27–73.

Louwe Kooijmans, L. P. (1993) 'Wetland exploitation and upland relations of prehistoric communities in the Netherlands', in J. Gardiner (ed.) *Flatlands and Wetlands: Current Themes in East Anglian Archaeology*, East Anglian Archaeology 50, 71–116.

Loveluck, C. (1999) 'Archaeological expressions of the transition from the late Roman to early Anglo-Saxon period in lowland East Yorkshire', in P. Halkon and M. Millett (eds) *Rural Settlement and Industry: Studies in the Iron Age and Roman Archaeology of Lowland East Yorkshire*, Yorkshire Archaeology Report 4, Leeds, 228–36.

Loveluck, C. (forthcoming) *Flixborough: the Character, Environment and Economy of a High-status, Middle to Late Saxon Settlement in north Lincolnshire, AD 600–1000*, Oxford.

Lowe, J. J., Coope, G. R., Harknes, D. D., Sheldrick, C. and Walker, M. J. C. (1995) 'Direct comparison of UK temperatures and Greenland snow accumulation rates, 15000–12000 yr ago', *Journal of Quaternary Science* 10, 175–80.

Lucy, S. J. (1988) *The early Anglo-Saxon Cemeteries of East Yorkshire: an Analysis and Reinterpretation*, British Archaeological Report 272, Oxford.

Lucy, S. J. (2000) 'Early medieval burials in East Yorkshire: reconsidering the evidence', in H. Geake and J. Kenny (eds) *Early Deira. Archaeological Studies of the East Riding in the Fourth to Ninth Centuries AD*, Oxford, 11–18.

Mackey, R. (1998) 'A Round Barrow at Easington, East Yorkshire: The 1996 Excavation', *Bulletin Prehistoric Research Section* 35, 1–4.

Macklin, M. G., Taylor, M. P., Hudson-Edwards, K. A. and Howard, A. J. (2000) 'Holocene environmental change in the Yorkshire Ouse basin and its influence on river dynamics and sediment fluxes to the coastal zone', in I. Shennan and J. E. Andrews (eds) *Holocene Land-Ocean Interaction and Environmental Change around the Western North Sea*, London, 87–96.

Maltby, E. (1986) *Waterlogged wealth: why waste the world's wet places?*, London.

Manby, T. G. (1976) 'The excavation of the Kilham long barrow, East Riding of Yorkshire', *Proceedings of the Prehistoric Society* 42, 111–160.

Manby, T. G. (1980) 'Bronze Age settlement in eastern Yorkshire', in J. Barratt and R. Bradley (eds) *Settlement and Society in the British Later Bronze Age*, British Archaeological Reports 186, Oxford, 307–70.

Manby, T. G. (1988a) 'Double ditched enclosure: South Kirby, West Yorkshire', in D. N. Riley (ed.) *Yorkshire's Past from the Air*, Sheffield, 24–5.

Manby, T. G. (1988b) 'Multiple ditched enclosure: Little Smeaton, West Yorkshire', in D. N. Riley (ed.) *Yorkshire's Past from the Air*, Sheffield, 26–7.

Manby, T. G. (1988c) 'The Neolithic in eastern Yorkshire', in T. G. Manby (ed.) *Archaeology in Eastern Yorkshire. Essays in honour of T. C. M. Brewster*, Sheffield, 35–88.

Margary, I. D. (1957) *Roman Roads in Britain. Volume II. North of the Foss Way-Bristol Channel*, London.

May, J. (1976) *Prehistoric Lincolnshire*, History of Lincolnshire 1, Lincoln.

May, J. (1996) *Dragonby: Report on Excavations at an Iron Age and Romano-British Settlement in North Lincolnshire*, Oxford.

McGrail, S. (1978) 'Dating ancient wooden boats', in J. Fletcher (ed.) *Dendrochronology in Europe*, British Archaeological Report 51, Oxford, 239–58.

McGrail, S. (1981) *The Brigg 'Raft' and her Prehistoric Environment*, British Archaeological Report 89, Oxford.

McGrail, S. (1987) *Ancient boats in N.W. Europe: the Archaeology of Water Transport to AD 1500*, London.

McGrail, S. (1990) 'Early boats in the Humber basin', in S. Ellis and D. Crowther (eds) *Humber Perspectives: a Region through the Ages*, Hull, 109–30.

McGrail, S. (1992) 'Prehistoric seafaring in the channel', in C. Scarre and F. Healy (eds) *Trade and Exchange in Prehistoric Europe*, Oxford, 199–210.

McGrail, S. (1997) 'The boat fragments', in *Excavations at Caldicot, Gwent: Bronze Age Palaeochannels in the Lower Nedern Valley*, Council for British Archaeology Research Report 108, York, 210–7.

McGrail, S. (2001) *Boats of the World*, Oxford.

Meddens, F. M. (1996) 'Sites from the Thames Estuary wetlands, England, and their Bronze Age use', *Antiquity* 70, 325–34.

Mellars, P. A. and Dark, P. (1998) *Star Carr in Context*, Cambridge.

Merrony, C. J. N. (1993) 'The archaeological assessment in advance of the Dearne towns link road (stage 4) development at Goldthorpe', *Archaeology in South Yorkshire 1992–1993*, 43–52.

Metcalfe, B. (1960) *Geographic Aspects of the Reclamation and Development of Hatfield Chase*. Unpublished MA thesis, University of Leeds.

Metcalfe, S. E., Ellis, S., Horton, B. P., Innes, J. B., MacArthur, J., Mitlehner, A., Parkes, A., Pethick, J. S., Rees, J., Ridgeway, L., Rutherford, M. M., Shennan, I. and Tooley, M. J.

(2000) 'The Holocene evolution of the Humber estuary: reconstructing change in a dynamic environment', in I. Shennan and J. E. Andrews (eds) *Holocene Land-Ocean Interaction and Environmental Change around the Western North Sea*, London, 97–118.

Middleton, R. (1995) 'Landuse in Holderness', in R. Van de Noort and S. Ellis (eds) *Wetland Heritage of Holderness, an Archaeological Survey*, Hull, 17–26.

Middleton, R. (1997) 'Landuse in the Humberhead Levels', in R. Van de Noort and S. Ellis (eds) *Wetland Heritage of the Humberhead Levels, an Archaeological Survey*, Hull, 13–18.

Middleton, R. (1998) 'Landuse in the Ancholme and lower Trent valleys', in R. Van de Noort and S. Ellis (eds) *Wetland Heritage of the Ancholme and lower Trent Valleys, an Archaeological Survey*, Hull, 15–20.

Middleton, R. (1999) 'Landuse in the Vale of York', in R. Van de Noort and S. Ellis (eds) *Wetland Heritage of the Vale of York, an Archaeological Survey*, Hull, 13–19.

Middleton, R. (2000) 'Landuse in the Hull valley', in R. Van de Noort and S. Ellis (eds) *Wetland Heritage of the Hull Valley, an Archaeological Survey*, Hull, 13–20.

Middleton, R. (2001) 'Landuse in the Lincolnshire Marsh', in S. Ellis, H. Fenwick, M. Lillie and R. Van de Noort (eds) *Wetland Heritage of the Lincolnshire Marsh, an Archaeological Survey*, Hull, 13–19.

Middleton, R. and Wells, C. (1990) *North-West Wetlands Survey Annual Report 1990*, Lancaster.

Miller, K. (1997) *The Isle of Axholme; Historic Landscape Characterisation Project*, unpublished Report, Countryside Commission, Leeds.

Millett, M. (1990) *The Romanization of Britain: an Essay in Archaeological Interpretation*, Cambridge.

Millett, M. (1999) 'New perspectives on the *civitas Parisorum*', in P. Halkon and M. Millett (eds) *Rural Settlement and Industry: Studies in the Iron Age and Roman Archaeology of Lowland East Yorkshire*, Yorkshire Archaeology Report 4, Leeds, 221–7.

Millett, M. and McGrail, S. (1987) 'The archaeology of the Hasholme boat', *Archaeological Journal* 144, 1–68.

Mitsch, W. J. and Gosselink, J. G. (1993) *Wetlands* (2nd edition), New York.

Mook, W. G. (1986) 'Business meeting: recommendations/resolutions adopted by the Twelfth International Radiocarbon Conference', *Radiocarbon* 12, 799.

Moore, P. D. and Bellamy, D. J. (1974) *Peatlands*, London.

Morris, R. (1989) *Churches in the Landscape*, London.

Murphy, P. and French, C. (eds) (1988) *The Exploitation of Wetlands*, British Archaeological Reports 186, Oxford.

Neal, P. G. E. (2001) 'Romano-British settlement, East Halton Skitter, North Lincolnshire', *Sixth Annual Report, Humber Wetlands Survey (1999–2000)*, 11–15.

Neumann, H. (1998) 'The palaeoenvironmental survey of the Ancholme valley', in R. Van de Noort and S. Ellis (eds) *Wetland Heritage of the Ancholme and lower Trent Valleys, an Archaeological Survey*, Hull, 75–101.

Nicholas, G. P. (2001) 'Wet sites, wetland sites and cultural resource management strategies', in B. A. Purdy (ed.) *Enduring Records. The Environmental and Cultural Heritage of Wetlands*, Oxford, 263–70.

Oelschlaeger, M. (1991) *The Idea of Wilderness: from Prehistory to the Age of Ecology*, New Haven and London.

Olivier, A. and Van de Noort, R. (2002) *English Heritage Strategy for Wetlands*, London and Exeter.

O'Sullivan, A. (1998) *The Archaeology of Lake Settlement in Ireland*, Dublin.

O'Sullivan, A. (2001) *Foragers, Farmers and Fishers in a Coastal Landscape. An Intertidal Archaeological Survey of the Shannon Estuary*, Dublin.

Palmer-Brown, C. (1993) 'Bronze Age salt production in Tetney', *Current Archaeology* 136, 143–5.

Parker Pearson, M. (1993) 'The powerful dead: archaeological relationships between the living and the dead', *Cambridge Archaeological Journal* 3, 203–29.

Bibliography

Parker Pearson, M. (1999) *The Archaeology of Death and Burial*, Stroud.

Parker Pearson, M. and Sydes, R. E. (1997) 'The Iron Age enclosures and prehistoric landscape at Sutton Common, S. Yorkshire', *Proceedings of the Prehistoric Society* 63, 221–59.

Parry, M. L. (1978) *Climate Change, Agriculture and Settlement: Studies in Historical Geography*, Folkestone.

Pedersen, L. (1995) '7000 years of fishing: stationary fishing structures in the Mesolithic and afterwards', in A. Fischer (ed.) *Man and the Sea in the Mesolithic. Coastal Settlement above and below Present Sea Level*, Oxford, 75–86.

Platts, G. (1985) *Land and People in Medieval Lincolnshire*, History of Lincolnshire 4, Lincoln.

Poulsen, G. (1840) *The History of the Seigniory of Holderness, volume 1*, Hull.

Pryor, F. (1991) *Flag Fen: Prehistoric Fenland Centre*, London.

Pryor, F. (1996) 'Sheep, stockyards and field systems: Bronze Age livestock populations in the Fenlands of eastern England', *Antiquity* 70, 313–24.

Pryor, F. (1998) *Farmers in Prehistoric Britain*, Stroud.

Pryor, F. (2001) *The Flag Fen Basin: Archaeology and Environment of a Fenland Landscape*, Swindon.

Raftery, B. (1990) *Trackways through Time. Archaeological Investigations on Irish Bog Roads, 1985–1989*, Dublin.

Raftery, B. (1996) *Trackway Excavations in the Mountdillon Bogs, Co. Longford, 1985–1991*, Dublin.

Richards, M. P. and Hedges, R. E. M. (1999) 'A Neolithic revolution? New evidence of diet in the British Neolithic', *Antiquity* 73, 891–7.

Richardson, W. (1981) *Some Useful Consumers of Waste: History in two Marshland Parishes, Adlingfleet and Whitgift*, York.

Ridgeway, J., Andrews, J. E., Ellis, S., Horton, B. P., Innes, J. B., O'B. Knox, R. W., McArthur, J. J., Maher, B. A., Metcalfe, S. E., Mitlehner, A., Parkes, A., Rees, J. G., Samways, G. M. and Shennan, I. (2000) 'Analysis and interpretation of Holocene sedimentary sequences in the Humber estuary', in I. Shennan and J. E. Andrews (eds) *Holocene Land-Ocean Interaction and Environmental Change around the Western North Sea*, London, 9–39.

Rieck, F. (1999) 'The Nydam sacred site, Denmark', in B. Coles, J. Coles and M. Shou Jørgenson (eds) *Bog Bodies, Sacred Sites and Wetland Archaeology*, Exeter, 209–16.

Riehm, K. (1961) 'Prehistoric salt boiling', *Antiquity* 35, 181–91.

Riley, D. N. (ed.) (1980) *Early Landscapes from the Air. Studies of Crop Marks in South Yorkshire and North Nottinghamshire*, Sheffield.

Riley, D. N. (1982) 'The frequency of cropmarks in relations to soils', in G. S. Maxwell (ed.) *The Impact of Aerial Reconnaissance on Archaeology*, Council for British Archaeology Research Report 49, London, 59–73.

Riley, D. N., Buckland, P. C. and Wade, J. S. (1995) 'Aerial reconnaissance and excavation at Littleborough-on-Trent, Notts', *Britannia* 26, 253–84.

Rippon, S. (2000) *The Transformation of Coastal Wetlands. Exploitation and Management of Marshland Landscapes in North West Europe during the Roman and Medieval Periods*, Oxford.

Robbins, G. (1999) 'Research and regionality: South Yorkshire as an example', in B. Bevan (ed.) *Northern Exposure: Interpretative Devolution and the Iron Age in Britain*, Leicester Archaeology Monographs 4, Leicester, 43–9.

Roberts, O. T. P. (1992) 'The Brigg raft reassessed as a round bilge Bronze Age boat', *International Journal for Maritime Archaeology* 21, 245–258.

Rohl, B. and Needham, S. (1998) *The Circulation of Metal in the British Bronze Age: the Application of Lead Isotope Analysis*, London.

Roymans, N. (1990) 'Late Urnfield societies in the Northwest European Plain and the expanding networks of Central European Hallstatt Groups', in N. Roymans and F. Theuws (eds) *Images of the Past. Studies on Ancient Societies in Northwestern Europe*, Amsterdam, 9–89.

Samuels, J. and Buckland, P. C. (1978) 'A Roman settlement at Sandtoft, South Humberside', *Yorkshire Archaeological Journal* 50, 65–75.

Samuels, J. and May, J. (1980) 'The excavations', in D. N. Riley (ed.) *Early Landscapes from the Air. Studies of Crop Marks in South Yorkshire and North Nottinghamshire*, Sheffield, 73–81.

Schadla-Hall, R. T. (1988) 'The early Post-glacial in East Yorkshire', in T. G. Manby (ed.) *Archaeology in Eastern Yorkshire. Essays in Honour of T. C. M. Brewster*, Sheffield, 25–34.

Schlichterle, H. (1979) *Pfahlbauten rund um die Alpen*, Stuttgart.

Scurfield, C. J. (1977) 'Bronze Age metalworking from the River Trent in Nottinghamshire', *Transactions of the Thoroton Society of Nottinghamshire* 101, 29–57.

Sheldrick, C., Lowe, J. J. and Reynier, M. J. (1997) 'Palaeolithic barbed point from Gransmoor, East Yorkshire, England', *Proceedings of the Prehistoric Society* 63, 359–70.

Shennan, I. and Andrews, J. E. (eds) (2000) *Holocene Land-Ocean Interaction and Environmental Change around the Western North Sea*, London.

Shennan, I., Lambeck, K., Flather, R., Horton, B., MacArthur, J., Innes, J., Lloyd, J., Rutherford, M. and Wingfield, R. (2000) 'Modelling western North Sea palaeogeographies and tidal changes during the Holocene', in I. Shennan and J. E. Andrews (ed.) *Holocene Land-Ocean Interaction and Environmental Change around the Western North Sea*, London, 299–319.

Sheppard, J. A. (1956) *The Drainage of the Marshland of East Yorkshire*. Unpublished PhD thesis, University of Hull.

Sheppard, J. A. (1957) 'The Medieval meres of Holderness', *Transactions of the Institute of British Geographers* 23, 75–86.

Sheppard, J. A. (1966) *The Drainage of the Marshland of Southern Holderness and the Vale of York*, York.

Sheppard, T. (1926) 'Roman remains in north Lincolnshire', *Transactions of the East Riding Antiquarian Society* 25, 170–4.

Simmons, B. B. (1999) 'General introduction', in A. Bell, D. Gurney and H. Healey (eds) *Lincolnshire Salterns: Excavations at Helpringham, Holbeach St Johns and Bicker Haven*, East Anglian Archaeology 89, ix–xi.

Sitch, B. (1989) 'A small Roman port at Faxfleet, near Broomfleet', in P. Halkon (ed.) *New Light on the Parisi*, Hull, 10–4.

Smith, B. (1985) *A Palaeoecological Study of Raised Mires in the Humberhead Levels*. Unpublished PhD thesis, University of Wales.

Smith, R. A. (1911) 'Lake-dwellings in Holderness, Yorkshire', *Archaeologia* 62, 593–610.

Spikins, P. (2000) 'GIS models of past vegetation: an example from northern England, 10,000–5000 BP', *Journal of Archaeological Science* 27, 219–34.

St. Joseph, J. K. (1969) 'Air reconnaissance in Britain, 1965–68', *Journal of Roman Studies* 59, 105–28.

Stead, I. M. (1976) *Excavations at Winterton Roman Villa and other Roman Sites in north Lincolnshire 1958–1967*, London.

Stead, I. M. (1979) *The Arras Culture*, York.

Stocker, D. and Everson, P. (2003) 'The straight and narrow way: Fenland causeways and the conversion of the landscape in the Witham Valley, Lincolnshire', in M. Carver (ed.) *The Cross goes North. Processes of Conversion in Northern Europe AD 300–1300*, Woodbridge and York, 271–288.

Stoertz, C. (1997) *Ancient Landscapes of the Yorkshire Wolds. Aerial Photographic Transcription and Analysis*, Swindon.

Stonehouse, W. B. (1839) *The History and Topography of the Isle of Axholme*, Gainsborough.

Stovin Ms., The Stovin Manuscript, C. Jackson (ed.) *Yorkshire Archaeological and Topographical Journal* 7, 194–238.

Straw, A. (1955) 'The Ancholme Levels north of Brigg', *East Midlands Geographer* 3, 34–42.

Stuiver, M. and Reimer, P. J. (1986) 'A computer program for radiocarbon age calculations', *Radiocarbon* 28, 1022–30.

Swinnerton, H. H. (1932) 'The prehistoric pottery sites of the Lincolnshire coast', *Antiquaries Journal* 12, 239–53.

Swinnerton, H. H. (1936) 'The physical history of Lincolnshire' *Transactions of the Lincolnshire Naturalists Union* 9, 91–100.

Switsur, V. R. and Wright, E. V. (1989) 'Radiocarbon ages and calibrated dates for the boats from North Ferriby, Humberside – a reappraisal', *Archaeological Journal* 146, 58–67.

Taylor, D. (1995) 'New pollen data from the Keyingham valley, southern Holderness', in R. Van de Noort and S. Ellis (eds) *Wetland Heritage of Holderness, an Archaeological Survey*, Hull, 121–7.

Thomas, G. and Fletcher, W. (2001) 'Prehistoric and Roman salt-making in the Lincolnshire Marsh', in S. Ellis, H. Fenwick, M. Lillie and R. Van de Noort (eds) *Wetland Heritage of the Lincolnshire Marsh, an Archaeological Survey*, Hull, 215–30.

Thropp, J. (1887) 'An ancient raft found at Brigg, Lincolnshire', *Association of Architectural Societies Reports and Papers* 19, 95–7.

Tilley, C. (1994) *A Phenomenology of Landscape: Places, Paths, and Monuments*, Oxford.

Tomlinson, J. (1882) 'The Isle of Axholme before Vermuyden', *Agricultural History Review* 1, 16–28.

Trump, B. A. V. (1985) 'A Middle Bronze dirk from Wilfholme, North Humberside', *The Yorkshire Archaeological Journal* 57, 7–9.

Turner, J. (1962) 'The Tilia decline: an anthropogenic interpretation', *New Phytologist* 61, 328–41.

Turner, R. C. and Rhodes, M. (1992) 'A bog body and its shoes from Amcotts, Lincolnshire', *Antiquaries Journal* 72, 76–90.

Turner, R. C. and Scaife, R. G. (1995) *Bog Bodies. New Discoveries and New Perspectives*, London.

Valentin, H. (1957) 'Glazialmorphologische Untersuchungen in Ostengland', *Abhandlungen der Geographische Institut der Freien Universität Berlin* 4, 1–86.

Van de Noort, R. (1995) 'West Furze: the reconstruction of a monumental wetland landscape', in R. Van de Noort and S. Ellis (eds) *Wetland Heritage of Holderness, an Archaeological Survey*, Hull, 323–34.

Van de Noort, R. (1997) 'Preservation of waterlogged sites in the Humberhead Levels', in R. Van de Noort and S. Ellis (eds) *Wetland Heritage of the Humberhead Levels, an Archaeological Survey*, Hull, 439–52.

Van de Noort, R. and Davies, P. (1993) *Wetland Heritage; an Archaeological Assessment of the Humber wetlands*, Hull.

Van de Noort, R. and Ellis, S. (eds) (1995) *Wetland Heritage of Holderness, an Archaeological Survey*, Hull.

Van de Noort, R. and Ellis, S. (eds) (1997) *Wetland Heritage of the Humberhead Levels, an Archaeological Survey*, Hull.

Van de Noort, R. and Ellis, S. (eds) (1998) *Wetland Heritage of the Ancholme and lower Trent Valleys, an Archaeological Survey*, Hull.

Van de Noort, R. and Ellis, S. (eds) (1999) *Wetland Heritage of the Vale of York, an Archaeological Survey*, Hull.

Van de Noort, R. and Ellis, S. (eds) (2000) *Wetland Heritage of the Hull Valley, an Archaeological Survey*, Hull.

Van de Noort, R. and Etté, J. (1995) 'The Humber Wetlands Survey: background, objectives and methodology', in R. Van de Noort and S. Ellis (eds) *Wetland Heritage of Holderness, an Archaeological Survey*, Hull, 1–7.

Van de Noort, R. and Fletcher, W. (2000) 'Bronze age human-ecodynamics in the Humber estuary', in G. Bailey, R. Charles and N. Winder (eds) *Human Ecodynamics*, Symposia of the Association for Environmental Archaeology 19, Oxford.

Van de Noort, R., Chapman, H., Head, R. and Dinnin, M. (1997a) 'The archaeological survey of West, Thorne and Hatfield Moors', in R. Van de Noort and S. Ellis (eds) *Wetland Heritage of the Humberhead Levels, an Archaeological Survey*, Hull, 369–81.

Van de Noort, R., Lillie, M., Taylor, D. and Kirby, J. (1997b) 'The Roman period landscape at Scaftworth', in R. Van de Noort and S. Ellis (eds) *Wetland Heritage of the Humberhead Levels, an Archaeological Survey*, Hull, 409–28.

Van de Noort, R., Fenwick, H. and Head, R. (1998) 'Introduction to the archaeological survey', in R. Van de Noort and S. Ellis (eds) *Wetland Heritage of the Ancholme and lower Trent valleys, an Archaeological Survey*, Hull, 123–40.

Van de Noort, R., Middleton, R., Foxon, A. and Bayliss, A. (1999) 'The 'Kilnsea-boat', and some implications from the discovery of England's oldest plank boat', *Antiquity* 73, 131–5.

Van de Noort, R., Fletcher, W., Thomas, G., Carstairs, I. and Patrick, D. (2001) *Monuments at Risk in England's Wetlands – Final Report*, Exeter.

Van den Broeke, P. (1995) 'Iron Age salt trade in the Lower Rhine area', in J. D. Hill and C. G. Cumberpatch (eds) *Different Iron Ages: Studies on the Iron Age in Temperate Europe*, British Archaeological Reports 602, Oxford, 149–62.

Van den Broeke, P. W. and Van London, H. (1995) *5000 Jaar Wonen op Veen en Klei. Archeologisch Onderzoek in het Reconstructiegebied Midden-Delfland*, Utrecht.

Van der Sanden, W. (1996) *Through Nature to Eternity: the Bog Bodies of Northwest Europe*, Amsterdam.

Van Es, W. A. and Verwers, W. J. H. (1980) *Excavations at Dorestad: The Harbour, Hoogstraat I*, 's-Gravenhage.

Van Gennep, A. (1908) *Les Rites de Passage*, Nourry.

Varley, W. J. (1968) 'Barmston and the Holderness crannogs', *East Riding Archaeologist* 1, 11–26.

Verhart, L. B. M. (1995) 'Fishing for the Mesolithic. The North Sea: a submerged Mesolithic landscape', in A. Fischer (ed.) *Man and Sea in the Mesolithic. Coastal Settlement above and below Present Sea Level*, Oxford, 291–302.

Vince, A. (ed.) (1992) *Pre-Viking Lindsey*, Lincoln.

Wacher, J. S. (1969) *Excavations at Brough-on-Humber, 1958–61*, Leeds.

Wacher, J. S. (1995) *The Towns of Roman Britain*, London.

Wainwright, G. J. (1979) *Gussage All Saints: an Iron Age Settlement in Dorset*, London.

Walker, M. J. C., Coope, G. R. and Lowe, J. J. (1993) 'The Devensian (Weichselian) lateglacial palaeoenvironmental record from Gransmoor, East Yorkshire, England', *Quaternary Science Review* 12, 659–80.

Walker, M. J. C., Bohncke, S. J. P., Coope, G. R., O'Connell, M., Usinger, H. and Verbruggen, C. (1994) 'The Devensian/Weichselian Late-glacial in northwest Europe (Ireland, Britain, north Belgium, the Netherlands, northwest Germany)', *Journal of Quaternary Science* 9, 109–18.

Waller, M. (1994) *Flandrian Environmental Change in Fenland. The Fenland Project, number 9*, East Anglian Archaeology Report 70.

Whiting, C. E. (1936) 'Excavations on Sutton Common, 1933, 1934 and 1935', *Yorkshire Archaeological Journal* 33, 57–80.

Whittle, A. (1985) *Neolithic Europe, a Survey*, Cambridge.

Whittle, A. (1996) *Europe in the Neolithic: the Creation of New Worlds*, Cambridge.

Williams, M. (ed.) (1990) *Wetlands, a Threatened Landscape*, Oxford.

Wright, E. V. (1990) *The Ferriby boats. Seacraft of the Bronze Age*, London.

Wright, E. V. and Switsur, V. R. (1992) 'The Ferriby boat fragment', *Archaeological Journal* 150, 46–56.

Wright, E. V., Hedges, R., Bayliss, A. and Van de Noort, R. (2001) 'New AMS dates for the Ferriby boats; a contribution to the origin of seafaring', *Antiquity* 75, 726–34.

Wylie, W. M. (1884) 'A note by A. Atkinson on the Brigg trackway', *Proceedings of the Society of Antiquaries* 10, 110–5.

Zvelebil, M. (ed.) (1986) *Hunters in Transition: Mesolithic Societies of Temperate Eurasia and their Transition to Farming*, Cambridge.

Index

This index is selective; it lists names of places, rivers and other wetlands (but not countries, counties or regions such as 'Holderness' or the 'Lincolnshire Wolds'). It includes the most important palaeoenvironmental and archaeological sites; references to sites discovered during the Humber Wetlands Project are listed under the name of the relevant mapview, e.g. 'Halsham–5' is listed under 'Halsham'.